NUREG-1262

I0439032

Answers to Questions at Public Meetings Regarding Implementation of Title 10, Code of Federal Regulations, Part 55 on Operators' Licenses

U.S. Nuclear Regulatory Commission

Office of Nuclear Reactor Regulation

Answers to Questions at Public Meetings Regarding Implementation of Title 10, Code of Federal Regulations, Part 55 on Operators' Licenses

Manuscript Completed: June 1987
Date Published: November 1987

Division of Licensee Performance and Quality Evaluation
Office of Nuclear Reactor Regulation
U.S. Nuclear Regulatory Commission
Washington, DC 20555

ABSTRACT

This document presents questions and answers based on the transcripts of four public meetings (and from written questions submitted after the meetings) conducted from April 9 to April 20, 1987 by the staff of the U.S. Nuclear Regulatory Commission. The meetings discussed implementation of the Commission's final rule governing Operators' Licenses and Conforming Amendments (10 CFR Parts 55 and 50). The rule became effective May 26, 1987 and is intended to clarify the regulations for issuing licenses to operators and senior operators; revise the requirements and scope of written examinations and operating tests for operators and senior operators, require a simulation facility; clarify procedures for administering requalification examinations; and describe the form and content for operator license applications.

TABLE OF CONTENTS

TABLE OF CONTENTS (Continued)

I PREFACE

On March 25, 1987, the U.S. Nuclear Regulatory Commission published in the Federal Register (52 FR 9453) revisions to 10 CFR 55 to meet NRC responsibilities under Section 306 of the Nuclear Waste Policy Act of 1982. The rule, Operators' Licenses and Conforming Amendments, became effective on May 26, 1987 and is intended to:

1. clarify the regulations for issuing licenses to operators and senior operators;

2. revise the requirements and scope of written examinations and operating tests for operators and senior operators;

3. require a simulation facility;

4. clarify procedures for administering requalification examinations; and,

5. describe the form and content for operator license applications.

From April 9, 1987 to April 20, 1987, the NRC staff held four public meetings to discuss implementation of the requirements of this rule and related issues. Those attending asked numerous questions which the staff answered. This document presents the answers to those questions taken from the transcripts of the four meetings, as well as to written questions which were submitted at the conclusion of the meetings. The questions are grouped to eliminate excessive duplication. However, where different questions addressed similar concerns, they were retained in this report if they provided clarification or a different perspective. Questions related to Regulatory Guides, industry standards, and other documents associated with the rule are included with the applicable portion of the rule.

This report attempts to retain the intent, tone, and nuance of each question without reproducing each verbatim from the transcripts. In some cases, questions submitted or recorded by the transcriber contained unintended or inadvertent factual errors. When identified, these errors were corrected. Similarly, verbatim answers in the transcripts have been edited where necessary for clarity and conciseness.

NRC staff discussions held since the final public meeting indicate that the answers provided to questions in the area of "Conditions of Licenses," specifically the proficiency requirements in 10 CFR 55.53(e), may have conveyed the impression that the staff advocated minimum shift staffing, and that this might have been construed to be counterproductive to safety. The apparent confusion stems from the definition of "Actively performing the functions of an operator or senior operator" in Section 55.4 of the regulation, which appears to tie the proficiency issue to a minimum staffing requirement in the facility licensee's technical specifications. The intent of the 10 CFR 55.53(e) requirements regarding maintenance of active operator or senior operator status is that personnel maintain proficiency by actively performing the functions and duties of the licensed operator positions. Because facility licensees assign to a shift more than the minimum number of operators required by their Technical Specifications, concerns have been raised since the public meetings that

10 CFR 55.53(e), if implemented in the manner discussed at these meetings, might discourage utilities from augmenting shift crews.

It is not NRC's intent to discourage augmenting shift crews; clearly, this practice can result in a significant safety enhancement. However, assigning a large number of operators to a shift could reduce the range of responsibilities of any one operator to a level where sufficient experience in directing shift operations and/or in manipulating controls is not being obtained. NRC's intent in 10 CFR 55.53(e) is that operators taking credit for watchstanding on shift to maintain an active license engage meaningfully and fully in the functions and duties of the positions required by the Technical Specifications. The intent is not to have licensees augment a shift with a contingent of operators whose main purpose is to acquire the minimum number of watches to meet 10 CFR 55.53(e) requirements. Their role is to fulfill the duties that the facility licensee judges are necessary and prudent for safe operations.

Facility licenses can take credit for more than the minimum number of watchstanders required by Technical Specifications provided that there are administrative controls which assure that functions and duties are divided and rotated in a manner which provides each watchstander meaningful and significant opportunity to maintain proficiency in the performance of the functions of an operator and/or senior operator as appropriate. Normally, more than one additional watchstander at each Technical Specification position would not be considered acceptable with respect to the proficiency issue.

Any answers to questions on this subject that were raised during the public meetings, and which might have conveyed the impression that NRC advocated such minimum shift staffing, have been revised in this report to reflect the staff's position as clarified above. Such answers are identified in this report by an asterisk next to the question number.

Similarly, NRC staff discussions held during the preparation of this report have identified a number of answers given during the public meetings which either misstated an NRC policy or may have been open to misinterpretation. These answers have been revised for this report and are identified by an asterisk next to the question number.

The views expressed in this report represent office practices and policies on how the staff will implement the rule. These views are intended as guidance and are meant to reflect the rule and its statement of considerations. The views expressed are not intended to interpret the rule or any of its provisions. Although any request for formal interpretation should be sought from the Office of General Counsel under 10 CFR 55.6, the NRC staff may provide informal guidance as needed and as appropriate. This report does not impose any requirements on facility licensees nor does it replace or supersede any existing regulations.

II INTRODUCTION

This rule (10 CFR 55) represents a significant move toward less prescriptive regulatory requirements for utilities that have accredited training programs and acceptable simulation facilities. It attempts to differentiate clearly between training programs sponsored through industry initiatives by the Nuclear

Utility Management and Resources Committee (NUMARC) and the Institute for Nuclear Power Operations (INPO), and Nuclear Regulatory Commission (NRC) licensing and examination requirements. One of the most important changes to the regulation is the flexibility it affords licensees in reviewing the content of continuing training (requalification) programs, and tailoring those programs to the needs of the job incumbents. This degree of flexibility represents a major change from the way NRC has implemented regulations in the past in that it relies on industry initiatives to provide both training and qualifications for license applicants. With this rulemaking NRC has moved out of the area of specifying training program content and qualifications for instructors.

INPO Accreditation

It is a precedent-setting move, and NRC is pleased that the industry has taken this initiative to improve its training of licensed operators and others. Although moving out of the training areas potentially leaves a void, particularly as it relates to some of the more prescriptive requirements used in the past, NRC has placed great importance in the INPO accreditation process. In its review of INPO accreditation criteria, the staff has concluded that they are equivalent to NRC's. If a utility implements an accredited training program, the accreditation will constitute the basis for NRC acceptance of that certification from a responsible utility officer, as indicated in Generic Letter 87-07.

The Appeal Process

NRC is also implementing a change to the appeal process for operator license candidates to clarify the process. The following figures describe the proposed appeal process.

Figure 1. NRC's appeal process has always permitted both informal reviews and hearing rights on issues which were in dispute between the candidate and the examiner. Informal reviews were conducted by regional management and, when requested, further review was conducted at NRC headquarters. The exercise of hearing rights, described in 10 CFR Part 2 of the Commission's regulations, becomes operable should there be a license application denial.

Figure 2. Informal reviews and hearing rights are available to the candidate for any adverse action, whether for a failure of the written examination or operating test, or for an application rejected for other reasons. The informal review will go first to the regional Division Director responsible for the operator licensing function, and then, should the candidate so choose, to the Director, Division of Licensee Performance and Quality Evaluation (DLPQE).

In the past, on occasion, NRC has not completed action on appeals in a timely manner and, in some cases, candidates have not submitted information that is necessary to review an appeal. We have tightened up the schedule by allowing 20 days for the candidate to decide to appeal and 30 days for informal management review.

Figure 3. Those schedules will work as follows. The day that the candidate gets the notification letter of a failure or notification of a rejected application, we have called day zero. He has 20 days to decide whether to request an informal review.

If the candidate does not act within that 20-day period, the notification letter automatically converts to a Proposed Denial of License Application, which will avail him of hearing rights under 10 CFR Part 2 of the Commission's regulations. If he requests an informal review, he submits the information to the responsible regional division director, who reviews it, and either sustains or overturns the examination failure or the rejected application.

If it is sustained such that the situation is still adverse to the candidate, he may, then, request another informal review. The second letter he received would, in the manner similar to the first, become a proposed denial after 20 days. If, during the 20-day period after he receives the letter from the regional Division Director, he decides to ask for an informal review, he submits the requested information to the Director, DLPQE, where another review of the merits of his contentions would be conducted.

If the candidate's examination failure or application rejection is sustained, a Notice of Proposed Denial of License Application will be issued. The candidate can then request a hearing under 10 CFR Part 2.

When a Proposed Denial has become effective, the applicant can choose to accept the Proposed Denial, waive his hearing rights, and have the denial become final. It takes an affirmative action by the candidate to waive his hearing rights through an NRC form letter which provides information about the date of his examination, his docket number, and the like. He simply signs the letter and returns it to NRC.

Or, the applicant may request a hearing. In order to implement the hearing process, he would have to notify the NRC Office of General Counsel. The Examiner Standards will contain sample letters and procedures that describe this process. The 80-day time frame for this process does not include mailing time. We will be using certified mail, request return receipts, and will place the correspondence associated with the appeal in the docket file.

In addition, we will provide copies of all relevant correspondence to the facility licensee's authorized representative who signed the application. This will be done at the time we mail it out to the individual. The reason for this is that the authorized representative is a part of this process, in that he certified the completion of training. Further, the facility reviewed a written exam and provided comments on the exam and the answers.

Figure 4. This figure shows the proposed denial/hearing process, beginning with the administration of the examination. NRC will complete the grading, make an initial determination within 30 days, and mail the results to the candidate.

If the candidate requests an informal review, he must send in a complete information package to the responsible regional division director. He has 20 days to decide to make the request, and 10 more days to submit the information. The regional division director would review the submittal and make a determination within 30 days. If the regional division director sustains the failure or the application rejection, the candidate could at that point request an informal review by the Director, DLPQE, a hearing, or accept the results. If the candidate accepts the results, NRC would issue a final denial and put it into his docket file. After the required length of time from the date of final denial (immediately in the case of an application denial) he could start the reapplication process.

Alternatively, if the candidate requests an informal review by the Director, DLPQE, he must submit the requested information within the prescribed time. The Director, DLPQE, would make a determination within 30 days. If the Director sustains the failure or the application rejection, NRC would issue a proposed denial. At that time the candidate would have the option of requesting a hearing or accepting the results.

This process is more formal than past practice. A candidate may not reapply under the provisions of 10 CFR 55.12 until he has a final denial in hand. The only way he can get a final denial is either to agree with the staff's proposed denial, waive his hearing rights and accept the outcome, or go to hearing, where an independent determination will be made in his case. The types of hearings under Part 2 may vary from informal to formal adjudicatory hearings. It is the candidate who controls the process. It is the staff's responsibility to ensure that the candidate understands his rights.

The review process as outlined is currently under staff review for ways in which it can be expedited.

INFORMAL APPEAL PROCESS AND HEARING RIGHTS

Can be stopped at any point by candidate accepting proposed denial and waiving hearing rights.

Candidate may reapply following examination failure only after application finally denied under 10 CFR 55.35.

— Candidate accepts Proposed Denial

— Hearing decision — Final Denial

Candidte may reapply at any time for rejection of application for reasons other than examination failure.

Figure 1

INFORMAL APPEAL PROCESS AND HEARING RIGHTS

Process has been clarified to assure candidate understands his rights

Applicable to any decision by the staff adverse to the candidate

Applicant always has the right to request
— informal regional management review
— informal headquarters management review
— formal hearing before an administrative judge

Schedule specified to ensure timely action upon informal review

— 20 days for candidate to decide
— 30 days for informal review

Figure 2

INFORMAL APPEAL PROCESS AND HEARING RIGHTS

0 DAYS   Notification of Examination failure
                or Application rejection

+ 20 DAYS   Request informal review by Region

+ 60 DAYS   Notification of Region's review results

+ 80 DAYS   Request informal review by Headquarters

+120 DAYS   Notification of Proposed License Denial

+140 DAYS   Request for Hearing

NOTE: Does not include mailing times

Figure 3

Figure 4

PROPOSED LICENSE-DENIAL/HEARING PROCESS

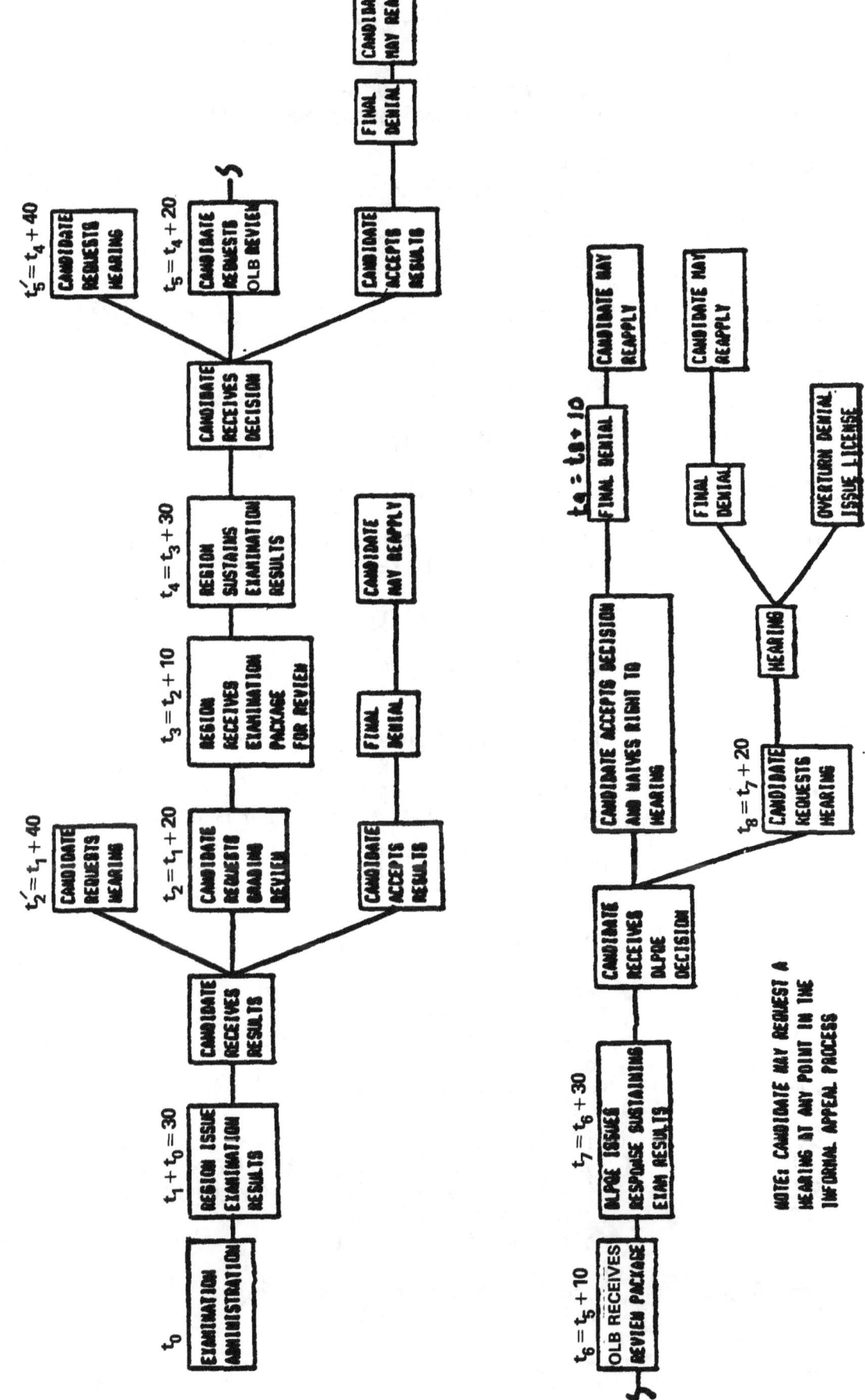

ACRONYMS AND INITIALISMS

ANS	American Nuclear Society
ANSI	American National Standards Institute
BOP	Balance of Plant
BWR	Boiling Water Reactor
CE	Combustion Engineering
CRD	Control Rod Drive
DLPQE	Division of Licensee Performance and Quality Evaluation
EOP	Emergency Operating Procedure
ES	Examiner Standard
FSAR	Final Safety Analysis Report
GE	General Emergency
IE	Office of Inspection and Enforcement (NRC)
INPO	Institute of Nuclear Power Operations
K/A	Knowledge and Abilities
LER	Licensee Event Report
NLO	Nonlicensed Operator
NRC	U.S. Nuclear Regulatory Commission
NRR	Office of Nuclear Reactor Regulation (NRC)
NTOL	Near-Term Operating License
NUMARC	Nuclear Utility Management and Resources Committee
OJT	On-the-Job Training
OMB	Office of Management and Budget
PWR	Pressurized Water Reactor
Reg Guide	Regulatory Guide
RG	Regulatory Guide
Requal	Requalification
RO	Reactor Operator
RWP	Radiation Work Permit
SAE	Site Area Emergency
SAT	Systematic (or Systems) Approach to Training
SFEP	Simulation Facility Evaluation Procedure
SRO	Senior Reactor Operator
STA	Shift Technical Advisor
Tech Specs	Technical Specifications
TSD	Training System Development
UE	Unusual Event

GENERAL ISSUES PERTAINING TO 10 CFR PART 55

Background to the Regulation

Q. 1. The Supplemental Information to NRC Generic Letter 87-07 states that, "These rules supersede all current regulations for operator licenses." Are training requirements from Mr. H. R. Denton's March 28, 1980 letter superseded by the new rule?*

A. The rule supersedes all requirements where those requirements are less restrictive. Where individual commitments are more restrictive, you must follow those commitments until you change them.

In some cases that change may require an amendment to the license. In other cases it can be done by yourself under 10 CFR Part 50.59, and you simply inform us of what you're doing. That would include any change within your authority to do under Part 50.59 that does not constitute a reduction in the effectiveness of the program, because it's being done to conform to the rule. Additionally, as a matter of interest, we are no longer, under the rule, permitted to certify instructors.

Q. 2. Will the revision to 10 CFR 55 cancel NUREG-0737, NUREG-0094, and the Denton letter? If so, will references to these documents be removed from NUREG-1021?

A. NUREG-1021, "Operator Examiner Licensing Standards," has been reviewed and the items left are required by the Regulation, or by Regulatory Guide 1.8. The items from NUREG-0737 and NUREG-0094 that are superseded have only to do with operator licensing. Items from Regulatory Guide 1.8 Revision 2, will be incorporated into NUREG-1021 when Regulatory Guide 1.8 becomes effective on March 31, 1988. Some items may be very similar to what was there in the past, due to NUREG-0737 or NUREG-0094. For example, four years of power plant experience are incorporated into NUREG-0737 and Denton's letter, and it's still in Regulatory Guide 1.8 and NUREG-1021.

Q. 3. Is it true that the NUREG-0737 requirements being incorporated in 10 CFR Part 55 are only those that relate to operator training and licensing?

A. The requirements pertain only to operator licensing, not training.

Q. 4. We also make commitments in NUREG-0737 for training and mitigating core damage of other work groups. Also, there is training related to STAs. For instance, Reg Guide 1.8 talks about the number of shifts that an STA must serve. So, nothing in this regulation affects these commitments even though there is some reference to it?

A. Yes, that's correct. It does not modify those prior commitments regarding training for STAs and other work groups.

---

*H. R. Denton, NRC, Letter to All Power Reactor Applicants and Licensees. Subject: Qualification of Reactor Operators, March 28, 1980.

Q. 5. If NUREG-0737 is still applicable in areas not applicable to regulations for operator licenses, are you going to publish a NUREG that supersedes NUREG-0737 in those areas?

A. No, we'll not issue a new NUREG that applies to the areas that have not been superseded.

Q. 6. Are experience requirements in NUREG-1021 for the RO and the SRO superseded by this change?

A. No. NUREG-1021 will be revised to reflect the changes that have been adopted in ANSI 3.1 as endorsed by Regulatory Guide 1.8. We anticipate these changes will be made in about one year.

Q. 7. Can licensees file an FSAR amendment for Commission approval to modify existing initial licensing and requalification training programs?

A. Yes. See Generic Letter 87-07 for guidance on how to file such FSAR amendments.

Q. 8. What other means are available for filing for program changes?

A. You can write a letter and say that you have substituted an accredited training program, which is performance-based, for the previously NRC-approved program, and indicate the date(s) your new program was accredited. See Generic Letter 87-07 for further guidance on how to submit such a letter.

Q. 9. Our FSAR commits us to ANSI/ANS-3.1-1978.

A. Recall that this Regulation and associated documents supersede all prior requirements. The rule identifies the Regulatory Guides that are part of the rulemaking package. The implementation of Reg Guide 1.8, which endorses, with exceptions, ANSI/ANS 3.1, 1981, takes effect March 31, 1988, to allow for a phase-in period.

Q. 10. Will we do anything different in the inspection of requalification activities due to the end of the two-year moratorium in INPO accreditation? Has the new rule been timed to coincide with the end of the two-year period?

A. This issue is currently under advisement by the Commission. No decision has been made to date. Publication of the regulation was independent of the two-year period.

Q. 11. Is failure to meet an INPO program requirement that was in the benchmark-accredited program grounds for issuance of a Notice of Violation?

A. Failure to meet INPO Guidelines, or loss of accreditation status through action taken by the National Nuclear Accreditation Board, will result in further evaluation by NRC. Such failure in itself would not be grounds for a Notice of Violation. However, per the "Policy Statement on Training and Qualification of Nuclear Power Plant Personnel" (50 FR 11147), "Nothing in this Policy Statement shall limit the authority or responsibility of the NRC to follow up on operational events or place any limit on NRC's enforcement authority when regulatory requirements are not met."

Definitions (Subpart A, Section 55.4)

Q. 12. Why did you change terms from "reactivity manipulations" to "control manipulations?"

A. For the purposes of Part 55, "controls" refers to the controls that affect reactivity or power.

Q. 13. By what means are utilities to determine NRC's interpretation of "reference plant" as it applies to multi-unit plants at one site (from the same vendor and vintage)? It seems that compliance with Part 55 is contingent on a clear interpretation of this term.

A. The definition of "reference plant" has been provided in Section 55.4 of the regulation. Section D, which is the implementation section of Regulatory Guide 1.149, provides clear guidance for the use of one simulation facility for more than one plant or unit, since each plant has a unique docket number.

The greater the similarity between the units, of course, the more likely it is that you'll be able to submit one certification form for each, identifying any exceptions as necessary against ANSI/ANS-3.5.

If your operators are dual-licensed, certification, with exceptions, would be considered satisfactory for multiple units or plants. If your operators are not dual-licensed, it is still possible to certify with exceptions, although more work may need to be done to justify acceptability of the simulation facility for the conduct of operating tests.

Q. 14. In the discussion of the term, "plant-referenced simulator," mention was made of the simulator being required to use controlled copies of procedures? What do you mean by the word control?

A. Controlled copies refers to procedures that are identical to those you use in the control room of the plant, and are maintained current through administrative control.

Q. 15. Do they necessarily have to be up to date to the minute or to the hour?

A. We expect them to be up to date.

Q. 16. As far as the references go?

A. Yes.

Q. 17. Revisions?

A. Yes.

Communications (Subpart A, Section 55.5)

*Q. 18. Section 55.5(b)(2)(iv) states that applications and correspondence should be submitted to the Regional Administrator. Should copies be submitted to the Regional Section Chief for Operator Licensing?

A. No. Copies of applications and correspondence under Section 55.5 need not be sent to the Regional Section Chiefs.

Q. 19. Is Form 474 to be submitted directly to the Director of the Office of Nuclear Reactor Regulation (NRR) in Washington, D.C., as opposed to Regional Administrators?

A. Yes. We made a conscious effort to ensure that Form 474 certifications and the applications for approval be submitted to NRR at Headquarters. Officially, they should be filed in accordance with 10 CFR Part 50.4, which specifies that those submittals go to ATTN: Document Control Desk, Washington, DC 20555.

Q. 20. Who specifically receives the certification referred to in Generic Letter 87-07, the region or headquarters?

A. Generic Letter 87-07 describes the form of notification to the NRC, which basically is a letter telling us that you have an INPO-accredited program, or an otherwise systematic approach to training at your facility. That submittal is made to NRC Headquarters in accordance with 10 CFR 50.4. It comes to the Director of the Office of Nuclear Reactor Regulation, and is to be submitted in accordance with 10 CFR 50.4, ATTN: Document Control Desk, Washington, DC 20555.

Q. 21. 10 CFR 50.4 is explicit regarding written communications and volume reduction; however, this part of the regulation seems to be inconsistent with 55.5. Which regulation do we follow?

A. For communications concerning 10 CFR 55, licensees should follow 55.5.

General Exemptions (Subpart B, Section 55.13)

Q. 22. With regard to Section 55.13, can you clarify the intent behind these exemptions?

A. Yes. There are certain skills and knowledge that an operator must have, for example, to perform a reactor start up. Hopefully, he would understand some reactor theory, the effects of subcritical multiplication, and other aspects of the controls he is manipulating.

If the candidate has not completed those phases of training, he should not perform reactor startup, whether or not it's included in the instruction. That's the concept. Now, if in your program, information is transmitted to him such that he is prepared to perform the function because he understands what he is doing -- he has either had the systems training, or he's had the theory training, or he's gotten it in some other earlier program, such that you are assured that the sequence of training is appropriate and the potential for him making an error is small--then the exemption applies.

We don't want to repeat an event which occurred a few years ago where an individual performed a startup soon after entering training. They had a high startup rate, short-period transient, and the individual did not understand what he was doing. He had no appreciation for the procedure because he had not received the appropriate on-the-job training for the evolution. There were two concerns with that event: First, they put the plant at risk because someone manipulating the controls didn't know what he was doing and, second, they provided negative training.

The sequence of training that leads to on-the-job-performance is important. That approach is consistent, by the way, with the INPO accreditation process and criteria. If you look at the objectives in INPO 85-002 for on-the-job training, you will find that they intend that the person adequately understand the task before performing it.

Q. 23. Can trainees manipulate facility controls under the appropriate supervision of licensed personnel?

A. If their training program leads to a license if carried to completion, they may manipulate controls under instruction if they have been properly trained. Properly trained means that the sequence of training that has led them up to that point is appropriate for the manipulations they perform.

Q. 24. In Section 55.13, Item 1, are you using training and education interchangeably?

A. No. Students at test or research reactors receive training on a reactor as part of a course of study to further their education. They may manipulate controls as a part of that course of instruction.

Q. 25. With respect to Section 55.13, is someone who is in a course, but from a visiting institution, considered a student? Would a group of high school students visiting a university for a couple weeks to familiarize themselves with the school be considered students; that is, could I sit them down at the control panel and tell them what steps to go through to operate the panel?

A. Both groups are considered students. There are colleges and universities that have exchange programs with high schools and other institutions where you bring students in to attend courses. If these students attend some part of classroom training, and as a part of that activity they manipulate the controls, then that's part of their instruction as students.

We want to avoid the situation where an individual comes in off the street without any training and starts manipulating the controls.

Q. 26. If the facility career path program considers all nonlicensed operators to be license candidates, can nonlicensed operators manipulate the controls under the direction and in the presence of the reactor operator's senior operator if the candidate is not currently in a hot licensed class?

A. No. The candidate must officially be enrolled in the hot license class. Simply being a nonlicensed operator on a designated career path is not sufficient to meet the intent without being enrolled in the hot license class. More importantly, the candidate must have completed the necessary classroom or simulator training in accordance with the appropriate training sequence prior to manipulating the controls of the facility.

Q. 27. If the operator is in a licensing class, has completed the classroom and the simulator portion, and has an opportunity to take part in an unplanned evolution, can he receive credit toward the training program for that participation?

A. Yes.

Q. 28. Is a senior operator license required to move fuel in a dry storage area, or away from the reactor vessel?

A. The Regulation doesn't specifically talk about the dry storage area or the refueling pool. It specifically talks about moving fuel in and out of the vessel. If there is a potential for criticality, a senior operator would be required to be there, as in some instances in a refueling pool. If not, no.

Q. 29. Can the licensed senior operator who supervised fuel handling be a senior operator licensed for fuel handling only?

A. Yes.

APPLICATIONS

Q. 30.   For a person who has dropped his license, what, if anything, must be done to later upgrade his status to an SRO beyond meeting the requirements of an accredited SRO training program?

A.   He must submit completed Forms 398 and 396 and be examined as an SRO.

Q. 31.   Has Form 398 changed?

A.   Not yet, but a change is in process.   It is scheduled to be available for ordering by the end of May 1987.

Q. 32.   Will the current Regional requirements for complete licensee history on Form 398 for license renewal be reduced to the data included in the OMB approval, 8150-0090?

A.   If you have an INPO-accredited program with an acceptable simulation facility (approved or certified), you can eliminate giving us information under blocks 11, 12, and 13, with the exception of the five significant control manipulations.   Those still must be included.

For renewal, the same rules would apply; there is a block specifically on the Form for renewal.   You will only have to provide information on candidate training, education, and experience dating from that last application for a license renewal.

There will be a block on the Form 398 to indicate the number of on-shift hours, or the experience that has been received.   That's all you will have to provide if you meet the two other criteria, i.e., having been INPO accredited, and having an acceptable simulation facility.   If you do not meet these two check points, then you will have to provide the additional data on training, education, and experience.

Q. 33.   On Form 398, since test and research reactors don't have simulators, are we required to completely fill out the form?

A.   What you are currently doing will continue to be acceptable.   For all test and research reactors, there is no change to the process except in terms of license operators being re-examined during the six year license.

Your requalification programs basically stay the same.   We still intend for you to use ANSI 15.4 for selection, training, and medical certification.   We've also adjusted the requirements for resuming an active license to six hours of parallel watch-standing.

Q. 34.   I understand that the designation of the authorized representative for a facility is changing.   Is that true?

A.   We will accept, as the authorized representative, the senior individual on site responsible for operations.   Some companies have a vice president on site, some have a site manager.   Others may choose to designate someone at a higher level, and send it off site to the corporate office. That is acceptable to us. It is also acceptable for it to be done on site. It need not be the same authorized representative who requests license amendments under Part 50.

There is, under the facility license, only one authorized representative; generally that is somebody at the corporate level, a senior vice president. If that is the authorized representative for the facility, that's who signs Part 50 license amendment requests and makes other certifications. We will accept, for Part 55 licensing, the senior person responsible for operations on site.

Please note a new requirement on Forms 396, 474, and 398. Above the signature there is now a statement that any false statement or omission in this document, including attachments, may be subject to civil and criminal sanctions, to the person signing it. The statement says: "I certify, under penalty of perjury, that the information in this document and attachments is true and correct." That's why we're adjusting the requirement so that the person on site, who's closer to the information, can be absolutely sure when attesting to the accuracy of the information.

Q. 35. Is it the intent of the Commission to limit the number of licensees at a facility to a specific position?

A. No. It is the facility licensee's decision as to whether to have a person in a licensed position or not, and how many of them are needed. We will not question the judgment of facility management.

Q. 36. Is it the NRC's intent that the facility licensee identify organizational positions as needing an NRC Operator License beyond those required by Tech Specs?

A. No. The facility licensee determines the need for whom they want licensed beyond the requirements of the Technical Specifications. However, all individuals who are licensed must be enrolled in the facility licensee's requalification program.

Q. 37. Does an applicant for a license have to be a member of the shift crew to obtain a license?

A. No. An applicant doesn't have to be a member of the shift crew to obtain it, but the facility must certify that there is a need for him to have a license.

Q. 38. In answer to the question: "Are experience requirements in NUREG-1021 for the RO and SRO superseded," you said, "no, that there were experience requirements that would still apply." Is that still in effect even if you have an accredited program?

A. The accreditation process has its own experience requirements identified within that program. For those facilities which have an INPO-accredited program and a simulation facility acceptable to the NRC, you do not have to designate on the Form 398 those experience requirements for those individuals. You need only check the blocks associated with the simulation facility and the accredited program.

Q. 39. Other than as stated in 10 CFR 55, are there any other requirements that must be included in initial or continuing training programs for licensed personnel?

A. Yes. All previous requirements are in effect unless superseded by the rule, until the training program is accredited.

Q. 40. Is accreditation by INPO's National Academy of Training sufficient?

A. As indicated in Generic Letter 87-07, if it is based on a systems approach to training, it is sufficient. We believe that a program developed following the INPO guidelines for continuing operator training for licensed operators, issued in October, constitutes an adequate basis for concluding that the program has been developed in accordance with the systems approach to training. If you follow that, and you are accredited, that's sufficient.

Q. 41. Is the systems approach to training development referred to in the new 10 CFR 55 based on the systems approach described in NUREG-1220 or on INPO standards?

A. It's both. The Commission has specifically endorsed the INPO accreditation objectives and criteria as being a systems approach to training. NUREG-1220 simply repeats the criteria that are contained in the policy statement. It then has subordinate questions that we use for information gathering to determine whether a systems approach to training is in place.

There have been questions in the past about the level of detail we are looking for in some areas. They generally relate to conditions and standards associated with learning objectives and whether you need to develop K/As or not.

We've reached agreement with INPO on that process; on how you're back-fitting existing programs that do not have K/As but have learning objectives.

In general the agreement has been that if it's a new task or new training, it should be developed with K/As. If it's an existing task or training, a panel of subject matter experts (job incumbents) could conclude that the existing training programs adequately cover the material, and therefore, it need not be back-fit.

Q. 42. Generic Letter 87-07 speaks of substituting an accredited training program for initial and requalification training programs previously approved by NRC. What if the initial training program was never formally approved by the NRC?

A. By virtue of your having been issued a license, your training program, as described in your FSAR, can be considered NRC-approved. If you subsequently submitted a change to your program for NRC approval, you can assume it was approved, unless NRC has notified you to the contrary.

Q. 43. Is this true even if it's not currently in the updated FSAR?

A. Yes. See Generic Letter 87-07 for guidance on how to revise your current training program to conform to the new regulation.

Q. 44. Programs developed using a systems approach to training are, by intent of the systematic approach, subject to revision on the basis of feedback and input to the system from legitimate sources. Once a training program is accredited and appropriate certifications are made to the NRC, do subsequent revisions to these programs need to be certified to the Commission?

A. No. For accredited programs, the particular evaluation, feedback and modification of your program is part of the process. For those programs that are not accredited or SAT-based, then, in accordance with 50.54, you will have to notify the Commission when you make changes that would decrease the scope of that program.

The program of record is the program to be implemented until such time as you change it, whether it be an SAT-based program or an NRC-approved program. We do not intend for the change process to be used after the fact, to justify what training has already been done; that is, a failure to implement your existing program -- you cannot get out of that failure-to-implement loop by going back and changing it after the fact.

Q. 45. Is it the Commission's intention that approved training programs will continue to be approved until accredited, and that the use of the simulators referenced therein will be acceptable for use until May 26, 1991?

A. Yes.

Q. 46. If a facility licensee does not include an approved systems approach to training, can operators be trained and licensed?

A. Yes. Until the program is accredited, they still have to abide by their current approved program, as upgraded by the requirements of the Regulation. We will still license those individuals.

Q. 47. When the new rule becomes effective, will all training programs previously accredited by the National Nuclear Accreditation Board be considered approved in accordance with the final policy statement on training and qualification of nuclear power plant personnel?

A. Yes, but for clarification, they won't be approved in accordance with the policy statement; they will be approved in accordance with the regulation, with the intent as expressed in the Statement of Considerations that if you have been accredited by the National Nuclear Accreditation Board, you're considered to have NRC approval.

Q. 48. Will utilities with INPO-accredited training programs be required to submit these programs to the NRC for approval?

A. No. Programs that have been accredited by INPO are assumed to have NRC approval. All that is needed is an update to your FSAR in accordance with 10 CFR 50.71(e)(4). However, programs must be available for NRC review and inspection on site.

But since it is still Commission approval that you need, there may be cases where an accredited program is not implemented appropriately and, therefore, NRC approval might be removed.

Q. 49. If the utility has an INPO-accredited operator training program, but does not yet use a simulation facility acceptable to the Commission, will an application that states that the operator training program is accredited by INPO and gives details of the simulator instructions be adequate for the license application?

A. The Form 398 will have a block on it to indicate whether or not the applicant has graduated from an INPO-accredited training program. If the answer is yes, and the facility has an approved or a certified simulation facility, then the information on education, experience, and training need not be filled out on the Form 398.

On the other hand, if the individual is a graduate of an INPO-accredited training program and the facility does not have an approved or certified simulation facility, then all that information will need to be submitted.

We would like you to begin certifying simulation facilities early on, and since nearly everyone has accredited programs with graduates, the process gets much simpler when you reach those two major milestones; otherwise, it stays difficult with you providing all of the details, which we subsequently review to verify eligibility, training and experience.

Q. 50. If the facility certifies the training program as being based on the SAT process, will NUREG-1220, "Training Review Criteria and Procedures," audit findings and comments be considered violations of 10 CFR 55?

A. If we did go to an accredited program, and we used NUREG-1220 to do a post-accreditation audit, and found problems, they would be addressed in one of two ways. Depending on their severity, they would be either left to the utility to resolve with INPO or, if they were of a more severe nature, we might ask for a performance-based inspection. Depending on the results of that inspection, there may or may not be any need for enforcement action.

Q. 51. If the SAT process is evaluated to be unsatisfactory during inspection, can operators be trained and licensed?

A. That will have to be determined on a case by case basis. If your program is deemed unsatisfactory, it would obviously depend on what the problems are.

Q. 52. When filing an application, the facility is required to provide evidence that the applicant has successfully completed the facility licensee's requirements to be licensed as an operator or senior operator.

Part of the training program is not complete prior to filing the application for the license due to the Examiner Standard (NUREG-1021) guidance to file an application 60 days prior to the examinations. This has been acceptable in the past due to the statement on the application above the facility representative signature. It states that: "The individual has or will have completed by the time of the examination all the required training." Will this continue to be an acceptable approach under the new rule?

A. No. This will not be continued. The Form 398 will be revised to remove the words "or will have."

The Commission has stated in the rulemaking that the authorized representative certifies that the individual has completed all training. It's not a future completion, and we don't want to get into situations such as "at the time I signed it I thought he was going to complete, but he didn't." You are certifying that training is complete.

We have had some experiences in the past where commitments that were made were not completed, and they resulted in significant enforcement actions associated with the failure to complete training programs, even after examining, let alone at the time of examining.

Q. 53. The Regulation requires INPO accreditation for NRC approval, while Mr. Denton's Generic letter 87-07 requires that the training program be both accredited, and based on an SAT process. Which is the governing document?"

A. The Regulation governs. The Generic Letter just restated what was in the Regulation. To receive relief under the Regulation, the program must be based upon a systems approach to training. And some of the earlier plants, which were accredited very early, were based upon the INPO guidelines, and not upon the INPO accreditation objectives and criteria as endorsed by the Commission in the Policy Statement.

In that case, what they are doing now by way of updating their program and revising it, and the fact that they now understand the process, would be the basis for them to certify to us that they have, indeed, done it on an SAT basis. They need not go back and wait until the next time through with the Accrediting Board.

Q. 54. Is a Commission-approved training program defined as an INPO-accredited training program, or are there other criteria for approval by the Commission of a utility's training program? How is a training program approved by the Commission?

A. NRC is getting out of the approval process for training programs. If there is an INPO-accredited training program, it only needs to be certified to us as indicated in Generic Letter 87-07. If a utility wishes to submit a revision to the present NRC-approved training program and asks for an NRC review and approval of that, while we are not prepared to do that now, we would probably have to deal with that using the SAT-based, performance-based approach specified in NUREG-1220.

To clarify, if a utility has a program that has been accredited by INPO, we expect that it will be the program of record. The Commission endorsed this program based upon the industry commitments to improve training, and the Commission is moving out of the role of reviewing and approving training programs.

The staff does not see that there is any need for, or value in, doing a review to come up with a lesser regulatory standard, because SAT-based programs are now the standard of record with NRC. If you are accredited, we expect you to follow the accredited program. We have revised the approach to the inspection of training programs, and we do not expect you to maintain a lesser standard for licensing with NRC than you have for training the people.

Therefore, the staff would consider a review of amendments or modifications to the cold license training program, which is SAT-based, and we would use as guidance in doing that review the kind of information that is contained in NUREG-1220, or you could propose that you have done it in accordance with the TSD process, which INPO is using. If you show that it's comparable to that, we would also consider it. That is a vehicle for getting a Commission approval of a performance-based or SAT-based program on a case-by-case basis for a cold plant. We don't mean to exclude you from being able to do performance-based training.

Q. 55. Are you still going to want Form 398 60 days prior to an examination?

A. We want to get to the point where, if you are accredited and have an approved simulation facility, all that is required is the certification. No prior review of the application will be necessary to determine eligibility, so the time between submittal of the application and the conduct of the exam could be very short.

However, until then, the Region needs time to review applications to determine whether the candidate is eligible, and to have an opportunity to interact with the training department to supplement that application in some cases. In those instances, we're still going to want to see it on the order of 60 days prior to the examination to start the review. However, we cannot take action on an application until the final completed application is filed.

Q. 56. There is one situation where you say you can administer the written exam and operating test but not issue a license until required evidence of control manipulations is supplied. It would seem a logical extension of this to allow us to put somebody up who hasn't completed all the requirements, pass him, and make the request, "Do not issue a license until he's subsequently certified." Does that make sense or is that completely prohibited?

A. The exception for manipulating the controls to which you refer is only for the individual who has not had an opportunity to perform the manipulations because the facility has been in extended shutdown. It is a condition beyond that candidate's control. However, we are moving into the role of accepting facility certification, and we want that certification to be unconditional. So the two situations are not comparable.

Q. 57. With respect to the logistics of submitting NRC Form 398 only after all program requirements have been completed, and; in addition, having to submit it 60 days prior to the examination date, would a reasonable compromise be to submit the 398s, unsigned by the facility, merely for a screening by the region, given that the the 60-day requirement is due to the time involved in such a screening? We could then follow them up once the program's been completed, maybe a day or a week before the examination, for approval by the Region.

A. Although those types of issues need to be worked out on an individual basis, it is preferable not to have licensing decisions made upon draft materials, particularly when there may be changes to them during the 60-day time frame. Advance copies (unsigned) may be submitted on a case-by-case basis if there is a concern about a particular candidate's eigibility, experience, or training.

However, what we review and base our licensing decisions on should be the application as it is submitted. The R lation does not provide for review of drafts and other documents along thos ines.

The time between submission of the document and when the candidate takes the examination appears to be the issue that's of greatest concern. There is one way you can shorten that time frame. Certify your simulation facilities early. That's one of the things that we would like people to pursue. The other thing we can do is to expedite the review, give the applications a review when they first come in, and see if we can't shorten the time needed since we can shorten the submission times between the time it has to come in and when we finalize for the exam. In other words, we will reconsider the 60-day time frame that was in the earlier version of the examiner standards in light of this requirement.

Q. 58. If a facility has an accredited initial program that's SAT based and has a plant-referenced simulator acceptable to the staff, then the time between submittal of the application and the exam can be of the order of a couple weeks?

A. Well, we're going to need to know well in advance of that how many candidates there are for licenses, but the review for eligibility, training and experience requirements is significantly reduced if all we have to do is look at two blocks on the form.

The intent of the rulemaking is to make the application process easier, and to put the burden of the determination of completion and eligibility on the facility, rather than on the staff, and accept that certification.

The issue that is significant is one of managing our own resources and knowing how many candidates are going to be put up and how many examiners we have to arrange for. Because it's a resource-intensive effort, we have to know, at about the time of the 90-day letter, how many candidates you are going to have for an exam on a given date. However, we don't need to know the specifics of who is being scheduled for the exam at that point.

Q. 59. Is there any difference between an "approved simulation facility" and a "certified simulation facility?"

A. In the context of applications, there is no difference. An acceptable simulation facility is one that is either certified or approved.

*Q. 60. What is a significant control manipulation?

A. Significant control manipulations are defined in Regulatory Guide 1.8. Examples can be found in items A-F of 55.59(c)(3) (On-the-Job Training for Requalification), although that's not an inclusive list. Basically, "significant control manipulations" involve situations that affect either power or reactivity, and that require manipulation of controls. Therefore, the plant should not be shutdown when these manipulations are performed, except for those manipulations required for fuel handling.

Q. 61. Will manipulations on a simulator be adequate?

A. Those five control manipulations have to be performed on the plant, unless the plant has not completed preoperational testing and is in its initial start-up test program.

Q. 62. Where does the requirement for five reactivity manipulations on the plant come from? Why can't they be performed on the.simulator?

A. The control manipulation on the plant has been required for some time. That's not a change. We have now put it in the Regulation to make it explicit. In fact, for a long time, if you had not performed a start up and shut down of the plant, we actually had you perform them as a part of the NRC examination. So this is not, per se, a change in practice.

Q. 63. Must the five control manipulations be different?

A. Regulatory Guide 1.8 asks for diversity. Therefore, the intent is to have different manipulations; however, this is not necessarily required. If reactivity manipulations are repeated, this fact should be indicated in the comment section on the application.

Q. 64. As far as the five significant control manipulations are concerned, what's going to constitute evidence?

A. Documentation on the OJT qualification cards consisting of a simple "performed" code next to the signature of someone on shift is sufficient evidence.

Q. 65. What constitutes an extended shutdown?

A. An extended shutdown would be anything that is long enough to prevent an applicant from completing required manipulations or training prior to taking the examination.

As an example, if the plant is in a refueling outage that lasts for a year and the candidate did not get an opportunity to perform the control manipulations because the plant never got to Mode 2 or Mode 1, we would consider giving that individual an exam, and even issuing him a license limited to shutdown conditions.

When he completes the control manipulations on a hot plant, we would then remove the condition on his license that limits it to shutdown. We do not intend to penalize individuals because of an extended outage, but we also don't intend to give waivers for what's clearly a requirement of the regulations.

Q. 66. If you have to complete the initial simulator and classroom training prior to allowing a nonlicensed operator to manipulate the controls from the control room, how can a person get their initial license? After the time needed for your simulator and classroom training, and for the NRC exam, there is not much time left to complete the five reactivity manipulations.

A. This applies only to a hot license. If the individual has not had the opportunity to perform control manipulations on shift because of an extended shut down, we would consider examining him. And if he passes that exam, we may issue a license which is limited to shutdown.

Q. 67. Will startup and shutdown experience gained on a certified simulation facility be considered adequate experience for operator and senior operator candidates?

A. Yes. The same answer applies to the use of an approved simulation facility. The application goes to whatever is in your NRC-approved training program, or your INPO-accredited program for startup and shutdown experience.

Q. 68. How much time can pass before the five control manipulations must be completed before the written exam and operating tests are completed?

A. Up to six years. If, for example, we had given a shutdown license to a plant experiencing an extended shutdown, and we had given a license to a candidate who was constrained to shutdown mode, he could actually serve out the term of that license for a period of six years.

Q. 69. Does NRC intend to make start-up certifications a part of the operating test for every new licensed applicant? If so, what is the status of the present start-up certification?

A. Start-up certifications are done on an audit basis, and it is left to the chief examiner to determine which initial license candidates will be audited. Therefore, there are no changes from our past practice.

Q. 70. For NRC licensing examinations which have already been scheduled for the remainder of 1987, will relief be granted from the new requirement that all training program requirements be 100 percent completed prior to the submittal of NRC-398 and NRC-396 forms? These 1987 licensing exams were scheduled in the fall of 1986.

A. Forms 398 submitted after May 26, 1987 must comply with the new regulation.

Q. 71. What kind of "written request" is discussed in paragraph 55.31(a)(3)?

A. An authorized representative of the facility licensee is required to request that the written examination and operating test be administered to the applicant. This request may be included in the transmittal letter forwarding the applications to the NRC. In order for the NRC to approve such a request, the facility licensee must provide suitable facilities for the administration of the written examination and operating test.

Q. 72. If an approved training program based on SAT is used for initial or requalification training pursuant to 55.31(a)(4) and 55.59(c), are there any NRC imposed minimum training requirements? Of specific interest is the 3 months of on-th-job training for initial training and the annual requirements of 55.59(c)(3)(i) and (ii)?

A. There are no additional requirements provided that the response cited in Generic Letter 87-07 is filed and the facility plans to or has incorporated INPO guidelines 86-025 and 86-026. We are aware that INPO guideline 83-022 "PWR Control Room Operator, Senior Control Room Operator and Shift Supervisor Qualification" does contain the three months on shift training period.

Q. 73. Reg Guide 1.8 endorses ANSI/ANS 3.1 for ROs and SROs. In reviewing the ANSI/ANS 3.1 annual and biennial manipulation requirements, it was noted that the ANS 3.1 manipulation list does not agree with the 10CFR55 manipulation list for five manipulations. This deviation was not stated as an exception in Reg. Guide 1.8. Please clarify whether Regulatory Guide 1.8 should have taken exception to this deviation.

A. The five manipulations specified in the rule are necessary for <u>eligibility</u>, not for requalification.

Q. 74. At a minimum, five significant control manipulations must be performed which affect reactivity or power level. For a facility that has not completed pre-operational testing and the initial startup test program as described in its FSAR, the Commission may accept evidence of satisfactory performance of simulated control manipulations as part of a Commission approved training program by a trainee on a simulation facility. If the facility is in an extended shutdown, the NRC may administer the examinations, but may not issue the license until the required evidence of control manipulations is supplied.

Do we need to submit waivers since we don't have full power license yet? Does this apply only to initial license candidates, or to all license holders, e.g. renewal? Does the NRC accept in lieu of the above simulator manipulations the use of a research reactor?

A. If a plant has not completed the initial startup test program, successful completion of an approved training program on a simulation facility satisfies this requirement, and no waiver is required.

These requirements apply to initial and replacement license applicants. Requirements for renewal of licenses are covered in part 55.57. For plants that have completed their initial startup test program, applicants must complete the control manipulations on their actual plant.

*Q. 75. How will NRC evaluations of INPO-accredited programs affect NRC's willingness to allow use of a Commission approved program developed by using a systems approach to training? Notwithstanding the generality of this initial question, please address the following two specific situations within the answer.

(1) How would an "unfavorable" NRC review of an accredited program affect a facility's ability to use an approved program in lieu of paragraphs 55.59(c)(2), (3) and (4) pursuant to 55.59(c)?

(2) How will the NRC determine that a requal and/or initial program is based on a SAT during their evaluations? Of particular interest is the evaluation of element (5) under the 55.4 definition of SAT.

A. For clarification, an INPO-accredited program and an NRC-approved program are the same. (1) Unfavorable NRC review may be due to a number of conditions as outlined in the Commission Policy Statement of March 20, 1985, and continuing evaluations using NUREG-1220 or examinations administered by the region.

An unfavorable review would not have any direct effect on your program. NRC would work with INPO to resolve identified deficiencies. However, NRC has discretionary enforcement authority under the Policy Statement, and this could be imposed if continuing problems were identified as a result of performance-based inspections.

(2) The criteria used by NRC may be found in NUREG-1220.

Q. 76. Will any combination of significant control manipulations be acceptable as dictated by the facility's modes of operation during which the applicant is in training?

A. Refer to Reg Guide 1.8 Regulatory Position C.1.h for guidance on what the Commission considers to be acceptable.

The acceptability of any alternatives will have to be determined on a case-by-case basis by the facility and indicated in the comments sections of the application.

Obviously, some significant manipulations may not be possible in Mode 4 of a plant. It may be possible in Mode 5 or 6, whichever you use for refueling, in the case of a fuel-handling foreman, so it's going to have to be on a case-by-case determination.

Q. 77. In the staff's presentations under Training Program Approval, it was mentioned that in order to implement §55.31(a)(4) and §55.59(c), the next annual FSAR update could delete training program details. Please clarify what (event or achievement) is meant by "implementation" of §55.31(a)(4) and §55.59(c): what would the staff expect to see in the FSAR update different from that information which would be provided under Reg Guide 1.70 and the basis for development of the information sought (Reg Guide 1.70, Standard Review Plan, etc.). Should utilities assume that besides stating that the training program is INPO accredited the FSAR should retain revised program details in accordance with details sought under Reg Guide 1.70?

A. The staff plans to revise Section 13.2, Training of NUREG-0800 to provide guidance for information contained in revisions to the FSAR. There are no plans at this time to revise Regulatory Guide 1.70. In lieu of additional guidance at this time the staff recommends that the licensed training programs which are accredited and are based on a systems approach to training only need reference Generic Letter 87-07 and the dates the programs were accredited. Plans for certification of simulation facilities should also be included. With regard to other training programs contained in Section 13.2 of the FSAR, those training programs listed in the March 20, 1985 Commission Policy Statement on Training and Qualification of Nuclear Power Plant Personnel which are accredited need to reference the date of accreditation. For those facilities which are developing programs under the accreditation process the FSAR should identify the programs and provide the dates that SERs were or are planned to be submitted.

Medical Examination (Subpart C, Section 55.21)

Q. 78. How long before administration of a license exam must an individual have had a medical exam?

A. The form verifying the medical exam should come in at the same time the license application comes in. It will be good for six months from the date it is signed by the physician; waivers, as stated in ES-111, will apply.

Q. 79. Assume a physician may not desire to release personnel medical data due to a patient-doctor relationship. What does the utility do if the information is treated as privileged by the physician?

A. The Privacy Act Statement contained in NRC Form 396, "Certification of Medical Examination by Facility Licensee," does not allow for privileged information being withheld by the facility or the physician if it is requested by NRC. It is the utility's responsibility to ensure that the records can be made available for inspection. Utilities should ensure that the physician understands this requirement.

Q. 80. For individuals who are currently under either license conditions or letters from the regions to submit continuing medical follow-up information (e.g., quarterly blood pressure readings) for review and analysis, do these conditions continue to apply after May 26, or should the individual submit this information to the utility's physician for evaluation and analysis (without a copy to the regions)?

A. Continue to report quarterly blood pressure or other restrictions. High blood pressure or other restrictions are usually associated with some remedial programs (diet, medication, or a combination) and should result in normal or acceptable conditions. At that time the physician can request termination of these reporting requirements.

Certification (Subpart C, Section 55.23; NRC Form 396)

Q. 81. Has NRC Form 396 changed?

A. Yes. A copy of the new version has been distributed to everyone at the public meetings.

Q. 82. Must a Form 396 be submitted for every license application?

A. Yes, but the detailed medical information only has to be submitted when a conditional license is requested.

Q. 83. Under the new Rule will you receive a Form 396 only upon license renewal?

A. That is correct. We expect to receive a Form 396, "Certification of Medical Examination by Facility Licensee," at the end of the appropriate license period, when the renewal application is submitted.

Q. 84. Is the examining physician an authorized representative of the facility licensee and thus allowed to complete and sign an NRC Form 396?

A. No. The Form 396 does not have a place for the physician to sign. The physician's name and license number are required, but the authorized representative is the highest level of corporate management who signed the application. That will be the same person who signs the Form 398.

Q. 85. Can Form 396 be held by the licensees for the two-year update or do they have to be submitted to the Commission? If the latter, how often do they have to be submitted?

A. You don't have to keep the Form 396 on file, but you must keep some documentation that the medical exam was performed and that the operator meets the ANSI standard. The Form 396 is only the means by which you transmit that information to us upon renewal of a six-year license.

Q. 86. For a multiple-unit site, can the signature on the application be from the individual responsible for operations, the highest ranking individual at that site? So that you could have different signatures; i.e., Sequoyah applications would different signatures than those of Brown's Ferry?

A. Yes.

Q. 87. Will the Commission develop a protocol to ensure that detailed medical records will be forwarded to the NRC medical experts and not made available to lay persons?

A. This is an issue for which industry initiative may be appropriate, and it has been discussed by NRC, INPO and the accrediting board.

The staff needs to have assurance that the medical examination was done in accordance with the ANSI standard. The staff does not need to see the private medical record from the doctor, because it may include other medical information not related to the standard, or may get into the area of privileged information between doctor and patient.

It might be appropriate for the industry to develop an examination form which would track the standard, such that the doctor would provide a statement to the responsible officer that the examination had been completed and which would identify the areas evaluated. Such a report would be all that is necessary for the individual's file, and it would be available on site.

If, in the case of a request for a license condition based upon some medically disqualifying condition that can be accommodated through medication, therapy, or something else, the doctor would submit the examination form and any additional supporting information for the staff medical doctor to review to make a determination as to whether to issue a conditioned license.

That information would be handled in the same manner as we now handle confidential information that is covered by the Privacy Act. Once submitted to NRC, the information would be exempt from further public disclosure, and it would be the basis for our review.

We don't anticipate developing any new protocols for handling that type of information, but we recommend that you have evidence available on site showing that the medical doctors conducted the examination in accordance with the ANSI standard, or that you provide the physician a copy of the standard and let him complete whatever form you use now for that type of examination. It's only a suggestion. The actual requirement is that the examination be conducted in accordance with the standard.

Incapacitation Because of Disability or Illness (Subpart C, Section 55.25)

*Q. 88. Must the felony blocks on Form 396 be completed in order for the form to be considered complete and to be accepted by the NRC?

A. The form has been revised to delete the felony blocks. A certification is now required that the individual meets the safeguards requirements of the facility.

Q. 89. Will a standardized form be provided by the Commission for notification of disability or illness?

A. The intent is that licensees keep the records. We don't need to be involved when someone breaks an arm or may be out for an extended illness. If it's a temporary condition, no notification is required.

We ask the question, "can the operator perform licensed duties?" If the individual is going on shift, and there is any question in your mind, we would say submit a revised Form 396 to describe the condition/remedy. We may tell you it's not necessary to make a ruling on it. But you can have a problem if you don't notify us and some individual has a problem in performing licensed duties. If a person is to resume duties after a disabling condition, then we would need to be notified with a Form 396.

Q. 90. What is the relationship between the facility licensee and the individual with regard to responsibility for notification on medical issues? The Regulations indicate that we have a 30-day notification period upon learning the diagnosis. The question really is, what's the mechanism for the facility to become aware of the diagnosis; and what responsibility does the individual licensee have to make that notification to the facility? There's the potential to get into a problem if we don't learn of a licensee's medical condition.

A. It is the operator's responsibility not to operate that plant in a disabled condition. The Regulation says that the facility licensee shall notify the Commission, but we believe that, logically, the operator should have enough responsibility to tell you there's a problem. Facility procedures should be set up to ensure that that occurs.

There is nothing in the Regulation that obligates the operator, or the senior operator, to let the facility know. But there is an obligation for you, on the biennial medical examination, to identify and report disabling medical conditions.

Q. 91. If the individual has a medical problem during the period of the license, for instance a broken arm, does this need to be reported to NRC if the operator is not carrying on licensed duties? For example, if he is training individuals in a classroom, do we still have to report it, or only if he's carrying on licensed duties per the Tech Specs?

A. It's when that person serves on shift that we have to know about a disability. Usually, if he has a temporary disability that would preclude him from performing regular duties, he's not to perform those duties with that temporary disability. We need not know if it's temporary. When you return him to shift duties, if he has been absent for a period of time, you control that process with the 40-hour parallel shift duties and maintain the certification on file. It's only in case of a permanent disability that we would have to be notified. In that circumstance you want to include a qualification in the license to allow the operator to perform licensed duties with the medical condition if some compensatory measure effectively offsets that condition.

Q. 92. Can an individual be returned to active licensed duties after the medical disability has been corrected if a portion of the requal program has been missed?

A. The operator must be current in the requalification program before he returns to duty, and he must receive 40 hours of parallel watch standing.

Documentation (Subpart C, Section 55.27)

Q. 93. The utilities must maintain some records in fire proof vaults. I don't feel that the physician's offices meet those requirements. Yet this is a qualification record, as defined by that ANSI Standard. Are we going to have to provide physicians some type of fire proof storage? How do we handle that aspect of this record keeping?

A. We recommended to INPO, and they are considering the development of, an examination report form which would cover the areas in the ANSI Standard and which would be submitted from the medical examiner to the facility for retention.

Q. 94. Can private physicians maintain medical records for the facility licensee, as is currently practiced?

A. You may choose to delegate that responsibility to them, but it is, indeed, your responsibility to ensure that the appropriate records are available for inspection.

Regulatory Guide 1.8 and ANSI/ANS 3.1

Q. 95. When we want to go from a non-accredited status to an accredited status, what would the step-by-step progression, and the changes in the regulatory environment be for us?

A. The date you receive accreditation from the Academy, you would send NRC a letter that says "we've been accredited on this date." You then begin that program because the previous training program is superseded. You need not tell us about it until the next FSAR update, which is required pursuant to 10 CFR 50.71(e)(4).

Simply send a letter saying that you were accredited, and the date of accreditation, and certify that your requalification program is based on a systems approach to training; this supersedes any prior commitments to NRC by way of additional training.

Q. 96. For the FSAR update following accreditation, it would not be necessary to have the extent of detail in that update, as previously was the case, is that correct?

A. That is correct. It can be blank, except for the information about the date of accreditation. It need not say anything, other than you were accredited, and the date you achieved the accreditation. All records associated with your training program, following accreditation, are available to the staff on site for review; they need not be submitted.

Q. 97. If the facility does not certify its training programs in accordance with Generic Letter 87-07, when must FSAR Chapter 13 be revised and how do I do it?

A. The Rule becomes effective on May 26th, 1987, and at that time, you must comply with the new provisions in the requalification program. So, there would need to be a change to the FSAR submitted in accordance with 10 CFR 50.54(i) and 55.59(c), to conform to the regulation, if you chose not to certify the training program.

The Commission endorsed the INPO Program for accreditation in the Policy Statement. We said we would accept a program after it was accredited and certified to be based on a systems approach to training. A utility that perceives they get some advantage by leaving an old training program on the docket because that's all NRC is going to inspect is misguided. That is not consistent with the intent of improving training in the industry. We do not require that you tell us all the details about an accredited program, but we do expect you to implement them.

We have heard rumors that some facilities intend to have one standard for NRC, and a different standard for INPO. That is not the Commission's intent in the Policy Statement and we would bring such a practice to the Commission's attention promptly. We expect you to follow the accredited program when it is accredited. Failure to implement that program will be of concern both to INPO and to NRC.

Q. 98. Will NRC be prepared to approve or disapprove FSAR Chapter 13 changes within the 60 days allowed for implementing 10 CFR 55 requirements?

A. The approval is effective automatically, if you have an accredited program and have certified that it is based on a systems approach in accordance with GL 87-07. You shouldn't expect to see any response from the Commission on changes that are implemented as a result of this rule, with the exception of any license amendments which are required because of something in your Technical Specifications. There are a number of facilities that have a more restrictive requirement in their Technical Specifications than that for which they would have to apply; amending their Technical Specifications to obtain relief is permitted under the rule. It would be an administrative change in order to conform with the Regulation. But it would not have to be acted on within 60 days and would be processed as any routine change to the Technical Specifications.

If you do not plan to certify that your program is based on a systems approach, we cannot act on it until we receive it in accordance with 10 CFR 50.54(i).

It will then be reviewed in the usual way. In this case, it would not be reasonable to expect it to be completed by May 26, 1987.

Q. 99. But in the meantime, is Revision 1 of Regulatory Guide 1.8 our commitment, as approved in our FSAR?

A. Yes. Your commitment is that which is approved in the FSAR. It is binding, as are any of the more restrictive requirements in the Rule, until you are accredited and so inform us by letter. At that point, you can make changes pursuant to 50.59 to remove things from your FSAR and your program. When you need to amend a license, you submit the application for an amendment to strike the sections in the Technical Specifications or in the license which have been superseded by accreditation.

Q. 100. Upon achieving accreditation, would we then become committed to Regulatory Guide 1.8, Revision 2?

A. No. Regulatory Guide 1.8, Rev. 2, goes into effect for all facilities, as is indicated in the implementation section of the Guide, on March 31, 1988. However, if you have an accredited program, you are no longer obligated to follow the Guide. At that point, you can put the Regulatory Guide aside, but you now must implement your commitment to the Accrediting Board. We have looked at that information, and we've concluded that INPO guidelines in this area are equivalent to the staff guidelines in Regulatory Guides.

Q. 101. This question addresses NRC approval of training programs. Do revisions to requal programs which reduce their scope require NRC review and approval per 10 CFR 50.54.i-1 if the program is INPO accredited? And can the term "reduction of scope" be clarified?

A. NRC review is not required if the program is accredited and is certified to be based upon a systems approach to training. Element 5 of the SAT includes revision of training in order to meet the needs of the job incumbents; therefore, we expect you to update your program based on this feedback.

The intent is that if you are SAT based, and are revising the program based upon an evaluation of the needs of the trainees, that the result of that evaluation is the program you are going to conduct. And you have a basis for that evaluation. Reducing the scope does not apply. The intent is to give you the flexibility to modify the program in order to provide the training that you, the facility licensee, determines appropriate for your job incumbents.

We have seen that process work through the INPO-accreditation process. We have confidence in the process. And even though we are sure that there are going to be cases where there is content left out, where we are going to have some concerns about something not having been covered, the process is there so that you can cover what's needed.

The training and the feedback process you provide will permit the training to be job-relevant. It is training which the trainees agree is important.

Probably the only exception is for the instructor who has had that training. But the old test-out exemption is gone. You can't take an exam, do well on it, and eliminate training in a systems approach. If someone misses a portion of the training program because he has been ill or been away, you may use something like a required reading program and a test to ensure that he has covered the material. But when the Rule says training on a continuing basis, it refers to whatever cycle you have designed that has been accepted by the accrediting board.

NRC has separated itself from the training review. We would prefer, after you are accredited, that you certify you have a systems approach in place to us, and eliminate the details from your FSAR. Certification is all that we need because the periodic reviews through the accreditation process are the vehicle for keeping your training programs current. We think that the separation of training from examining is the most significant part of this rule-making.

Q. 102. There are a lot of documents involved with the accreditation process, so if an IE inspector came in and said, "We think that your program is less than the scope," what is he basing that on?

A. Regional inspectors are governed by inspection module IP 41701, which requires a performance-based inspection. If you make a change to your program through the accreditation process using the mechanisms for revising and updating your program, based upon feedback and need, and that's the reason that you're revising it, we don't see that that is an issue of lessening the scope.

The lessening of a scope issue had to do with the old program when it was regulatory-based, where we required a certain number of hours in the classroom and certain types of content. The approach now is one of modeling the program based upon performance and need, and the process is one that has been endorsed by the Commission through the policy statement. To the extent that you need to change the program based upon feedback of your own performance, that's appropriate.

If you have an approved program today that calls for administering a comprehensive written exam annually and you want to change that to a comprehensive written exam every two years, the regulation is the basis for concluding that that is acceptable; that is not reducing the scope. That is simply conforming to the regulation. You can make changes to match the regulation either through the 50.59 review process or by amending your license. There are a few facilities which have commitments to operator training programs associated with a staffing requirement section in Section 6 of the Technical Specifications. If you are in that category, you can submit an amendment request to the Commission for an administrative change to your Technical Specifications to conform to the requirements of the regulation, but you may not do less if it is, in fact, a requirement in your license now. You can't do less than what's currently in the license. If it's in your approved program, you can do a 50.59 review to conform to the regulation.

Q. 103. Let's say that in my systematic approach to training, I have determined that it doesn't take three years of experience to meet the requirements. I complete the program with whatever experience we determine is appropriate, and we've got an accredited program. Do we still have to have the experience requirements in our program? Do we still have to meet them if we have an accredited program?

A. The industry, through NUMARC, has made a commitment to NRC in both training and qualifications. We did not take exception to the three-year requirement for experience. In the past we have accepted two years for reactor operators.

On the effective date of Regulatory Guide 1.8, March 31, 1988, we would expect people to meet ANS 3.1 unless they have already committed to that.

Within the accreditation process, there is a hierarchy of guidelines just as within the regulations. An acceptable way of meeting the regulation, as it relates to experience requirements, is by conforming to ANS 3.1. Another way is through the accreditation process, which also has guidelines.

In the case of a review and approval by the Staff, we would look at any bases for waivers of those requirements and alternatives that are proposed. In the accreditation process, the mechanisms are already built in for you to do that yourselves on a case-by-case basis.

So accreditation criteria for entering into training as it relates to qualifications are described in the INPO training guidelines for each position. They articulate what the entry levels are for training and have in that process a mechanism for granting waivers to certain requirements.

The Commission, through this rule making, has said, "We will accept the candidate at the end of training if he is certified to have been a graduate of an accredited program." We have done that through promulgation of the policy statement on training and qualification and an endorsement of the accrediation program. That means that you control the review and waiver process, through your vehicle with INPO. Now, if you want to deviate significantly from the INPO guidelines, I would suggest that you need to contact INPO and they may need to contact NUMARC if you want to come up with a radically new interpretation.

But, in fact, if you have a basis for what you're doing which is documented, and you do that on an individual basis, we do not intend to second-guess your judgement. In fact, we would not see it on the application when you have both an accredited program and a simulation facility acceptable to the Commission for the conduct of operating tests.

That's a major change in the way we have done business in the past; it puts a lot of trust in the industry through the self-initiative of INPO and NUMARC in order to provide both training and qualifications.

Q. 104. Have the experience requirements to sit for an RO or SRO exam stated in Reg Guide 1.8 and NUREG-1021 changed?

A. Yes, in that the experience requirements are not operative if you have an accredited program and have certified your simulation facility. ES-109 will be changed under the revision to NUREG-1021 and under Regulatory Guide 1.8, which becomes effective March 31, 1988 for nonaccredited programs.

Q. 105. Will NRC change any of the eligibility requirements in the Examiner Standards for taking the SRO exam discussed as a result of implementing 10 CFR 55? This question is being asked in light of the fact that 10 CFR 55 supersedes previous regulations. Specifically, will NRC require that someone have one year of experience as an RO before entering the training program for an SRO? ANSI/ANS 3.1-1981 requires a minimum of six months.

A. Yes, there is a change to the eligibility requirements except if a facility has an accredited program and an acceptable simulation facility. In that case, the requirement goes away because it becomes part of your accredited program.

Q. 106. The way I understand the Examiner Standards presently, the experience requirement to take a reactor operator exam is two years of power plant experience, one of which is nuclear. ANSI Standard 3.1-1981, specifies three years of power plant experience, one of which is nuclear. The two remaining years should be as a nonlicensed operator, and of that, six months should be as a nonlicensed operator at the facility for which you seek the license. So, that would be, in my interpretation, a three-year requirement now, whereas in the past it was a two year. Is that correct?

A. That is correct. The standard had not been imposed across the board in 1981. There are some facilities that have committed to that standard in their application, and were reviewed against that standard. A previous version of the Examiner Standards was based upon ANSI N18.1-1971, because we had not endorsed ANSI 3.1. This rule making process endorses ANSI 3.1.-1981.

Q. 107. And the same applies for the senior operator. Examiner Standard 109 says four years, and ANSI 3.1 says three. So, you will be changing that one also?

A. The Reg Guide takes exception to the ANSI Standard. Reg Guide 1.8 cites a four-year requirement for experience for the SRO.

*Q. 108. Reg Guide 1.8 endorses certain positions through ANSI 3.1-1981 for training and qualifications. The ANSI Standard has experience requirements which are different from those in the Examiner Standards. For instance, for a reactor operator, ANSI 3.1 of 1981 requires three years power plant experience, one of which is nuclear. And I believe it says two years as a nonlicensed operator, with six months as a nonlicensed operator at the facility. Is the Reg Guide endorsing those eligibility requirements also, or just training?

A. We have not taken exception to three years of experience for reactor operator. We have endorsed the ANSI Standard with respect to three years for RO, but have taken exception by requiring the four years for SRO. That's the same as the practice has been. We recognize the difference between the Examiner Standards and the Reg Guide in this area. The Examiner Standards will be changed to coincide with the implementation date of the Reg Guide, which is March 31, 1988.

Q. 109. Are the experience requirements for operator licenses applicable also to research and training reactors?

A. The requirements for test and research reactors have not changed. Whatever has been approved in the past, in terms of eligibility requirements, continues for test and research reactors. The eligibility requirements in Regulatory Guide 1.8 refer to power reactors.

Q. 110. I have an accredited SAT-based program. The simulator should be available next year and will meet ANSI/ANS 3.5 Standards. It's my understanding that we are okay because we meet those three elements, SAT, INPO accredited, and our simulator should meet your standards. Am I correct, that in meeting those standards, I don't have to worry about the ANSI Standards requiring two years as a nonlicensed operator with six months at the plant?

A. No, that's not entirely correct. While you don't have to submit that information to NRC, the industry, through NUMARC and INPO's training guidelines and accreditation, has standards comparable to those in the ANSI standard. Therefore, we feel that the qualification requirements are still being met. The only difference is that you don't have to submit all that information to us.

We had a case recently where an individual was a graduate of an accredited program but did not meet the experience eligibility requirements. His plant experience was that of a chemist, a position not comparable either to that of a control room operator or a shift engineer. We denied the application, and it was denied on appeal. We aren't going to see that kind of information in the future, and we expect the industry to police itself with respect to ensuring that the NUMARC commitments are, indeed, met. Because we are stepping out of that area, and not requiring it to be submitted, does not mean that you can relax your standards.

Q. 111. In the example that you just gave you were apparently talking about an SRO candidate, and I was referring, primarily, to RO candidates. In the past, particularly for those who weren't committed to the 1981 version of that ANSI Standard, there was no requirement for RO candidates to have been nonlicensed operators. Now we are faced with the new requirement, and I've got a group of people who are in training now, who don't necessarily have that background.

A. There is one aspect of the accreditation process that you may be missing. And it's a part of the process that pertains to meeting NRC eligibility requirements. The accreditation process does include a mechanism for you to exempt, or waive aspects, based upon having performed an evaluation of the candidate's experience and/or testing. That is the same kind of process that we use in making a judgement, on a case-by-case basis, about eligibility, where a person didn't cross all the "t's" and dot all the" i's".

We are looking for you to use that same process. You may choose, for a documented reason, as a part of your program, to waive a portion of the requirement, based upon experience and/or testing. That is a part of the accreditation process, and we understand that, and we expect that to continue. And the only difference is, you don't have to submit it to us to request a waiver.

Q. 112. Will NRC continue to accept one year as a Navy reactor operator, engineering watch supervisor, etc., as meeting the one-year reactor operator experience requirement, if one year remains as a requirement?

A. Yes.

Q. 113. The definition for related technical training in ANSI/ANS 3.1 says, "Formal training beyond the high school level in technical subjects, associated with the position in question, such as acquired in several programs, including utilities, and others. Such training program shall be of a scheduled and planned length, and include text materials and lectures." All of our programs meet that definition of related technical training, and yet we can't count it for experience. Why not?

A. Experience is an eligibility requirement. If the person has the experience and the qualifications, then he goes into a training program. You have mechanisms, through your accreditation process, where you look at the entry level into your training program. You can count time and training prior to that program, but we have not been giving credit for experience for the training which is required and has been approved by NRC as a part of the specific program leading up to license eligibility.

Q. 114. Do radiation protection personnel now require three years experience per ANS 3.1-1981, even if Tech Specs require less experience?

A. The requirements for radiation protection personnel in Reg Guide 1.8 are the same as those included in ANSI Standard 18.1 of 1971.

Q. 115. About five years ago, we all wrote our response to the Denton letter and said that we would do specific punch list items to train our STAs. Now if we have an approved STA training program, per INPO, the old prescriptive hours that we committed to no longer apply. However, if that punch list item is in our FSAR, we need to remove it "per the INPO-accredited program." Is that correct?

A. That is correct, as it relates to licensed operator programs and other programs for which you have made training commitments which are covered by the Commission's Policy Statement on training and qualifications. And in both cases, it is simply a 50.59 type review to amend or update your FSAR to indicate the date on which you received accreditation, for instance, for the STA position. The only exception relates to the Commission Policy Statement on engineering expertise on shift or the use of the dual role SRO/STA compared with a separate STA, as indicated in Reg Guide 1.8, Regulatory Position C.1.j.

Q. 116. When an applied science degree is being considered, what constitutes an acceptable degree? How do we know what specific degree allows someone to be an instant SRO or whether he must first be an RO?

A. The staff reviews those and we use our best judgment, as do the people in the regions, in making a determination based on an application. If you feel that an application has been unfairly rejected, you can request reviews by regional and headquarter's management. If you want to bring it up through a review, we can certainly do that on a plant-specific basis.

Q. 117. Is it true that in the future it won't be a problem, because you won't check up on us? If we send an application in saying someone's an SRO, will you accept the application because you won't know what degree he has because it won't be listed?

A. It's our understanding that the determination will be made in accordance with guidelines that have been established under your INPO-accredited program.

The Commission has made a determination that we're going to trust the industry and let the industry programs be operative in the area of training and qualifications under the policy statement. We understand generically what those commitments mean, and we've reviewed them quite closely.

If we find that they're being abused, either through an inspection program or through any other vehicle, that's going to cause grave concern as to whether the industry is able to police itself and act responsibly, given what we have delegated to you through those programs.

We've been on team visits and at board meetings and we've seen utilities being put through their paces to describe what mechanisms they use to review and make determinations about the eligibility for candidates to enter into training and whether they are qualified to perform in that job position.

What we're saying is that we believe that process is the appropriate one to use. If you do that in a straightforward, rigorous manner, that's what we're looking for. We're not going to nit-pick and second-guess your judgments, provided you have an adequate basis for them and provided they are consistent with what has been approved generically through the accreditation process and the guidance that INPO has issued.

Q. 118. Are documents referred to, such as NUREG-0737, still required as references?

A. Revision 2 of Regulatory Guide 1.8 supersedes NUREG-0737 as it relates to operator licensing. However, there may be some aspects of NUREG-0737 which have been committed to in a facility training program, and the initial program may not yet have been accredited. Those commitments are still in effect. They are part of the approved program, and remain so until that program is superseded by an accredited program, and you provide the letter to the staff, as is described in Generic Letter 87-07 which forwarded the Rule.

Q. 119. It seems that Regulatory Guide 1.8 says a diploma or equivalent is required only for the shift supervisor and senior operator. ANS 3.1 requires only a high school diploma for licensed operators. Is that what you intend?

A. Yes. The intent of the exception taken in regulatory position C.1.d. was to eliminate the 30 and 60 semester hours of college-level education from the shift supervisor and SRO positions. The definition section in ANS 3.1 includes the General Education Development Test as the equivalent to a high school diploma, and it would be acceptable for all three positions.

Q. 120. 10 CFR 55 provides allowable training exceptions from this rule if a systematic approach to training is used. Reg. Guide 1.8 however, does not state that there are allowable training exceptions from following ANSI/ANS 3.1 for ROs and SROs. Please explain why exceptions were not allowed for RO and SRO training when a systematic approach is used.

A. Exemptions are allowed under Section D, Implementation, of Regulatory Guide 1.8, which states that the guidance in Section C does not apply to those training programs which have been accredited under an accreditation program which has been endorsed by the NRC.

WRITTEN EXAMINATIONS AND OPERATING TESTS

General Issues (Including Learning Objectives and Examination Question Bank)

Q. 121. Will the format of the written exams change? If so, how?

A. At the present time the format of the examinations is not expected to change, although there are numerous initiatives under way which may lead to format changes in one way or another as we refine the process.

Q. 122. The exam content states that Licensee Event Reports (LER) will be included in the exam. How is the scope of LERs determined and communicated to the individual taking the examination?

A. We expect your training program to include relevant LERs. We would sample from your learning objectives, but we would not necessarily be limited to those.

We would not take an LER from a significantly different plant and try to adapt it to your plant. But if there were LERs that reflect either training needs or operational safety, we are going to include those in the exam process. It may be in the written exam or on the operating test.

Q. 123. Will there be any effort by NRC to ensure a consistent level of detail in the facility's learning objectives?

A. Yes. We have a major effort under way to evaluate the quality of learning objectives that are submitted for an exam. This is a significant issue because we have seen a large spectrum of differences in learning objectives.

As a part of our examination development efforts, we have been reviewing the quality of the learning objectives submitted with materials for the 90-day letters. We're evaluating their quality and using that as a feedback mechanism into the evaluation process for how well accreditation is working.

Where we find that the learning objectives are not adequate, we'll use other materials. Where they are adequate, we will use them. We intend to evolve over time to the point where we can construct an NRC exam solely using the facility learning objectives.

We have also opened our examination development training program to INPO and others, providing information to them on how we construct examinations and on the training that we're providing to examiners. There are also activities underway within INPO to improve development of testing objectives.

Q. 124. How does the Commission intend to implement written examinations based upon the knowledge, skills, and abilities identified in the learning objectives derived from the systematic analysis of licensed operator duties?

A. It's our intent, as expressed in the Statement of Considerations, to reach the point where the training program's learning objectives become the major source for our examination. We want to sample according to a scheme that looks at the most important job performance, knowledge, and abilities, and we have that area documented with our K/A Catalogs. In fact, there's a supplement to the PWR Catalog being published that has the same sections as the BWR Catalog.

In addition, we asked a PWR and BWR panel of subject-matter experts to rate the testing emphasis they thought we should have. That rating forms the basis of NRC's sampling plan, so we will sample the most important job content. What we expect in terms of conditions and standards of performance will be driven by the learning objectives, and that will form the basis of our testing objectives. The only slight difference between testing and learning objectives has to do with the context in which you judge performance, because one is a time-limited testing situation, and the other might allow a longer training or job performance period.

We don't want our exam to be devoid of contact with your training program. The purpose is to get to the same spot. Of course we reserve the right to look at LERs and other events, and to further investigate other questions, with your assistance, manuals, license amendments, or other materials, because even if we judge our question in terms of your learning objectives, the material to develop the question and the answer has to come from something other than the learning objective.

Q. 125. What, if any, utility actions will NRC require to incorporate utility learning objectives into the NRC testing objectives?

A. The better your materials are, the more closely they are keyed to our K/A catalog, the easier it is for us to use them. But we're not going to require any actions. In the 90-day letters that go out prior to the administration of an exam, we're requesting that learning objectives be submitted, and we're evaluating them, and if they are appropriate for use in our exam, both the written and the operating test, we would employ them to the extent that they are consistent with our sampling plan in the Examiner's Handbook and the K/A Catalogs.

We've been training examiners to look at learning objectives and to use them for testing objectives. To the extent that you can provide material to the examiner where the learning objectives provide a standard of performance and you key the training materials in which the material to develop that question is available, and if you know a K/A in the catalog with an importance rating that's above 2.5, you will have provided the basis for developing a good question and a good examination.

Our experience is that the learning objectives may have conditions and standards of performance, but the supporting training materials are not there to develop the appropriate questions or they're cast in such a way that it's unclear whether they are related to a K/A associated with job content having a relatively high safety significance.

We also did not want to see the "enabling objectives," because these are for training purposes and are not grounded in job performance. We want objectives that are "terminal," and have to do with job performance; and the better the material is that you supply, the closer our exam will mirror those objectives.

We've spent a great deal of time looking at how one judges a question based on the learning objective so that the question will elicit the kind of performance or knowledge or response that lets us infer that the person has mastered that particular aspect of the job.

There's a related issue. We issued Generic Letter 87-01, which announced the availability of the NRC Examination Question Bank, and indicated the mechanisms by which utilities could request the information on what's contained in the bank on their facility or similar facilities. It also indicated a mechanism for you to update questions on the bank, either where we have inaccurate references or the design of the facility has changed.

We purged the bank of questions that were more than two years old because some of the older questions did not meet today's quality standards. In some cases, we have only four or five examinations on the bank for a particular utility. We want to improve that and are interested in your comments and/or questions for the bank. We'll also provide the bank to you for creating your own questions. To the extent you provide us information that's in a format which is compatible with loading into the bank, we can do that directly, either through hard copy or electronically. But for security reasons, we can't give you direct access to the bank. We have discussed with INPO the need for an industry initiative to validate a set of plant-specific questions that could be a source for NRC exams.

Q. 126. If the utility has established some internal guidelines of what they expect of the individual, will you accept those guidelines for the purposes of written examinations?

A. Yes. We would have an issue that we would discuss with the utility, that we would want to revise the guidelines if they did not conform to our testing blueprint based on the job-related knowledge and ability statements with high safety significance.

Q. 127. Can we submit that in advance of the written examination, and then come to an agreement somewhere up front?

A. It can be part of the materials that you submit in accordance with the 90-day letter, and we would consider that in developing the exam.

Q. 128. You mentioned a training program for the examiners on writing the learning objectives. How is that program being instructed; who's teaching that?

A. We started several years back working on writing multiple choice questions, and have been doing one-week training sessions in all the regions, twice at headquarters, and once each for contractors. During the one-week training session, examiners converted learning objectives into testing objectives and practiced writing testing objectives.

We've shared that information with INPO and have had INPO staff participate and take the materials back with them, so the information that we're using to develop examinations is available to you through INPO, or even through the staff if you want to request it.

Written Examinations and Operating Tests (Statement of Considerations)

Q. 129. In the Statement of Considerations, under Part D, Written Examinations and Operating Tests, it says: "Learning objectives derived from job-task analyses should form the basis for licensing written examinations and operating tests at a facility. Ultimately, the NRC testing objectives will reflect facility licensee-developed learning objectives. In the interim, while programs are being developed and reviewed for accreditation, the NRC has activities underway to improve the content validity of NRC examinations and operating tests." Will NRC commit to solely using the learning objectives for plants that have accredited operator programs?

A. No. The rule states that the learning objectives will be used in part, but that other things, like LERs, etc., will also be used.

Q. 130. Why are written examinations only taken in part from learning objectives?

A. The hope is, eventually, to take the entire written examination from learning objectives. However, at this time, there are many places where the learning objectives are somewhat incomplete or inadequate. So, we utilize LERs and other training materials, such as lesson plans, system descriptions, and procedures, to supplement the learning objectives.

Q. 131. When will NRC activities underway to improve the content validity of NRC examinations and operating tests be complete?

A. We view this an an ongoing activity. We have a number of initiatives scheduled for completion in this fiscal year, including the revised Handbook (NUREG-1121), passing-point workshop, and the supplement to the PWR K/A Catalog (NUREG-1122) to conform to the BWR K/A Catalog (NUREG-1123).

By the end of this fiscal year, a number of milestones toward meeting that objective will have been met. But this is a continuing process, as we work toward a common understanding of what's necessary for assessing job performance. With the advent of the K/A Catalogs, we've made significant improvements in basing test content on the operator's performance-based job requirements: that is the essence of content validity. We have used a systematic process involving subject matter experts. We have supplemented the PWR Catalog, which now has a theory and component section similar to that in the BWR Catalog.

In addition to that, we have been looking at alternate ways to sample the content of the NRC written exam. At present ES-202 and 402 weight all four sections of the exam equally. We've looked at a way of sampling according to the sections in the Catalog. The differences would reflect differences between RO and SRO positions. We'll sample more heavily in plant systems for ROs and more heavily in emergencies that have fewer normal and more integrated plant responses for SROs. The final decision on that will be made based on the recommendation of a Panel made up cf industry representatives and NRC contractor personnel that will meet May 18th through the 22nd.

We will consider the panel's recommendations to us before we make any recommendations to change the format of the NRC exam. That sampling plan from our Catalog and your input on your learning objectives should, in fact, be the essence of a content-valid exam.

Q. 132. I've heard different people say that all NRC exams are now based on the K/A Catalog. Are all NRC Examiner-Contractors held to that Catalog as a standard?

A. Examinations prepared by Contract Examiners are reviewed in the Region so the standard for the regional Examiner and the Contract Examiner is not different. Like regional examiners, the Contractor Examiners are required to write an examination which meets the requirements of the Examiners' standards, which now reference the Catalog and will, in a future revision, also reference the handbook.

We are sensitive to feedback from the exam process. We look at the facility comments generated during the exam review process. We intend to be very responsive to comments that point out any differences between a contract exam and one administered by NRC examiners.

*Q. 133. Is the new rule going to change the format of the exams (e.g., largely essay-type)?

A. The new rule does not alter the format of the exam. The current Examiner Standard, ES-202, permits a maximum of 25 percent objective-type questions (e.g. multiple-choice, true-false), a maximum of 25 percent longer essay-type questions, and a minimum of 50 percent short-answer questions in Sections 2-4 and 6-8 of the exam. Exam Sections 1 and 5 (reactor theory and thermodynamics) can consist of a greater portion of objective-type questions.

We're working on the issue of a generic exam--a prototype, objective exam for theory and component operation.

Q. 134. Have you pilot-tested Form 157 or have you had any practice with it?

A. No. The new Form 157 will be available after May 26. We'll be revising it as necessary, based on our feedback from field use.

Written Examination: Operators (Subpart E, Section 55.41)

Q. 135. The items in 55.41(b)(10) and (13) have previously been for senior operator knowledge. What level of knowledge is expected for the reactor operator?

A. Part of 55.41(b)(10), has been for operator knowledge in that it concerns normal, abnormal, and emergency operating procedures for the facility. For the administrative part, the reactor operator would be tested for the depth of knowledge required for his job position in the administrative area because operators get involved with administration at times. And Part (13), "Procedures and Equipment Available for Handling and Disposal of Radioactive Materials and Effluents," would also be geared to RO job requirements at your site.

Q. 136. Part 55.41, "Content," does not specifically address that licensed operator candidates need to know Technical Specifications, yet the examiner standard, Section ES-202, discusses the need to know Technical Specifications. What is the reason for this difference? Is ES-202 correct in its application for Technical Specification knowledge?

A. Section 55.41(5) addresses the Technical Specifications. We expect operators to use Technical Specifications as appropriate to their job. Reactor operators, as in 55.41(5), are expected to know limiting conditions, particularly
those things they should recognize and communicate to the SRO in a timely manner.

The same thing goes for the SRO. We don't expect SROs to be engineers. So
required job performance in your systematic evaluation, plus our K/A Catalog,
should give you an idea of the level of specificity. We intend to revise the
examiner standards to give our examiners better guidance. Right now, it's not
as clear as it could be, but required job performance is the key, and if, for
some reason, you feel you use Technical Specifications differently than we can
interpret, you should call that to the Region's attention and discuss it long
before the exam occurs.

There is clearly a difference between our expectations for ROs and SROs by virtue
of SROs directing the activities of others. The SRO must know all aspects of
license conditions. He approves work, work orders, and other things which
require a knowledge of Technical Specifications beyond the material covered in
the operator's written exam.

We don't expect the SRO to be able to develop a basis for a requirement on his
own. We expect him to understand what the requirement is, and be able to carry
it out. That's the difference that we tried to articulate in these two sections.
An RO doesn't have to know about approving surveillances, yet surveillances are
covered in the Technical Specifications. An RO does need to know about limits
on operation of the plant, as they relate to the list of items under the written
examination.

Q. 137. For facilities that have an approved INPO-accredited performance-based
training program, what percentage of the written and/or oral exam questions
administered by NRC will come from the facilities' objective-based exam bank,
or at least from the facilities' training objectives? From Attachment A (to
Generic Letter 87-07) it appears that all the exam questions for accredited
facilities will come from the facilities' training objectives.

A. Eventually, we'd like to use the facilities' learning objectives. But,
it's our experience that we have varying degrees of polished objectives. We've
also found that even when there is a good objective, where the conditions of
performance and the standards of performance are explicit, and the learning and
the mastery is all tied to job performance, the supporting materials submitted
with the 90-day letter do not allow examiners to develop the kind of question
that will elicit the appropriate material to decide whether the candidate has
mastered that objective. So while the objective may be good, the supporting
material isn't sufficient to develop the right kind of question.

We're working on this. And we key the content of our exam right now to the K/A
Catalog. We do not sample those items that have been found to have a low importance to safety. But we have to rely on your analysis to help determine
what's important on a plant-specific basis.

And this is where there's some breakdown at the moment. The better the learning
objectives in terms of their explicit statement of conditions and standards, the
better the supporting material, and the better it's tied to our Catalog, the
better the whole system works.

But don't read into that that we would be limited to those objectives. We would sample, we would tie it to those objectives; but if there isn't an objective in the safety-related system that we think is important, we may create our own test objective and cover it on the exam.

We're going to try very hard to ensure that it is safety related, it is operationally oriented, and it is performance based. Obviously we would want to have good justification for asking that kind of a question.

Many of you have used the INPO Job Analysis in your own plant-specific analysis. And part of the reason that we tied our analysis at the generic level to the INPO Analysis was so that the system names and numbers, and the resulting material, would be easily keyed at the plant-specific level to the K/A Catalog.

Q. 138. What will the Commission do to ensure that operator exams are both valid and reliable from a psychometric perspective?

A. Many things. One: We're working on a sampling plan developed by subject-matter experts that will better reflect the job of the operator as opposed to the four evenly weighted written exam sections currently in the Examiner's Standard.

Two: We'll be sampling only those items that received a high importance rating to ensure the exam's content validity.

Three: We have a meeting on May 18th in which we're bringing together another panel of experts first to evaluate our proposed sampling plan and document the basis for our passing point.

Four: We are conducting continuous, extensive training with our examiners on writing and reviewing questions, and we are evaluating feedback from the industry on the quality of our examinations.

Finally, we are continuing to make improvements to the exam question bank, which will include a validation process using statistical techniques to eliminate poor questions.

Q. 139. The statement of considerations makes the following statement: "Ultimately, the NRC test objectives will reflect facility licensee developed learning objectives..." With an INPO-accredited program already developed from a job-task analysis (JTA), does our training standard (site-specific learning objectives) supersede the NRC Knowledge and Abilities Catalog? How do we get regional concurrence that they will test to our training standard?

A. It's our intent to use site-specific learning objectives as the basis for our testing objectives. However, if we detect errors of commission or omission in the site-specific reference material (including learning objectives), we obviously will not shape our exam content to those errors.

Q. 140. Criminal violation only covers persons who willfully violate the Atomic Energy Act or NRC's regulations, and does not apply to situations such as discussions after an examination is administered or when a previously administered examination is used as a practice exam. What is the attitude of the NRC concerning distribution of the facility's examination bank to the examinees?

A. NRC has no specific policy concerning the distribution of the facility's own examination bank to their examinees. While some portion of training may be given using previously administered examinations as references, this should not be interpreted as NRC endorsement or acceptance of such a practice exclusively.

Written Examination: Senior Operators (Subpart E, Section 55.43)

Q. 141. The Commission Policy Statement on Technical Specifications and improvements may result in a substantial increase in scope and documentation. Will any effort be made to limit the knowledge required of senior operators to those elements of the Technical Specification basis that are essential for safe operation?

A. Yes. We have an ongoing program looking at the issue of what needs to be examined at the SRO level, as opposed to the RO level. And we are working with the people developing these new Tech Specs and intend to make sure that we are producing a performance-based exam.

That's not to say that there won't be some additional exam material that comes from the new Technical Specifications. But, again, it will be performance based, job relevant, and safety-significant material, and we will provide ample guidance to the examiners, in the examiner standard, as this program develops.

Q. 142. When we were developing standardized Techical Specifications, the requirement was that an operator know from memory, and be able to apply "one-hour-or-less," action statements from the Tech Specs. Since standard Tech Specs have come in, there are now well over a hundred one-hour or less action statements from Technical Specifications. Is the policy, or the guidance from the Commission still the same, to commit those to memory, recognizing that the utilities do not rely on nor require the operators to act from memory in that situation?

A. We are dealing with performance-based knowledge that an operator needs to know. Specifically, if the information is appropriate to the job, if it is in the K/A Catalogs with a high importance rating, he should know that information. If there is not a specific knowledge or ability associated with it or those that are have a low importance rating, then normally it would not need to be examined. However, there may be procedual steps or other indications that cause him to look into the Technical Specifications. The method you use procedurally in the plant for these indications, through performance-based testing under certain circumstances, such as procedural or event-related problems, would be the method that would be followed by NRC. We don't have any blanket rules that require memorization of everything in Technical Specifications that has to be done in less than an hour. That is not our policy. Ensuring that our examinations are operationally oriented and job related is our policy.

Q. 143. Senior operators are required to know the facility operating limitations in the Technical Specifications and their bases. If and when the Westinghouse Owner's Group completes development work and gains acceptance for the Technical Specification MERITS program, this will vastly increase the bases section of the Technical Specification. Will the NRC position change regarding the requirements to know the Technical Specification bases if this new program is implemented?

A. No. As we implement improvements to Tech Specs, we hope to reduce their size substantially as a result of this program and to do a better job of describing the why's associated with the limits and the underlying assumptions that relate to them.

We hope that in the long run we will better define the knowledge that a senior operator should have related to the Technical Specifications and their bases. We don't expect that the volume of the bases to increase to several three-inch notebooks. It should be significantly reduced compared with what's contained in the FSAR. It's going to require a topical report submission and an approval by the staff before it can be implemented on a plant-specific basis. We will be looking at generic bases, and there will be an opportunity for utilities to comment.

Our intent is not to add superfluous information; it needs to be related to the job.

Q. 144. Section 55.43(b)(3) refers to the facility licensee procedures required to obtain authority for design and operating changes in the facility. What is the intent of this? Should the SRO understand the process the licensee goes about in obtaining a design change?

A. There may be administrative procedures which would allow, for example, two SRO's on a back shift to change a procedure, as long as they don't change the intent of the procedure. Or, there may be other aspects of the 50.59 review process which an SRO is held accountable for knowing. He may be the shift supervisor, on shift at the time, responsible for those activities. And it's that type of administrative procedure we are addressing.

Q. 145. Therefore, are we talking about temporary alterations, not design changes, or permanent license changes?

A. He needs to understand what he's approving when he approves the work to be done in the plant. We're looking principally at those things which he can approve; deviatation from a procedure, an alternative approach, etc. The 50.59 type process, how those changes are controlled, and what it means when he signs off to approve a work package, is likewise important. This process may change the design of the facility, or change the way the facility is operated by a procedure. For clarification, there has been no change in this area from the previous Part 55.

Q. 146. What maintenance activities are included in 55.43(b)(4)?

A. Section (b)(4) talks about radiation hazards that may arise during normal and abnormal situations, including maintenance activities, and various contamination conditions. A common item may, for example, be a radiation work permit (RWP). He may be responsible for signing off, either in concurrence or approval, depending on the facility, on the RWP, so he would be expected to have site-specific knowledge in that area.

Q. 147. Part 55.43 does not specifically address emergency plan implementation. This is addressed in Part 55.45. Will the senior operators continue to be asked to classify events, given a specific scenario, into four categories (UE, Alert, SAE, GE) from memory on the written examinations?

A. Item 5 in Section 55.43(b), stipulates that SROs must be able to address the "assessment of facility conditions and selection of appropriate procedures during normal, abnormal, and emergency conditions." However, neither ROs nor SROs are required to classify events from memory.

Operating Tests: Content (Subpart E, Section 55.45(a))

Q. 148. Is there a definition of plant equipment that could affect the release of radioactive materials to the environment, per 10 CFR 55.45(a)(8)?

A. There are many systems and many controls that an individual can operate that could cause a release; operators are required to understand these systems and controls, which are the responsibility of licensed personnel.

Q. 149. Does 10 CFR 55.45(a)(10) imply that operators must perform exposure shielding calculations?

A. That depends on how these calculations are made at your facility. If you have an on-shift health physicist or, in an emergency, an STA, then we would not ask operators to do the shielding calculations. But if the SRO typically checks such calculations, then we may ask the SRO to check one.

Q. 150. Items 12 and 13 of Section 55.45(a), were reworded to include the phrase "as appropriate." What is the significance of this phrase for the Commission to classify this change as "major" in the final Regulation?

A. The comparison that we're making in the Statement of Considerations, Section IID(2), is between the proposed rule published in November 1984 and the final rule. Items 12 and 13 were significantly rewritten between the proposed and the final rule. To clarify, we have made sure that you're held accountable for performing as appropriate to the assigned position. So ROs are not expected to pass a test at the SRO level.

Q. 151. How will you evaluate Item 13, "Teamwork," in the operating test? I'm talking about the operating test itself, when you have to evaluate one single candidate on how he reacts and interreacts with the team?

A. You could put some licensed operators on the team with him, and we would just put an examiner with the individual taking the exam. You could have one of your instructors standing there, as we have done in the past.

Q. 152. How would you evaluate this if we didn't have a simulator?

A. It is the responsibility of the examiner to structure his operating test scenarios for the Integrated Plant Operations portion of the test that would create situations that would challenge the candidate in competencies G (communication/crew interface) and H (responsibilities/supervision). Obviously this would require a discussion format since the operating test without a simulation facility is a one-on-one test. For example, a scenario could have an SRO candidate evacuate the control room. He would then be expected to shut down the reactor from the local shutdown panel. He should be able to talk through how he would utilize his resources, including direction, communication, and report backs. Questions would be phrased as follows: What would you direct the BOP to do? What reports do you expect to receive from the RO upon reactor trip? How would you verify a questionable report from the BOP/RO? How do you evaluate the licensed operator's use of nonlicensed operators during local operation of an auxiliary feed pump?

Q. 153. Part 55.45(a) contains a new evaluation criterion which requires an applicant to demonstrate the ability to function within the control room team as appropriate to the assigned position and in such a way that the facility licensee's procedures are adhered to and so that the limitations in its license and amendments are not violated. Is this criterion intended to be evaluated using the manipulation criteria addressed on the operating examination report contained in ES-302 which requires that an applicant: (1) follow procedures, (2) observe and check instrumentation, (3) exhibit dexterity and a feel for console operations? Or, will this evaluation be addressed in a future revision of ES-302?

A. This criterion is addressed in the operating test using the existing ES-302 with the new Form 157. Specifically, the form identifies, in competencies G and H (both with and without a simulator), the evaluation of communication/crew interaction and responsibility/supervision.

Waiver of Examination and Test Requirements (Subpart E, Section 55.47)

Q. 154. In 10 CFR 55.47, what is a comparable facility?

A. This question addresses the waiver of written examination and operating test requirements. We would look at each waiver on a case-by-case basis, and make a determination as to whether or not the facility was, for licensing purposes, "close enough."

SIMULATION FACILITIES

Q. 155. Will NRC continue to examine operators on plant-referenced simulation facilities following the effective rule date, but prior to the submittal of the simulator certification?

A. Yes. If we're giving exams on your simulator now, we will continue to do so.

Q. 156. Will NRC examine operators on nonplant-referenced simulators for those utilities that have accredited training programs and use a nonplant-referenced simulators between the date that the new rule becomes effective and simulation facility approval by NRC is achieved?

A. We anticipate no change from what we're doing today.

Q. 157. Our facility will not have a plant-referenced simulator available for training until the first quarter of 1990. It is assumed that operating tests will consist entirely of plant walk-throughs until such time as a plant referenced simulator is certified. Is this a correct assumption?

A. Yes, but in the event the utility were to start using that simulator to evaluate candidates prior to the time at which they chose to certify it, we'd have no problem with the examiners using it to conduct operating tests.

Q. 158. Are the provisions of 55.45(b)(2)(i), and 55.45(b)(2)(iii) mutually exclusive? In other words, if the utility plans to meet the provisions of 55.45(b)(2)(iii) by purchasing a simulator during the 46-month period, does the utility need to submit a plan per (b)(2)(i) for the simulator to be used until the plant-referenced simulator is certified?

A. No. If you intend to certify a simulation facility on Form 474, you have 46 months from the effective date of the Rule to do that, and you do not need to submit to us a plan, or an application, prior to that time. If, however, we do not see any evidence that there are plans in the works for a certified simulation facility, and if we have not seen a plan from you for a noncertified simulation facility, we'll probably get in touch with you to find out what your intentions are.

Q. 159. We currently have a site-specific simulator, and it has been used to administer the simulator portion of the operating tests. Do we have 46 months from the effective date of the rule to submit Form NRC-474, "Simulation Facility Certification"? Will the simulator tests continue to be administered on our noncertified simulator before we submit the Form 474? Under what conditions would NRC refuse to administer operating tests on the simulator?

A. Yes, you have 46 months to submit Form 474, and, yes, the simulator will continue to be used for the conduct of exams until you submit that Form 474 or until you reach the four-year deadline. NRC would refuse to administer operating tests if the simulation facility has not been certified by the deadline or if, after it has been certified, an inspection proves that it is unable to meet the requirements of conducting an operating exam. And, if certification is pulled, then it needs to be recertified.

Q. 160. For simulators that are not plant specific, when the regulation goes into effect in May, are you going to start giving nonplant-specific simulator exams?

A. No. We do not intend to administer such exams. Those few plants without plant-referenced simulators will be handled on a case-by-case basis.

For clarification, once a utility begins to use a simulator to evaluate its operators, we would retain the option to use it to conduct our operating tests, even though it may not yet be approved or certified.

It's our intent to continue with business as usual from the effective date of the regulation until such time as you either have an approved simulation facility, or you have certified a simulation facility. Or, of course, the four-year deadline arrives.

In other words, if we presently conduct operating exams in a walk-through because you do not have a plant-referenced simulator or you do not have an acceptable simulation facility, we would continue to conduct exams on a walk-through basis. But if you do obtain a simulation facility between now and the date that you chose to certify it, if you find the simulation facility is acceptable for your use in evaluating operators then we will find that same simulation facility acceptable for our use in evaluating operators, even prior to the time it is certified or approved.

One other clarification. It does not matter who owns a simulation facility, or where it is located--the key is the plant to which it is referenced. And the facility licensee is the one who must certify that simulation facility for use regardless of whether that facility licensee is the owner of that simulation facility or not.

Q. 161. Several simulators are still in the manufacturing pipeline, to be delivered in the next two years, while a few are still just beginning their procurement activities. Is this plan required within one year regardless of whether the utility is in the process of procuring a simulator?

A. The plan referred to is required only for those utilities which are not planning to submit a certification on Form 474. If you are procuring a certified simulation facility, there is no plan required and there is no application for approval required, regardless of where in the pipeline your procurement is.

If you are not procuring a simulation facility that is to be certified on Form 474, then there is a plan required and there is an application for approval. Then the answer is yes, we would expect that plan to be submitted to us within one year of the effective date of the regulation, regardless of where you may be in the procurement cycle.

Q. 162. Consider the utility undergoing the simulator procurement process right now. There is certainly the realistic possibility that that simulator will not be delivered and declared ready for training until sometime in 1990. At that time it will be approximately two and a half years since design data freeze.

In that period it's reasonable to expect that the utility would not be able to meet the requirement of ANSI/ANS 3.5, 1985 that the plant reference simulator be current within 12 or 18 months of the reference plant, to which you are attesting when you sign the material-false-statement on Form 474. Does this mean that this utility would have to submit a plan for an alternative within 12 months of May 1987?

A. We would still expect a certification from those utilities on Form 474, rather than the application for approval. If necessary, you would take exception to meeting some of the requirements of ANS 3.5. These would have to be identified and described, along with a description of when and how they would be resolved. There is a provision on Form 474 for this information to be supplied.

Q. 163. In other words, they would not be held to the statement that says they are or are not in compliance with ANSI 3.5?

A. That is correct. The facility licensee would address them as exceptions to ANS 3.5.

Q. 164. I didn't see on the proposed Form 474 an area that addresses exceptions.

A. There is such a block on the form. It might not have been on an early version of the form; but on the final version you will see an area near the top which indicates exceptions taken to the standard.

That's not an unusual circumstance just for those who are buying new simulation facilities. Because design modifications are made in the plant, you may at the time of certification have modifications made in the plant that you have not yet put into the simulation facility.

The process provides for reference plant data and design data for the simulation facility, and there can be as much as two years' difference between the time these two conform with one another. If you're not in conformance at the time you certify, if there's some exception, identify that in the exceptions sections and indicate on what schedule you're going to correct it.

If we disagree with the exceptions, we'll visit you. But if you've done a reasonable job of identifying them and we still conclude that we can conduct an operating test, we'll accept that certification.

Q. 165. In Section 55.45, implementation schedule and simulation facility certifications, what is the relationship of the two timetables provided in (b)(2)(iii), which is 46 months, and (b)(3)(iii), which is 60 days?

A. There is no relationship between them. The 46-month requirement in (b)(2)(iii) refers to facility licensees, which includes anyone who has a docketed application. The 60-day requirement in (b)(3)(iii) refers only to what we call facility applicants, which includes only those without docketed applications. So you can ignore that 60-day requirement.

Q. 166. Do we have a requirement to certify a simulation facility to NRC prior to its being used for an operating exam?

A. No. You have a requirement to certify a simulation facility to NRC no later than four years after the effective date of the regulation. Prior to that four-year deadline, it can still be used for conducting operating exams whether it is certified or not.

Q. 167. Due to the extensive use of the simulator for training, there may be times that meeting the 25 percent performance testing requirements within 12 months of the last set of tests is not possible. What is the allowable time table tolerance regarding this situation? For example, is it permissible to perform 50 percent testing in one year and no testing in the next year, as long as 100 percent testing occurs every four years?

A. The regulation provides, in 55.45(b)(4)(vii) and (b)(5)(vi), that performance testing be done at the rate of approximately 25 percent per year on a continuing four-year cycle. The goal is to ensure the ongoing testing and upgrading of the simulation facility, and to assure that it is maintained on a consistent basis with the status of the plant. You must present to us, on Form 474, your performance testing schedule. To the extent that it must deviate from 25 percent per year, if it must deviate, you need to let us know just what those deviations are and we will have to evaluate it case-by-case. It's safe to say that performing 50 percent of the tests in one year, and no tests in the next year would not meet the intent of the regulation.

For clarification, we really don't want to see the minutiae of your performance testing schedule, which tests are to be run on which days of which months. We're looking at an annualized 25 percent per year basis, and that's the block of time in which we would like to see your performance testing scheduled. Any changes that may need to be made to that schedule, you need to tell us about, based on that annual block.

Q. 168. What is the required retention period for simulation facility test procedures, modification documentation, and discrepancy reports?

A. Four years is the record retention period. But at any given time, you may have accumulated and held on to more than four years' worth of data, because you are performing your performance tests at the rate of 25 percent per year. So if you certify, hypothetically, at time zero and then you submit your first four-year report on the four-year anniversary of that initial certification, at that time in year four you can discard the results of the performance testing that you had for the initial certification. Then when you submit your next four-year report at year eight, you can discard all the performance testing documentation that you used to submit the first four-year report.

So it's a four-year period, but as you accumulate the tests at 25 percent per year, you're going to be retaining these test results until the time comes at your next report to discard it.

Q. 169. Regarding decertification of a plant-referenced simulator: What process will be used to decertify a simulator? Will an NRC examiner be able to decertify a simulator based on his observations of simulator performance during an NRC exam?

A. No. An examiner will not be able to decertify a simulation facility based upon his observations. He will report those observations to NRC, and the staff may use that information to perform an audit or an inspection. "Decertification" can occur only as a result of an inspection which finds that the simulation facility is incapable of being used for the conduct of an operating test.

Q. 170. Section 55.45 requires that within one year after its effective date, each facility licensee proposing to use a simulation facility must submit a plan detailing how and when their simulation facility will be developed and submitted for approval. Must a utility that operates dual units at the same plant and that currently obtains a multi-unit operator license from the NRC submit this plan for the unit not being replicated?

A. The key issue is the similarity of the two units. The availability of current multi-unit licenses would lead us to believe that you do not need to submit an application for approval for the simulation facility for those units. We in all likelihood will accept certifications on Form 474 with the exceptions noted for each unit.

Q. 171. If a utility with multiple units believes that the units are too dissimilar to support Form 474 certification, what format requirements, if any, does the Commission wish to see in the application for approval?

A. Here is an example of what we'd expect. Let's assume that you have a dual unit control room and that the control rooms are identical with the exception that they're mirror images of each other. Your physical fidelity comparison in accordance with the standard would identify as an exception the mirror-image layout.

One Form 474 would indicate that the mirror-image issue was a difference, but you conclude that's acceptable for an operating test. And you'd reference the certification form for the other unit; that is, you'd identify all the other exceptions that you may have. So one is tied to the other. That way we get a form that says it's certified for each plant to which it's referenced.

Where you have a simulator now which is on site and which replicates two units, we would expect you to use the certification process.

Q. 172. Several utilities are not planning to obtain plant-referenced simulators. They prefer to use other simulation devices. Assume that a facility licensee has constructed and is operating a plant-referenced simulator that meets the provision of Regulatory Guide 1.149 and ANSI 3.5 and has been certified to the NRC for use for operators and senior operators who operate the reference plant or are candidates for a license at that plant. A second utility wishes to use the simulator as their simulation device rather than construct and operate a plant referenced simulator. What procedure must the second utility follow to obtain approval to use that simulator?

A. The answer assumes that the utility who wants to use it is treating it as a noncertified, nonplant-referenced simulator. It does not matter who built the simulator, who owns it, where it's located. The facility licensee who wants to use a particular simulation facility for conducting operating tests is the organization that is required to file a certification or to apply for approval to use it. So in this case, the procedure that the second utility must follow would be to submit a plan within a year, followed by the application for NRC approval to use that simulation facility, whether they are the owner of it or not.

Q. 173. Has the staff developed guidance and/or criteria regarding the use of a certified plant-referenced simulator by individuals other than those from the referenced plant?

A. It is possible for any particular simulation facility to be certified as referenced to more than one plant, to the extent that those plants are similar. But only the facility licensee who wishes to use a simulation facility for its reference plant should submit the certification for its use. So if one simulation facility is intended to be used by several different licensees for different plants, then we would expect to see several different certification forms coming in, one for each of those facility licensees.

Q. 174. Does this guidance apply to facility licensees that wish to use another facility licensee's plant referenced simulator?

A. Yes, but there are some very practical issues that utilities are going to have to address in the area of configuration control, plant design changes, and getting those plant design changes referenced back into the simulator.

Some of those can be taken care of with software, by having a different data pack, tapes, etc. Others are going to be very difficult to take care of where they relate to control board location or systems that you have on the device that are different. Clearly, where two utilities want to use the same simulation facility, they are going to have to work out agreements with each other as to how they are going to maintain configuration control such that the same device can be used for the operating test at each utility.

We have not precluded that a facility may certify a simulation facility owned by someone else to its reference plant; but the requirements for having an appropriate configuration control system still exist, and you must still follow the ANSI standard. So that if you get into that mode, you may find it difficult over the long term.

Q. 175. Assume that an entity has constructed and is operating a plant-referenced simulator that meets the provisions of Regulatory Guide 1.149 and ANSI/ANS 3.5-1985, and has been certified by NRC for use by operators and senior operators at the reference plant, or who are candidates for license. A utility wishes to use the above simulator as their simulation device rather than construct and operate a plant-referenced simulator. What procedure must the utility follow to obtain approval to use the above simulator?

A. Only facility licensees are to certify simulation facilities to NRC or request approval for simulation facilities. If an entity means a facility licensee under 10 CFR Part 50, then that's fine. If it means some other organizational body, then that would not be acceptable for certifying, or applying for approval of a simulation facility. It does not matter whether that utility owns that simulation facility. It does not matter where that simulation facility is located, but it is the utility who must certify, or apply for approval to use it.

If that simulation facility referred to is referenced to a facility licensee's plant, then the process to be followed is certification on Form 474. If it is not referenced to the facility licensee's plant, then the proper approach would be submittal of a plan within a year, followed by application for NRC approval.

Q. 176. Title 10 CFR 55.45(b)(4)(i) states, "In accordance with the plan submitted pursuant to Paragraph (b)(2)(i) or (b)(3)(i) of this section, as applicable, submit an application for approval of the simulation facility to the Commission, in accordance with the schedule in Paragraph (b)(2)(ii) or (b)(3)(ii) of this section, as appropriate." What performance tests are required and what standard is used to evaluate whether the tests are satisfactory or not?

A. To the extent applicable even to those simulation facilities that will not be certified, ANS 3.5, as endorsed by Reg Guide 1.149, is the standard to be used. The performance tests include the malfunctions identified in Section 3.1.2 of the standard to be done at a rate of approximately 25 percent per year over an ongoing four-year cycle; the performance tests that are specified in Appendix A of the standard, also at the rate of 25 percent per year; and the operability tests identified in Appendix B to the standard that are to be done annually.

The criterion for the performance of these tests is that the simulation facility must be capable of being used for the conduct of the operating tests which are identified in Section 55.45(a) of the regulation, and the staff will inspect simulation facilities against that requirement.

Our definition of "plant-referenced simulator" differs from the ANSI standard definition in that we require that a simulation facility be capable of being used with the plant's control room procedures, and we would inspect against the ability to use those procedures as well.

Q. 177. Sections 55.45(b)(2)(i) and (ii) state that within one year a plan shall be submitted for a simulation facility (other than a plant-referenced simulator), and within 42 months an application for use of the simulation facility must be submitted. When will the facility licensee know if the plan for the simulation facility is acceptable to the NRC? What criteria will NRC use to determine acceptability? Can the plan be modified after the first submittal?

A. The minimum acceptance criteria for nonplant-referenced simulators as simulation facilities include the capability for conducting the operating tests identified in Section 55.45(a) and their ability to operate under the use of the control room procedures.

The nonplant-referenced simulator alone or in combination with other devices must demonstrate acceptability for conducting these operating tests using control room procedures.

The staff will review the plans for such simulation facilities against the criteria specified in the regulation for the conduct of the operating tests; and to the extent applicable, we will also apply the requirements of ANS 3.5 as endorsed by Regulatory Guide 1.149 even for nonplant-referenced simulators.

The staff intends promptly to inform any facility licensee if the staff's review of the plan or the application submitted is not satisfactory for being able to conduct these exams.

We plan to meet with the small group of facility licensees who have indicated an intention to request staff approval of simulation facilities during the year following the effective date of the regulation and prior to the deadline for their submittal of a plan for application for approval.

Finally, although we expect that our initial meetings with these few facility licensees will result in sufficiently specific guidance that modifications to plans won't be needed after submittal, we don't want to preclude such modifications if the facility licensee judges them to be necessary or desirable.

Q. 178.   The preparation of a simulation facility plan will cost money and resources.   If an submitted simulation facility plan is not acceptable, the NRC should let the utility know it is wasting its time as soon as possible.   If a utility submits a plan for an "approved simulation facility" before May 26, 1988 will the utility receive an indication of whether or not the NRC will approve the simulation facility?   Or, will the NRC approve the simulation facility only after application within the 42-month period stated in the rule?

A.   The NRC will review the plan submitted by each facility licensee which proposes to use a simulation facility pursuant to Section 55.45(b)(1)(i).   The facility licensee will be provided the results of such review.   However, approval of a simulation facility (in accordance with Section (b)(4)(ii)) proposed pursuant to paragraph (b)(1)(i) will only be considered after receipt of an application submitted in accordance with Section 55.45(b)(4).

Q. 179.   When a simulation facility evaluation is conducted by the NRC, plant operators may be used to perform the operations using plant procedures.   In this case, are the operators performing on a "no risk" basis to their licenses? If not, will the operators receive credit for an operating test?   Could certified instructors be used to demonstrate the simulation facility evaluation test instead of plant licensed operators?

A.   During a simulator evaluation, no evaluation will be made of plant operators.   If clearly unacceptable performance is identified, the operators and specifics of their performance will be identified to the facility licensee for appropriate action.   Qualified simulator instructors would be acceptable for demonstrating simulator performance.

Q. 180.   When a malfunction is used during training can we take credit for it as a performance test?

A. If all of the requirements of the Perfomance Test including planning, scheduling and documentation as required on Form 474 are met, credit may be taken for completion of the Performance Test.

Q. 181. Paragraph 55.45(b)(4)(i)(B) states "A description of the components of the simulation facility which are intended to be used for each part of the operating test" must be included as part of a facility's application for approval of simulation facilities. Please elaborate. Does "intended" mean "can?"

A. The word "intended" means that the listed component is that which the facility licensee plans to use for the evaluation of a specific one of the 13 items specified in 55.45(a).

Q. 182. Assuming that a utility were to submit a plan to certify a non-reference plant simulator as a simulation facility, what minimum criteria would this facility be required to meet (since operator testing using reference plant procedures would be limited or not possible) and what aspects of the non-reference simulator would disqualify the device from certification as a simulation facility?

A. The minimum criteria for approval of simulation facility are contained in 55.45(b)(4)(ii), which requires that it be suitable for the conduct of operating tests for the facility licensee's reference plant. The operating test requires that the 13 items listed in 55.45(a) be able to be adequately evaluated, and that plant procedures be used. Further details of simulation facility characteristics necessary for NRC certification are contained in Regulatory Guide 1.149 and ANSI/ANS-3.5-1985. For clarification, a non-plant-referenced simulator would be developed following a plan and then an application for NRC approval. It would not be certified using NRC Form 474.

Q. 183. For utilities which have not yet received simulation devices from their respective vendors, when will they be <u>required</u> to undergo simulator examinations as part of their operating examination? When ready for training? When certified by the utility? When utilized by the facility as an evaluation tool?

Does the above answer change for any facility which currently possesses a simulation device, but asks that it not be used for NRC examinations until such time that it is certified?

A. No simulation facilities will be required to be used in the conduct of operating examinations until May 26, 1991, unless they have been certified to the NRC or approved (after application) by the NRC earlier. However, if a simulation facility is used by the facility licensee as an evaluation tool, the NRC will use it for exams as well. This would hold true despite any request by the utility that it not be used until certified.

Regulatory Guide 1.149

Q. 184. In order for a utility to comply with ANSI/ANS 3.5-1985, it would have to use a full-scope nuclear power plant control room simulator. The standard states the following under Section 1, Scope: "Also excluded are part-task or limited scope simulators intended for specialized training or familarization."

This means that non-full-scope simulators would clearly be excluded from the Standard, and, hence, a simulation facility that does not consist solely of a full-scope simulator has no guidance or standard which a utility may use to obtain NRC approval. The previous statement leads us to the following conclusions: If Reg. Guide 1.149 and ANSI/ANS 3.5-1985 become the only standard for determining the acceptability of a simulation facility, the simulation facility must be a full-scope simulator, is that correct?

A. No. Regulatory Guide 1.149, in regulatory position (c)(2), takes exception to those segments of the Standard that were just cited. The Reg Guide says that simulation facilities, as defined in Section 55.4 of the Regulation (and that includes the plant, and potentially other simulation devices) should meet applicable requirements of the Standard. Also remember that Regulatory Guide 1.149 is only one acceptable means of meeting the requirements of the Regulation, and that facility licensees may propose other approaches to meeting the Regulation.

We intend to evaluate those simulation facilities which are other than certified plant-referenced simulators on a case-by-case basis, once we get to the point of dealing only with the applicable portions of the Standard.

Q. 185. If Regulatory Guide 1.149 and ANSI/ANS 3.5-1985 do not represent the only standard for determining the acceptability of a simulation facility, will NRC identify the minimum standards and criteria that are acceptable to them for non-full-scope simulators?

A. Those two documents do describe the only standards. But Regulatory Guide 1.149 is a Guide, it is not a regulation. A facility licensee may propose alternative ways to comply with the regulations in Part 55, other than the submittal of the information in Regulatory Guide 1.149.

Q. 186. Does NRC continue to endorse the requirement in ANSI/ANS 3.5-1985 to perform annual operability tests? If so, should this be part of the 25 percent testing, or should it be done annually?

A. Yes. We endorse Appendix B on operability testing, and as the standard requires, this must be done annually. This is not a part of the 25 percent performance testing.

Q. 187. Section C4 of Reg. Guide 1.149 specifies that reference plant modifications be reviewed annually against the simulator and that the simulator update design data be revised as appropriate, and that the first such annual review and update should take place within one year following the facility licensee's certification. Does this mean we have until a year after certification to match the simulator update design database to the reference plant or 18 months after simulator operational date, as specified in ANS 3.5, Section 5.2?

A. No. According to Section 5.2 of ANS 3.5, you start with a database which may, for nonoperating plants, be based on predicted data. Eighteen months after the simulator is ready for training, your simulator update design data must include available plant data, unless the simulator is on line before the plant, in which case you have 18 months from the date that the plant becomes operational. In accordance with the standard, it's whichever is operational later, the plant or the simulator.

Section C4 of Regulatory Guide 1.149 refers not to the development of this update design database, but rather to the annual review of reference plant modifications that are called for in the same Section of the standard, the results of which must be added to the update design database.

The standard says, "Reference plant modifications shall be reviewed at least once per year, and the simulator update design data shall be reviewed as appropriate." Section 5.3 of the standard goes on to say that the simulator shall be modified as required within 12 months. It is this cycle of the annual review of plant modifications, followed within 12 months by simulator modification as required, that we expect will begin with your certification on Form 474.

The rest of Section 5.2 addresses when your database must include actual plant data. And the two time schedules are somewhat independent.

You must still base the simulator update design data against the reference plant within 18 months after the simulator is operational. But you must begin your cycle of annual plant review of reference plant modifications when you submit the certification.

Q. 188. Section D, "Implementation," of Regulatory Guide 1.149, outlines a procedure to be followed for a facility licensee that wishes to utilize a simulation facility at more than one nuclear power plant. Does this guidance apply to facility licensees that wish to use another facility licensee's plant-referenced simulator?

A. Yes. But the facility must certify that the simulator meets the requirements of ANSI/ANS 3.5-1985, as endorsed by Reg Guide 1.149, for his plant. In reviewing such certifications, we would be particularly concerned about how you handled configuration control. Because you would have the potential for multiple design changes at a facility, we would have to understand how you are going to ensure that the simulation facility tracks the different plants.

Q. 189. What procedure must be followed to determine whether a two-unit site will require only one plant-referenced simulator?

A. There is considerable guidance on this in the "Implementation" section of Regulatory Guide 1.149. It says that if a facility licensee wishes to use a simulation facility at more than one nuclear power plant, it must demonstrate to NRC in its certification, or in it's application, that the differences between the plants are not so significant that they have an impact on the ability of the simulation facility to meet the regulations in 10 CFR Part 55.45(a), and the guidance of ANSI/ANS 3.5-1985.

There is a list of indicators that can be used to demonstrate that there are not such significant differences. One of the key areas that we will look at is whether we issue multiple licenses for your operators of those facilities.

ANSI/ANS 3.5, 1985

Q. 190. ANSI/ANS 3.5-1985 requires that performance tests be conducted in the event a design change results in a significant simulator configuration or performance variation. What is the NRC's definition of significant?

A. Our operational definition is any change to the simulation facility, its models or software that might cause the results of performance tests to fall outside the acceptable performance criteria set within the standard. The standard does not define "significant," and for an official definition, or an official clarification, you need to seek guidance from ANS itself. It's possible that this definition will be clarified in the next revision to the standard, but unless and until it is, we will use our operational definition.

Q. 191. This question concerns the list of required malfunctions in performance testing and ANS 3.5-1985. Are those not more "events" versus "malfunctions"? Do you understand that this causes confusion on the part of the simulator vendors in that if I was to go to a vendor and tell him that I want a reactor trip malfunction, he's going to wonder what I'm talking about? Do I want power to the CRD breakers? Do I want to lose all reactor coolant system flow? How do I want to do this to create the abnormal event that ANSI 3.5 is asking me to perform? Isn't that really referring to a list of abnormal transients?

A. Yes.

Q. 192. ANSI/ANS 3.5 Section 3.1.1(7) requires that the simulator be capable of performing startup and power operations with less than full rated reactor coolant flow. If the facility licensee is not allowed by Technical Specifications to conduct such operations, is this capability still required?

A. No. If a plant is constrained in any particular area by its Technical Specifications, then the simulation facility need not possess that capability as it applies to routine operations.

Q. 193. The Technical Specifications clearly bind the conditions under which the plant is allowed to operate. Am I correct that the simulator only needs to be bound by the same parameters?

A. No. For normal startup and shutdown practical-factor evolutions, in accordance with your procedures, you need not model those to be outside the bounds of the Technical Specifications. The question came up in the context of "N-minus-1 loop operation"; for instance, continued operation with a recirculation pump out of service or continued operation with one reactor coolant pump out of service. You need not model the simulation facility for operation in that mode if you are not permitted normally to start up in that mode. It was with respect to the context for startup.

Clearly, emergency procedures, for example, which go into function restoration guidelines and go beyond design basis accidents are not covered by Tech Specs, but we expect the simulation facility to be able to reasonably model those events. The same holds true when you insert malfunctions. If you turn off power to a panel, you're clearly outside the bounds of the Technical Specifications. You would not be operating with that panel de-energized. So in general, if you are conducting malfunctions, you may be in that mode.

Q. 194. ANSI/ANS 3.5 Section 3.1.1(9) states that measurement of reactivity coefficients and control rod worth using permanently installed instruments be performed. What is meant by "permanently installed instrumentation?"

A. The question of the meaning of the term "permanently installed instrumentation" is in ANS 3.5, and official definition or clarification really has to come from ANS and not from the Commission.

Our operational definition essentially says that portable or temporary instrumentation that is brought into the control room for specific modes of operation, such as startup, would not be required as part of the simulation facility.

We intend that you use the normally installed instrumentation available in the control room and not instrumentation associated with special tests.

So if it's part of your normal plant operating procedures and it's instrumentation you rely on (and we expect that you have instrumentation that falls into that category for calculating rod worth for doing startups) that's what we intend you to use. You need not simulate other instrumentation that is outside the scope of your normal procedures.

Q. 195. ANSI 3.5 Section 3.1.1(10) states that the simulator be capable of performing operator-conducted surveillance testing. Are you only considering the remote shutdown panel?

A. Any surveillance that cannot be performed from the control room need not be modeled. For example, if you're doing a diesel startup from the local panel for the diesel and that's the way you conduct the surveillance, you need not model anything that's done on a routine basis from outside the control room.

Q. 196. Would it be wise to evaluate, for example, the plant's surveillance procedures and identify which of those we think would be applicable to being done on the simulation facility? In other words, generally the operator from the control room would be doing that evolution. Naturally, all of those valves exist on the control board and so on, and you can legitimately perform that. Would that be acceptable in meeting the intent of Item 10 in the standard?

A. That would be one way of doing it. But if you look at the performance testing, particularly when you're getting out of component testing and into system testing, and you're evaluating your capability to actually model the system, a way of doing that would be to see if you can model the surveillance procedures on that.

What you describe is acceptable. You may choose some subset of the surveillances that you can perform on those particular systems to show that those systems are operating within the bounds expected by the plant.

After all, that's where you have a source of data on the actual performance of the system: the records from the surveillance tests that you've conducted on those systems, particularly where they have specifications for flow or pressure or some other characteristic which is modeled in the control room.

Q. 197. Plant data, simulator update design data, and simulator design data: I interpret their relationship this way. Plant data represents the current plant configuration including installed and functional modifications. Simulator update design data, call it Data A, is an accumulation of plant data for a fixed time period, such as one year. At the end of the data accumulation, the simulator update design data is evaluated and appropriate data is incorporated into the simulator design data by the simulator modification process. We have one year to match the simulator design data to the simulator update design data, Data A. In the meantime, a new accumulation of data into the next simulator update design data, Data B, is begun. Is this a correct interpretation?

A. That interpretation is reasonable. The key thing is that you have up to two years according to the standard to incorporate a plant modification into the simulator. You have one year in which to identify the need for a simulator update; based upon the required annual review of plant modifications; and then you have one more year during which you have to get it incorporated into the simulator modification. So we have possibly two years from the time you recognize the need from a plant change to update the simulator until it must be in the simulator.

Simulation Facility Certification (Including Performance Testing, NRC Form 474, NUREG-1258)

Q. 198. When will the official simulation facility inspections start? Will they start before certification takes place?

A. No. There are two minimum criteria. They will not start before the SFEP guidance has been out for six months, and they will not start until we have received your certification on Form 474, or your application for approval.

Q. 199. What level of simulator capability must be reported and tested if a simulator has considerable simulation capability, much greater than ANSI/ANS 3.5-1985 requirements?

A. We are requiring that the capability of the simulation facility be such that it meets the requirements of 10 CFR 55, and ANS 3.5, as endorsed by Reg Guide 1.149. To the extent that any simulation facility has capabilities that exceed those minimum requirements, you need not tell us what they are. You need not certify them to us, and we will not inspect against them.

Q. 200. In the event we had capabilities beyond ANSI/ANS 3.5-1985 and Part 55 that we did not test and certify, would those capabilities be utilized in examining the operators?

A. Possibly. For example, let's say that ANSI/ANS 3.5-1985 for a transient requires a parameter to move in a certain direction so that you don't get spurious alarms, etc. The standard is rather loose with respect to modeling for transients. And if you have something which is closer to an engineering tool, such that you cannot only predict the direction of the parameters, but also have a rather good tolerance on its value as compared to what you would expect from simply meeting the standard, that does not mean that we're not going to examine that particular transient or say that it's outside the scope of our examinations. On the other hand, if you are able to go into the area of, say, severe accidents, which we don't currently cover in the requirements, we may not be examining in that area. The issue is whether that's appropriate for the control room crew, or the technical support center, the accident assessment function, and that's the difference.

Q. 201. That's the real question. When our vintage simulator was purchased, the limitation on the vendor was to build it to plant design. Sometimes some of the NRC scenarios go beyond design basis, and I can't say whether the simulator's performance is correct or incorrect, I have no basis to certify it.

A. We will still be examining on the design basis, because you must do that in order to get into symptom-based procedures and function-restoration guidelines. And we want to be able to see an operator's ability to use those emergency operating procedures, in particular.

That already puts you beyond the Chapter 15 design-basis transients and evaluations. There is one requirement in ANSI/ANS 3.5-1985, which is endorsed in our Regulatory Guide, and is also contained in our Simulation Facility Evalution Procedure, for some means or mechanism within the simulation facility to notify the simulator operator when the simulation facility has exceeded the capability of its modeling. And that's one of the things that we would be looking at in our inspections.

Q. 202. In order to get into the emergency operating procedures on most plants, you have to have a variety of different types of failures that are compounded, which go beyond the design scope of the plant as single-failure-proof and would be very difficult to run on a simulator. We have found that in using the emergency operating procedures (EOP), we can quickly get outside the bounds of simulation. How do you propose that we address that issue on EOPs?

A. There are two ways: First, the standard indicates that when you go beyond the bounds of modeling, it should indicate that in some way during the simulation. Second, we conduct examinations that go outside the bounds of your Chapter 15 accidents and transients. That's necessary in order to get you into the function-restoration guidelines.

We intend to see and the regulations require that we understand that an operator can effectively implement those procedures. The tolerances, however, for those procedures are quite large. When you get into casualties, ANS 3.5 essentially requires that the parameter go in the same direction it would go during the actual transient in a plant; that you don't get spurious alarms and that the alarms that are supposed to come in are the ones that you get. It's not time dependent. It's really the ability to look at the parameter and decide, based upon that parameter, what procedure you're supposed to be using, and then implement that procedure. We are not looking for a high-fidelity severe-accident simulator in order to be able to exercise the emergency procedures.

Q. 203. This question relates to the definition of "site-specific plant-referenced simulator." What is meant by "it's been designed and uses plant procedures?" With this explanation, could you give me a feeling for whether I have to delete some steps as inapplicable because of non-modeled systems? Does that need to be highlighted in my performance testing exceptions?

A. What we mean by "use of procedures" is simply that the procedures that your operators use in the control room should be capable of being run on the simulation facility without change. You must be able to use controlled copies of the control room procedures, not copies modified in some fashion or by pen-and-ink changes. They actually need to be controlled copies. You can indicate which steps cannot be performed, then you must certify to that. NRC must be able to use the facility emergency operating procedures during the conduct of operating tests. A suitable alternative must be provided in the event of non-modeled systems that are involved with the execution of such procedures in the control room. Depending on the extent and degree of such discrepancies, it is possible to certify with exceptions as opposed to applying for NRC approval.

Q. 204. In other words, I can't take exception to any step in the procedure because of non-modeled systems?

A. Let's assume that it is a step in the procedure that's used in the control room, but it directs an activity outside the control room. Say the reactor operator tells the auxiliary operator to do something, and you have not modeled that capability in the simulation facility. That would be not applicable.

If it is a step normally conducted from the control room, it is part of the operating procedures for the control room, and it falls into one of the categories appropriate for the operating test, then you need to model and describe it as a part of your certification of the simulation facility.

If that step need not be used as a part of the operating test, if it's for an ancillary system outside of what we would test on -- you may have something associated with fire suppression or some other system, for example, that's not explicitly covered in the items for the operating test -- then that need not be included.

So you have to look at the scope of the operating test in view of the required capabilities of the simulation facility as described in the ANSI standard.

Q. 205. Let's assume that in the absence of a modeled system or a modeled cabinet within the control room area, I believe it would be permissible to use the plant to train on that particular component. In essence, I have an exception on my performance test plan, which would normally require the use of that cabinet. But through on-the-job training in the actual control room, I can give the equivalent of that training that I would have performed on the simulator. Have I gone beyond the plant-referenced simulator category and moved into the other category here? If so, how do I address that?

A. Not necessarily. You need to look at whether that system is, for instance, a safety system. If it's not a safety system and it's not otherwise called out in the categories under the operating test, then you need not model that system as a part of the control room. The safe-shutdown panels in some facilities aren't modeled. They are outside the control room. We do not require that you model that in the simulator.

There are radiation monitor panels in the control room and things like that that you may not have modeled in your simulation. We understand that. That should not preclude you from using certification with exception.

You need not necessarily go through the application process. It's when there is some portion of the operating test which requires controls in the control room that are not replicated on the simulation facility that would require you to submit an application for NRC approval.

Q. 206. Will the operator/examiner feedback form that was discussed be used to determine the status of current simulators?

A. The guidance to the Examiners is that the form will be applicable only to simulation facilities that have been certified, or have applied for approval. However, even today, with the present vintage of simulators, you still are experiencing feedback reports, although informal, in the exam review process. And that will continue. If the Examiners have a problem in conducting the operating test at your simulator, you can expect some feedback in that regard, even though it won't be the formal process that will occur for certification or approval.

Q. 207. So, is it true that if I wait for 46 months to certify, that is an advantage to me?

A. No. It's not an advantage because you will to have provide substantial additional information for every application that you submit and we are going review that information and make determinations on individual applications and candidates.

Q. 208. But, yet, you won't inspect us?

A. We won't inspect your simulator, but we're certainly going to be keep close tabs on your applicants. And every time you receive an NRC operating test using your simulator, you can expect feedback through the exam report on the performance of your simulator.

Q. 209. This refers to the accelerated update of the simulation facility that may be required as a result of performance testing. What systems, events, or procedures are we trying to exercise during the simulator exam?

A. The intent was to identify any potential system, operation or scenario that we could not conduct on the simulator exam because of the simulation facility and which we could not readily implement another way during the examination, so that the exam could potentially be compromised or considered invalid. We would need to see that that system, or procedure or event had been corrected before we could develop an appropriate exam using it. For example, one simulator was unable to adequately represent flow coast down on a loss of coolant. The response was very unusual as compared to what was expected, and on how the procedures were to be used, because there was no coast down. It would not have been appropriate to conduct an examination which involved a loss of flow event in that case. We would not want that situation to exist for the next two years, because we may want to conduct a loss of flow scenario as a part of an exam within that time. So, we would require that that be corrected on a schedule that is faster than the normal two-year correction schedule provided in the standard.

Q. 210. I think clearly, that's the intent. But I see opening some areas of disagreement in the future. None of us know what the next round of the "topic of the day" is going to be. And we may find that our present machines were not designed to handle whatever that issue is. And, so, when you say any event, that can be troublesome.

A. We suggest that you look at NUREG-1258 that describes the Simulation Facility Evaluation Procedure (SFEP) and the pilot tests. That should allay some of the apprehension.

Also remember that this system, operation or event is something that you have already certified that your machine is capable of doing. We're referring to something we discovered during the course of our inspection that contradicts something you've told us on your certification.

Q. 211. This question addresses performance tests to be performed on the simulator in compliance with 10 CFR 55. What are those set of performance tests, the specific scenarios and malfunctions? Could you clarify that?

A. We're talking about Appendices A and B of ANSI/ANS 3.5-1985, and the list of 25 malfunctions that are contained in Section 3.1.2 of the Standard. There is a defined list of malfunctions that the simulation facility needs to perform.

Q. 212. Is it just that list that's in 3.5, only?

A. Yes.

Q. 213. Or is it that list, plus the diesel generator that's covered in Regulatory Guide 1.149?

A. There was a specific list of malfunctions in an earlier draft of Regulatory Guide 1.149, but it is gone from the final version. The equivalent paragraph that's in the final version endorses the paragraph in the Standard that lists the 25 malfunctions. Recognize, however, that some of those malfunctions are quite broad. We talked about the loss of power. That could mean loss of power to a panel, to a system, to a component, or loss of all power. Small break LOCAs can be initiated from a reactor coolant pump seal, from a steam generator, a tube rupture, a lot of different ways. What we are interested in is a representative sample of those things. You need not do all possible permutations and combinations.

But you are going to have to look at what you are certifying to, that's the reason that you are submitting test abstracts, and you describe what your testing program is.

Q. 214. So we will determine which specific scenarios we will run, as long as we cover those areas?

A. That is correct. And you describe that in your abstract, with your certification, and you describe the performance tests that you will conduct in the future to maintain the simulation facility.

Q. 215. Would the Commission find a formal simulator facility review board/ committee (consisting of training management, operations management and senior reactor operators) a suitable forum for making judgments regarding the simulator scope requirements versus training value? For example, ANSI/ANS 3.5-1985 states that all accidents analyzed in the facility's FSAR must be included in plant malfunctions in the simulator's scope. It then later states that this is required only when the simulator is determined appropriate for training.

However, in a few cases the accidents provide little, if any, training value to an operator. Can a board, such as that proposed, be considered a legitimate forum for making these decisions?

A. We are concerned with the applicability of your simulation facility for the conduct of operating tests, and not as it applies to your training programs. Generally speaking, when you look at the ANS 3.5 document, you can safely substitute the term "operating tests" wherever the term "training" appears.

Although we recognize that your simulation facility's scope, when applied as part of your training program, may exceed that which is necessary for its applicability to use in operating tests, it doesn't matter to us what process you use internally to identify those differences.

We have tried to indicate clearly the minimum requirements for use of your simulation facility to conduct operating tests, and it must meet those minimums. These include the evolutions and malfunctions identified in Section 3.1.2, in the performance test appendix, and in the operability test appendix of the standard, using the required operating test requirements in Section 55.45(a) as the criterion.

However you meet those requirements is your decision to make; and as to whether you need to certify or provide additional performance testing data for anything additional, that's also your decision to make.

You will be submitting performance test abstracts with the Form 474 that describe the testing that you're going to perform.

When you look at the list of malfunctions and you see a malfunction that says "loss of power," that's very broad. Which ones do you choose in developing the test abstract for various losses of power?

You should look at the testing that you propose and, if possible, combine some of those malfunctions so that you have a smaller number of performance tests than would otherwise be the case and describe how those tests in your abstracts meet the intent of the standard.

In doing that, we would use those tests in making a judgment as to what the capabilities are. That does not mean that we would limit our examinations, however, to those particular tests or scenarios.

Obviously, if you demonstrate that the simulation facility works well for an event at high power and for some tests at low power, we may be able to mix those just as we do now. You have a substantial amount of control in deciding what testing you want to propose for the performance tests and that list of malfunctions is quite general.

In the case of using the panel, that could be an appropriate vehicle for deciding what tests are going to be proposed as performance tests. They could be a subset of all the malfunctions the simulator is capable of performing. You may literally have hundreds of malfunctions which you can implement.

We don't want to see a performance test for each malfunction. We do want to be sure that all of the malfunctions that are listed in the standard can be performed.

Q. 216. Section 55.45(b)(5)(vi) says a certification report need only include a description of performance testing completed, performance testing planned, and the schedule for conducting 25 percent of performance tests per year for the next four years. Is this sufficient, or must the document conform to ANS 3.5-1985 Appendix A?"

A. This question addresses two different issues. The first is the testing that is required, and the second is the reporting. The reporting itself need not be in the format of Appendix A, ANS 3.5, although that's not necessarily a bad idea. But it must cover those items that are called out in the Regulation in Section 55.45(a), specifically a description of the performance tests conducted, and the schedule for future performance tests, if that schedule differs from one that was previously submitted with the certification.

The actual testing must include not only the Appendix A performance testing, as called out in the standard, but the specific list of malfunctions that are identified in Section 3.1.2 of the standard, both at the rate of 25 percent per year. Also, the operability testing that's shown in Appendix B of the standard is to be performed annually. So, testing and reporting are separate issues.

Q. 217. When does the Commission project that their guidance for conducting simulation facility audits will be made public?

A. That guidance is available now in draft NUREG-1258, and we will accept your comments on that NUREG until the 26th of May.

Q. 218. Will simulator certification audits be performed by NRC headquarters staff, regional NRC staff, or some combination?

A. In all probability, the simulation facility inspection program will combine headquarters and regional staff, starting largely as a headquarters function and over time becoming more region-based as we move into the inspection procedures.

Q. 219. NRC released a final draft of "Handbook for Software Quality Assurance Techniques Applicable to the Nuclear Industry," dated February 1986. This handbook addresses the applicability of 10 CFR 50 Appendix B requirements associated with computer uses in the nuclear industry.

It specifies that training simulators require stringent software quality assurance. This requirement seems to imply that the simulator's software should be treated as though it were safety related, with the appropriate programmatic and procedural controls applied. What are the Commission's plans in this area and what relationship, if any, will the draft handbook have to simulator certification?

A. The draft handbook to which you refer imposes no requirements on the industry. It is under consideration by the staff, but there is no intent for us to review your software development or quality control procedures as they apply to Part 55 and to simulation facility certification.

You, of course, have to manage your own simulator software program in order to meet the regulations in Part 55 as required to certify that the simulation facility is suitable for conducting operating tests. And we will review the simulation facility's adequacy using the performance testing program, after you submit your Form 474.

We will take a look at the handbook to determine its status, but we think it is safe to consider it not applicable to these regulations.

The best way of determining whether the software is any good or not is to see whether it performs in accordance with the plant's design characteristics. We don't need a very prescriptive software control program protocol that is subject to NRC review and evaluation.

We've described how we intend to inspect the simulation facilities and we have put that into the Simulation Facility Evaluation Procedure. The evaluations will be based upon running things like Licensee Event Report scenarios and seeing how the simulation facility compares with the plant.

But if you start modifying the software in one area, you may affect other areas. So you need to understand what impacts such changes will have to the overall performance tests. If a modification causes a performance test to fall outside of its acceptance values -- that is, the 2 percent and the 10 percent -- you need to rerun that test to ensure that the simulation facility is still performing in accordance with the design specification. We're looking for a machine that will replicate what we expect to happen in the plant. We're not looking for developing a software control system which is appropriate to a reactor protection system where you cannot test by operation how effectively the performance of the reactor protection system works. Title 10 CFR 50 Appendix B requirements would appear to be appropriate in such safety-related applications. That's the difference.

Q. 220. This question concerns a simulation facility consisting of other than a plant-referenced simulator, and the performance testing related to such a facility. What performance tests are required and what standard is used to evaluate whether the tests are satisfactory or not?

A. We intend to follow the guidelines in the ANSI standard as applicable to the simulation facility which you have proposed.

Let's say that you want to use another plant's simulation facility for reactor startup and that you can effectively model the controls and indications that would be used for reactor startup. We would expect you to follow the ANSI standard as it related to startup modeling. You may not be able to model it for controls and indications because you don't have that capability on the simulation facility. You would not have to follow ANS 3.5 guidelines in that instance because they are not applicable.

Q. 221. If the standard for performance tests is ANSI/ANS 3.5, as modified by Regulatory Guide 1.149, will it be possible to deviate from the standard in certain areas or must it be adhered to in its entirety?

62

A. We recognize that there will be a number of outstanding discrepancy reports on the simulation facility against its reference plant. We expect that, for certified simulation facilities, as well as for those that achieve approval after application, exceptions will have to be taken from the requirements of ANS 3.5. There is a block on Form 474 for certified simulation facilities to address the exceptions that you take at any given time. The same would apply to noncertified simulation facilities where you would address those exceptions in your application.

Q. 222. Does a simulation facility certification form, NRC 474, have to be submitted prior to each operating examination?

A. No. Assuming that you maintain the acceptability of the simulation facility, it is a one-time certification.

Q. 223. Will the guidance document be limited to auditing the provisions of ANSI/ANS 3.5-1985?

A. No. It will be limited to auditing certification against the requirements of Section 55.45(a) of the regulation, which delineates the 13 components of the operating test, and ANS 3.5-1985, as endorsed by Regulatory Guide 1.149.

Q. 224. Will the performance testing documentation maintained for NRC review be limited to those items addressed in ANSI 3.5?

A. No. The performance testing and its documentation will use Section 55.45(a) of the regulation as its criterion, and must employ the malfunction testing of Section 3.1.2 of ANS 3.5, as well as the standard's two appendices, and the endorsement by Regulatory Guide 1.149.

To amplify, the operability test identified as Appendix B in the standard is done annually. We have not taken exception to that. Performance testing, which appears in Appendix A, plus the repeat of the malfunction testing, which is described in Section 3 of the standard (that set of testing at approximately a rate of 25 percent per year over four years), will constitute the additional annual testing to be done.

So you have an annual operability test, and then 25 percent of the performance tests that are described in the first appendix, plus 25 percent of the malfunctions that are listed. To the extent the operability test itself duplicates a portion of the performance test, that's sufficient. You don't need to do it twice, but that's the scope of the testing we are expecting to be done on an annual basis, and the term annual is used in its common meaning. We are interested in you doing the performance tests regularly over a period of four years, and not putting them off for the last year.

Of course, before you submit your certification or your application for approval, you should have completed 100 percent of the operating tests and the performance tests. After that, the 25 percent per year cycle will begin.

Q. 225. It was indicated that when we submit the Form 474, we should have 100 percent of the performance tests completed. Can we count performance tests, specifically malfunction tests, that were performed as part of an acceptable test procedure, say, three years ago, towards having performed that part of the performance test one time, or do we have to redo it before we submit the form?

A. There is not necessarily any need to redo those performance tests. The concern, if any, is the difference in time from when they were done, and any changes to the plant configuration that would be required by the ANSI standard to bring the simulation facility up to date. If there have been no changes that would require you to repeat some performance tests to make them in compliance with the standard, then those tests should be acceptable.

Q. 226. So if we conducted an acceptable test program, and since then have had a program in place to test all the modifications to the software, including malfunctions, if appropriate, then we've got a basis for starting, anyway?

A. Yes. We intentionally did not specify a time prior to certification by which you had to have them all completed.

But the situation you have is that once you do certify, then you start performing those same performance tests over again on a 25-percent-per-year basis over the 4 years to ensure that configuration changes are, indeed, incorporated in the simulation facility. But the rule itself is silent on how long before certification these tests may have been performed.

There were some changes in the standard between the 1981 version and the 1985 version. You have to show that you have met the 1985 version, and that any design changes or software changes that you have made since then have not affected the validity of those earlier tests. It may be easier to repeat them than to repeat the entire process, but that's up to you.

Q. 227. Is there any intent to include remote shutdown panels in any of the simulation facility requirements?

A. No. However, if these panels are provided as part of the simulation facility, they may be used in the NRC operating test.

Q. 228. What does the Commission consider an adequate schedule to correct performance test failures identified in the four-year anniversary certification?

A. Although the rule requires a report on every four-year anniversary of certification, or four-year anniversary of application, we intend to have a much closer working relationship with you so that we will know on an ongoing basis about any such performance test failures, and there are several mechanisms to do that. One is the 90-day letter prior to examinations, in which uncorrected performance test failures would be identified. Another would be simulation facility fidelity reports from our examiners, and the third would be the results of our periodic audit and inspections of simulation facilities.

The schedule to correct performance test failures is really based upon the seriousness and the magnitude of the failures that are discovered. It may range from purely an NRC recommendation that the failures be corrected, to a recommendation that a failure be corrected within the normal update cycle required by ANS 3.5. The next level would require a correction on an accelerated schedule. The most serious failures require that the simulation facility essentially shut down until the failures are corrected.

Q. 229. What detail of description is the Commission anticipating in the report? Should the report be revised if a schedule for conducting a performance test changes year-to-year during the four-year period?

A. If your schedule for performance testing changes between the time you submit a certification and any subsequent four-year report, you should advise us of that change on the Form 474.

There are three documents for certified simulation facilities that address the level of detail. The rule, specifically the operating test in 55.45(a), lists 13 items that make up the content of the exam; ANS 3.5, which sets out the requirements for the simulation facility's capabilities, as well as the performance testing requirements; and Form 474, which indicates that we want performance test abstracts and performance test schedules.

We don't want reams of material on the details of all your performance tests and all the results. If we need additional information in the course of conducting an off-site or an on-site simulation facility evaluation we will request it from you; we are really looking for summaries and abstracts submitted with that certification form.

Q. 230. Will an NRC certification team be sent to the facility to conduct a simulator performance audit using the new simulator certification criteria?

A. Essentially yes. The NRC staff will conduct the review and the inspection. It will be a two-phase process, an offsite review, followed by an onsite inspection, if necessary. Only as a result of onsite inspection might certification be removed, as a last resort. For further clarification, a certification is not removed as a result of an inspection. It's removed as a result of failing performance tests which are required by the regulation. During the inspection we conduct performance tests where we audit the ability of the simulation facility to perform as described in the performance tests that you submitted. So if the machine does not work during an inspection, the criterion is still the failure of a substantial number of performance tests, such that you cannot perform a meaningful operating test as described in the regulation.

The conclusion is based upon the requirements for the operating test, not just on failing some fraction of the performance tests. You have to fail performance tests, but it's got to be a substantial enough number of performance tests that it impacts on the simulation facility's ability to conduct an NRC operating examination. So one performance test failure does not necessarily mean that the simulation facility would be decertified. It has to be a gross enough set of failures that we can't conduct a test.

Q. 231. We presently have two years before a plant modification must be incorporated into our simulator. Can we certify the simulator to the NRC without having incorporated all plant modifications?

A. We always anticipate that even when you certify a simulation facility, there will be exceptions if you haven't been able to bring it up to date with plant modifications. The ANSI standard allows a two-year period from the date you identified the need for making modifications until those are fully incorporated into the simulation facility. So the answer is yes, you can certify prior to the date you've incorporated the modifications.

Q. 232. Where specifically would that be on Form 474?

A. There is a block near the top of the form that says "I hereby certify that the simulation facility meets 10 CFR 55 and ANSI 3.5."

It then says: "If there are any exceptions to the certification of item two above [that is, the ANSI standard], check here and describe on additional pages if necessary."

Q. 233. In earlier discussions mention was made about using controlled copies of procedures for simulators. What do you mean by the word control?

A. Controlled copies means those procedures identical to the ones that you use in the control room of the plant. The copies should be up to date, including references and revisions.

*Q. 234. When an examiner conducts an exam on the simulator, are we going to be able to take a look at some of the fidelity questions that they have on a simulator prior to them leaving or prior to their exit interview?

A. Yes. The examiner will provide any comments that he or she has about the simulator's fidelity on a "Simulation Facility Fidelity Report," which has been added to Examiner Standard ES-104. Those thoughts will be shared with the facility licensee along with the rest of the examiner's comments, before he or she leaves the site.

Q. 235. Are licensees required to submit exemption requests per the ANSI Standard or the Regulatory Guide, and they are to be issued per the requirements of 55.45?

A. If any one of the requirements of the operating tests in Section 55.45(a) cannot be met with the simulation facility, you would require an exemption from the Regulation. A failure to meet all of the requirements of the ANSI standard does not require an exemption. It simply requires an identification of what it is that you cannot meet. And it must include a conclusion on your part that that difference would not preclude the conduct of an operating test as it's described in the Regulation.

That's why the certification on Form 474 is a certification to the Regulation with an identification that you follow the ANSI standard with some exceptions. We recognize that there will be exceptions. There are exceptions on new licenses on the day they're issued and we issue a number of license conditions.

We don't expect that the number of discrepancy reports on a simulation facility is ever going to get to zero. It's anticipated that there will always be some feedback, some necessary correction. The standard itself provides a schedule for incorporating those corrections and revisions.

Q. 236. I'm unclear as to how much we have to put into our simulator with regard to back panels.

The simulator we have is what's called a main horseshoe. We have 50 to 60 back panels in the simulator which are used during surveillance testing, and recently there have been a lot of bypass switches that we use during our emergency plan training. Must we have all those back panels in our simulator or can we substitute the plant for that part of the training? It's a very big main control room, and we put all our back panels in there instead of outside the main control room.

A. Our intent is not to have you model the entire plant, but if the evolutions you are citing are your operating and emergency procedures for the facility, and it's an evolution which is conducted from within the control room by the regulation, we would expect that to be modeled or you would have to show us how that could be done without modelling and identify that as an exception.

But for facilities that have a large number of back panels or other equipment available in the control room, it's not the intent that you mock up all those panels. Generally, they are merged in the main control boards. For example, those that control the reactor, safety systems, electrical line-up, and balance of plant are the typical ones that we're looking for.

Q. 237. Would it be safe to assume that you have in mind the area that the operating shift typically does not leave during normal operation of the facility?

A. It's those portions of the facility where the individual is defined as being "at the controls," which is described in Regulatory Guide 1.114. Some facilities mark it off with a red line on the floor or with a fence or whatever. It's that area where the individual is at the controls as defined in the Regulatory Guide that we're interested in simulating.

LICENSES

Special Senior Operator Licenses (Including Instructor Certification)

Q. 238. What is the impact of the new rule on instructor qualifications? Are the requirements of NUREG-0737 superseded?

A. The new rule supersedes the requirements for instructor qualifications in NUREG-0737. The responsiblity for ensuring that instructors are qualified now rests with the accreditation process. INPO has established the qualifications for technical instructors, which would be reviewed within accreditation. NRC's role is to monitor the accreditation program to ensure that it maintains the standards that have been endorsed by the Commission.

Q. 239. Instructors who have been certified or who have held a license previously may instruct students in courses needed to prepare applicants for NRC licensing examinations. Are these instructors required to participate in a requalification program?

A. If you have an accredited program or systems approach to training (SAT) program, then that program will define the continuing qualification and re-training requirements for instructors. If you do not have an accredited program, then the instructors will have to meet the commitments of the approved program as defined under Part 55 and commitments contained in the FSAR. NRC will no longer issue instructor certifications. If a licensee is using vendor-certified instructors in a requalification program that has not been completely converted to an SAT program (performance-based), it is conceivable that a 50.59 change could be made to support such an approach in the interim until such time as the requalification program is converted to an SAT-based program.

Q. 240. As I understand it, only people that hold a license for a facility may instruct license-type material to a hot license class. Would consultants who were previously licensed and certified by General Electric be able to teach such material?

A. If your program is accredited, then you determine subject matter expertise and instructor skills in accordance with the accredited program. If your program is not yet accredited and you were previously under the commitment in the Denton letter to assure subject matter expertise for instructors -- which was that those instructing integrated plant operations have a level of knowledge comparable to that of a senior reactor operator -- then the process we've allowed in the interim permits you to certify your instructors based upon their successful completion of your senior operator training program.

We have also allowed that those examined and certified by NRC in the past can continue, but they should receive additional training on plant or procedure changes, that portion of the requalification program which is applicable to what they're teaching.

Now, the practical aspect is that those people who are instructing have to learn that material to a depth greater than that which they instruct, and your program also has mechanisms for evaluating instructor performance.

We are trying to move out of the area of specifying training program content or qualifications for instructors. So depending upon your commitment in the presently approved program, you may need to review that in accordance with 50.59. NRC will not need to certify it; you may do that under your own program.

Q. 241. How would that apply to vendors such as Westinghouse? We cannot get accredited by INPO. Therefore, if we hold a staff of instructors, are they then going to have to go to the utility and the utility is going to have to either license or certify them?

A. For contractors that are providing instruction for facilities, it is the responsibility of the facility to ensure that the contractors have the appropriate subject matter expertise and instructor skills to meet the requirements of their accredited program. The staff will not be certifying or approving instructors who are contractors, nor will we be certifying or approving instructors who are facility employees.

Q. 242. Did I understand correctly that you said that if you're not accredited, that you would have to license instructors?

A. Some facilities in their existing training programs have committed in the FSAR to have either licensed senior reactor operators or individuals who were certified instructors. The old instructor certification, which was comparable to a license (the eligibilty requirements were relaxed), required that the instructor go through the same examination, although he was not authorized to manipulate the controls. We no longer issue such certificates, which would imply that you would be obligated to have licensed operators conduct your program.

We also indicated that you could perform a 50.59 type of review that would meet the same intent. Having your instructors complete and be examined by the standards of a program comparable to your own senior reactor operator program, such as a vendor certification program, would be sufficient in the interim. When we get to the point where everyone has been accredited, that issue is superseded. The accreditation process covers instructor qualification and training.

Q. 243. I do not have my programs accredited yet. I hope we will have them done by the end of the year. But I have people who are in a program right now, the same one we've been using all along, and they are being examined by us next week. And the Region is not going to come in and give them an NRC exam. My intention is to certify them as I have done in the past and put them right into a classroom. They will also be in a requalification program. Do I understand that to be a correct procedure?

A. Yes. If you are getting ready for accreditation, you probably have completed the self-evaluation report, and are getting ready for a team visit. As preparation for that, you look at how you train and certify instructors. We want that to be a part of the accreditation process, and not a part of the NRC review.

Q. 244. Can trainees participating in a systems training program for instructor certification manipulate controls on the facility under the appropriate supervision of licensed personnel?

A. If that training program can lead to a license if carried to completion trainers may manipulate controls under appropriate supervision if it occurs in the proper sequence within the training program. The trainee may also manipulate controls (under proper supervision) without being involved in a course that leads to a license if the systems that are being manipulated do not affect power or reactivity (e.g., feedwater). However if the systems that the trainee will teach, and therefore the controls he would manuipulate, do affect power or ractivity, then he must be enrolled in a course that leads to a license.

Q. 245. As I understand it, in the accredited utilities, instructors will be considered to be certified to teach licensed operators after they complete the accredited training program. In the case of a utility that doesn't have their operations programs accredited yet, could you outline what the requirements will be?

A. The requirements are basically those which were in existence before the effective date of the Rule, and that is to either have an individual who has completed a training program comparable to that of an SRO, and been examined on it (we used to call that instructor certification), or be a licensed senior operator, who is currently enrolled in a requalification training program.

Because of the fact that we no longer are going to be giving instructor certifications, you then have only the option of using a licensed operator to teach those courses. We are not going to give any further instructor's certifications, that's not permitted under the Rule.

For NTOLs and facilities that are in the accreditation process, the Commission's Policy Statement in Training and Qualification of Power Plant Personnel of March 20, 1985 allowed facilities to make the transition from FSAR commitments to accredited programs. Therefore NRC instructor certifications which, as a policy, were discontinued in Mid 1985, relied on facility certification of instructors. We believe this policy will continue and eventually be reflected in Revisions to Section 13.2 of NUREG-0800, the Standard Review Plan.

Q. 246. So, training instructors must be licensed operators?

A. Yes, until such time as you get accredited, or have some other way of getting subject matter expertise through your accredited program, including instructor training. We are not going to specify that for an accredited program. But you may have a program on record today, in which you have committed to the requirements to the Denton letter, which said you were going to do certain things to ensure subject matter expertise in instructors. And that was to either use a licensed senior reactor operator or an individual who has been examined by the NRC to the same level as a senior operator.

We are not going to examine without issuing a license.

Q. 247. Will people who are currently certified by virtue of the fact that they have previously passed a senior reactor operator examination somewhere, and thus demonstrated their competency, be considered as certified to teach?

A. Yes. But when they come to us after the effective date of the Rule requesting to have their certification renewed, that's not going to happen, because there is no longer such certification.

Q. 248. So, then, is someone who has passed an SRO exam given by the NRC at some point in the past, considered certified or not?

A. For the purpose of meeting your training program commitment of having an individual who has a knowledge level comparable to that of a senior reactor operator, the answer is yes, provided the individual is maintaining currency in the requalification program, with respect to any changes which would affect his knowledge base. That is consistent with what INPO is looking at in the instructor training and as identified in Technical Instructor Training and Qualification Guideline, INPO 82-026 at 7.1.

Q. 249. Can you tell us how you expect to treat people under the new rule who are currently SRO instructor certified? What kind of credit are they going to get because they are SRO instructor certified, if any?

A. The answer is none. Obviously they have completed the same training program and taken the same exam as an SRO, but because of eligibility requirements or time on shift or some other requirement they did not meet the SRO requirements.

In the past, there have been individuals who successfully converted an instructor's certification to an RO license.

Additionally, there is the provision for waiver of certain portions of the NRC examination, based on operators having: (1) extensive actual operating experience at a comparable facility within two years, (2) discharged his or her responsibilities competently and safely and is capable of continuing to do so, and (3) learned the operating procedures and is qualified to competently operate the facility designated in the application.

If you want these individuals to become licensed, you will need to submit a complete application, and if applicable, request a waiver under the Regulation. This application would then be reviewed by the Region as to what portion, if any, of the examination would be waivered.

"Actively Performing the Functions of an Operator or Senior Operator"

Q. 250. What guidance will the Commission provide to the facility licensees and the staff that Section IIF(2) is Commission policy?

A. Section IIF(2) is part of the Statement of Considerations that summarizes public comments and describes the staff's final actions in response to them. This Section discusses the definition of "actively performing the functions of an operator or senior operator," which is part of the regulation, contained in Sections 55.53(e) and 55.53(f).

*Q. 251. The regulation for active participation states that "an individual has a position on the shift crew that requires the individual to be licensed as defined in the facility's Technical Specifications, and that the individual carries out and is responsible for the duties covered in that position." How does this rule accommodate plants with RO and SRO licenses on shift that exceed the Technical Specification minimum staffing requirements?

A. The rule does not preclude having additional people on shift beyond the minimum staffing requirements. That is a utility decision. However, in order to take credit for the proficiency of such personnel standing watch above the Technical Specification minimums, as a condition for maintaining a license under 10 CFR 55.53(e), the facility licensee must maintain administrative control over these designated watchstanders, and must be satisfied that these individuals are maintaining their proficiency by manipulating the controls of the facility in the case of an operator, or by manipulating the controls and directing the licensed activities of licensed operators, in the case of a senior operator.

So that if you operate a single unit with three reactor operators on shift, two of those individuals are in positions required by the Technical Specifications. One is usually the reactor operator and the other is the balance of plant operator. The third person would need to rotate into one of those two positions over the course of a quarter to obtain the requisite number of shifts to maintain his license active, so he would need to sign the logs, on occasion, as the reactor operator or the balance of plant operator. So it's clear that you must be in the position on shift required by the Technical Specifications, and additional personnel on shift to perform other duties do not meet the requirement for directing the activities of licensed operators or for manipulating the controls. There are alternatives built into the regulation to provide ample flexibility in obtaining proficiency for licensed duties, e.g., 40 hours of parallel watch standing.

Q. 252. Our Technical Specifications do not address the individual's responsibilities for each position in order to satisfy the active participation requirement--it says you have to have an RO and two SROs, one SRO as a shift supervisor and one that's another RO. Can you rotate that SRO position from a shift foreman position to another senior reactor operator position? It doesn't say who is required to fill those positions, so the complication is that if we have a senior control operator who has an SRO license and he's clearly directing the operator's activities, can we give him the responsibility for the day and say the shift foreman no longer has the responsibility, because both of them hold an SRO license?

A. For the case that you've described, the individual who is on shift directing the activities is the one who's in the position required by the Technical Specifications. Whether he is the shift foreman for that shift because that's the title that you use to describe other responsibilities he may have, it is the senior operator in the control room who directs how the other two operators manipulate the controls and who is there fulfilling the requirements of the Technical Specifications to be supervising the activities of the licensed operators. That's the position that qualifies for the eight hours on that shift, independent of title. Your administrative procedures should be clear as to who has authority to direct licensed operators so that if the shift foreman is relieved there is another senior operator in the control room carrying out those duties. The Technical Specifications don't refer to shift foreman; they say senior operator directing the activities of other licensed operators.

There is a related question that concerns the extra person on shift who may not be in the licensed role. It is possible for that individual to complete 40 hours of parallel watch standing; that is, he's not in the position required by the Technical Specifications, as long as he is being supervised and his activities are being closely monitored by the person responsible. He could accrue 40 hours of parallel watch standing for that quarter and not be actually in a position required by the Technical Specifications to meet the seven shifts at eight hours each, or the five shifts of twelve hours each.

It would require in that case, that the authorizing representative of the facility certify that he has completed that duty. From a practical standpoint, it's easier to rotate the people through the watch to maintain their proficiency. The active license status is intended as a way of maintaining the proficiency of the people who are performing the functions. If you're dual licensed, the active status requirement can be met by standing watch on only one plant, or on some combination of the plants.

Conditions of Licenses (Subpart F, Section 55.53)

Q. 253. With regards to fuel handlers, in the case where you may refuel once a year, it's probable that the requirement won't be maintained. Subparagraph 55.53(f)(2) suggests that one shift of supervised duty is required before the fuel handling foreman with the license can assume his full duties. Is the intent that that supervision be performed by another fully qualified SRO who may not be a fuel handling specialist?

A. That is correct. An active SRO license includes the capability and responsibilies associated with monitoring fuel-handling activities.

Q. 254. The Operations Manager and Operations Supervisor are required by Technical Specifications to be licensed as Senior Reactor Operators. These individuals do not have a position on the shift crew. They are involved in the day-to-day direction of Licensed Operator activities. Are these positions considered as actively performing Licensed Duties?

A. No, unless they stand the seven 8-hour shifts per quarter, or five 12-hour shifts per quarter. That does not mean that the Ops Manager and the Ops Supervisor cannot keep a license. The requirements to maintain a license are that they continue in requalification.

If the Operations Manager must hold a license, then he must participate in requal, but he need not stand watch on shift in a position where he is directing the activities of the Reactor Operators. A license, whether it's active or not, may meet some Technical Specification requirement.

Q. 255. What if you have an SRO stand a shift assignment as an RO? Does the SRO get credit for standing watch in that position for renewal purposes?

A. The SRO is not performing Senior Reactor Operator license duties. Unless he is also standing SRO's duties during that quarter, then his SRO license would not be active. Where an SRO is standing an RO watch, his license would continue to be active insofar as it deals with his operating or manipulating the controls as an RO.

In order for him to direct others, he would have to stand a 40-hour parallel shift in order to be proficient and go back into an SRO's duties. He could, however, continue to maintain an SRO license if he's current in requal. If he wants to assume an SRO's capacity, he must go back to a 40-hour shift under instruction as an SRO.

Q. 256. When the operations manager is licensed, should technical advisors or licensed instructors have to become members of a shift crew to maintain an active license?

A. Yes, to maintain an active license, they do. To maintain an inactive license, they don't.

Q. 257. Do personnel seeking to maintain an active license have to replace a member of a shift crew to meet the watch requirements of 10 CFR 55.53?

A. Yes, they do, with the understanding that there may be additional people on shift beyond the minimum technical specification requirements.

Q. 258. Although there is only one Technical Specification SRO position on shift (Shift Supervisor), our Technical Specification reflects the 10 CFR 50.54 requirement of a second SRO on shift. Would standing a watch as a designated second SRO meet the definition of actively performing the function of a Senior Operator?

A. If he is filling an SRO position under the Tech Specs then he would be maintaining his active SRO license. A number of people have asked, can we have two or three people come in to get their on-shift time? Our position is that those meeting the minimum staffing Technical Specification requirements for whatever operational mode get credit, although there can be other people on shift who are also eligible for credit.

For clarification, this question seems to imply that at this facility the Tech Specs do not conform to the Regulation for a single-unit site for having two Senior Operators on shift during operational modes. That's understandable because the Rule itself supersedes the Technical Specification requirement, and is a higher order requirement. That is, you must conform to the Rule even if your Tech Specs permit something less. We would suggest that the next time you have an administrative change to that section of the Technical Specifications, amend it to conform to the Rule.

Q. 259. If the Operations Manager does not hold an active license, what duties may he perform or not perform in that status? For instance, we all have Technical Specifications that require licensed Senior Reactor Operators to approve changes to procedures. Would an inactive license allow him to do those administrative functions?

A. Yes. He can do everything but direct a Reactor Operator in manipulation of controls, or himself manipulate the controls.

Q. 260. All stations have engineering expertise on shift in the form of a shift engineer, who is the STA. STAs hold a current SRO license. They direct activities and integrate schedules. Are they not actively performing the functions of an SRO license by those duties, or are they going to have to come back and perform as a shift supervisor, on shift?

A. If they are one of the two individuals required by Technical Specifications to staff the shift, then what you just described is acceptable. If one is there as an engineer on shift who happens also to hold an SRO license, and is only fulfilling the role of an STA, then he is not responsible for directing the activities of licensed operators. There are many cases of extra people on day shift, who do support functions, such as reviewing tags, procedures, line-ups, records, etc., and do not require an active license to perform them. It is only when he is performing the functions and duties of an operator or a senior operator that an active license is required.

*Q. 261. Our Technical Specifications require two senior reactor operators and two reactor operators for mode one and two operation. Typically, though, we'll have others assigned to the shift. Is it NRC's intention that only the two people assigned as the balance of plant operator and the reactor operator are receiving credit for being on shift? Or are the others manipulating the controls getting credit for being on shift?

A. If utility management has determined that they are necessary for safe operation, the decision about the number of additional watchstanders is that of the facility licensee. However, in order to take credit for the proficiency of such personnel standing watch above the Technical Specification minimums, as a condition for maintaining a license under 10 CFR 55.53(e), the facility licensee must be satisfied that they maintain their proficiency by manipulating the controls, in the case of an operator, or by manipulating the controls and directing the licensed activities of licensed operators, in the case of a senior operator.

Q. 262. Do candidates with an RO license in training to be upgraded to senior operator lose their active license status per 55.53(e) while standing watch as an extra operator for three months?

A. Yes. If the operator does not maintain the requirements of an RO, he loses his active status.

Q. 263. This question is related to actively maintaining a license. Could someone stand 40 hours in January and then again in June to meet the active license requirement by calendar quarter.

A. No. The 40-hour requirement does not pertain to maintaining a license, but is part of the requirement for resuming active status. Maintaining an active license means standing the necessary shift watches.

*Q. 264. This question concerns active license status at a dual-unit plant. The shift supervisor is the SRO who normally directs the activities of the operators. We also have an SRO on shift who is over both of the shift supervisors. He does not normally direct the activities of the operators, but he may. Would his supervisory time on shift count as active time?

A. Yes. If you look in the Regulations on staffing for a dual-unit site, you have three SROs for the two units. If he is in one of those positions, that qualifies him. If he is not in one of those positions, you may still take credit for his proficiency if you are satisfied that he is maintaining that proficiency by manipulating the controls and directing the licensed activities of licensed operators.

Q. 265. If an operator gets sick in the middle of February, and has been actively on watch in January and February and has this requirement met but is sick for three months before he goes back on the watch, does he have to stand a 40-hour watch? You don't have to demonstrate in the prior three months he has served 40 hours; isn't it by calendar quarter?

A. Correct. But during the remainder of that quarter he's going to have to complete the required number of shifts to be considered actively performing the functions.

Q. 266. What records will the Commission require to ensure that a licensee has maintained active status per 10 CFR 55.53(e)? What will be the record retention period?

A. It's up to the facility to determine how it wants to be able to document the active status. Shift turnover logs would be appropriate documentation. The key is that the documentation be retained and available for review.

There are two answers to the question of record retention. If the record is the control room log, it has its own record retention requirement, which is essentially for the life of the plant. If you are using the control room log to determine whether the guy was signed in, that's adequate.

The certification for his returning to duties is based upon his standing 40 hours of parallel watch. On parallel watch, however, he need not sign the control room log. Under those conditions, the responsible official onsite could create a form which would go into your records onsite and be available for audit. That form would have a record retention requirement equal to that person's license; that is, six years.

Q. 267. The proposed rulemaking said nothing about the five 12-hour shifts or seven 8-hour shifts. What is the basis for this, and why weren't we given an opportunity to comment?

A. The previous practice has been for a minimum of one shift, essentially per month, three per quarter. That was deemed by the Commission to not be sufficient, as a part of their review and determination of the final Rule, and they increased it to the current requirements in the Rule.

Q. 268. Would it be possible for an operations superintendent to direct activities from off his shift, and if so, then would that individual be required to maintain an active license by actual shift time for a calendar quarter?

A. Let me give you what I think is the most practical example: in an emergency, typically, the operations superintendent is the individual who goes back and forth between the Tech Support Center or provides assistance in an emergency. He gives directions to whoever it is, the Shift Superintendent or the other SROs; so he is not directing the manipulation of the controls; he's providing guidance on how he wants the event to be handled.

Someone else in the decision process is actually deciding whether he agrees or doesn't and directs the activities of the licensed operators in manipulating controls.

So in that case he is not on shift in the position; he is off shift, responding in accordance with the emergency plan, which is covered by a different portion of the regulations.

So the operations superintendent need not hold an active license unless you intend him to go on shift as a shift superintendent.

Q. 269.   That same logic would apply to day-to-day operations, then, if I under-stand you correctly?

A.   There is no day-to-day operations issue. He's there fulfilling the posi-tion that's required by the Tech Specs as the operations superintendent; that is, independent of proficiency in manipulating controls. We would not expect the operations superintendent to go in, for instance, and line up systems or manipulate controls on the board.

He needs to be proficient in order to be consistent with the requirements of the regulations, so he would either have to stand 40 hours of parallel duty or maintain proficiency or keep his hands off the controls.

In the process of examining him for requalification, we would examine him both at the RO and the SRO level. Your continuing training program should ensure that he doesn't lose those manipulative skills because he is not required to maintain an active license.

Q. 270.   If our Technical Specification defined the STA position as an SRO on shift, would filling that capacity satisfy the requirements?

A.   Yes.

*Q. 271.   Consider a plant in cold shutdown with lowered minimum shift manning requirements. Are the licensed operators assigned to that crew who are in excess of the minimum cold shutdown staffing requirements actively performing licensed duties?

A.   Yes, if you have determined that they are necessary for safe operations, you maintain administrative control over these positions, and if you are satis-fied that they are maintaining their proficiency in accordance with the regulation.

Q. 272.   How, and to whom, is certification made under 55.53(f)?

A.   This section has to do with returning the individual to an active status. A certification must be made and available on file for inspection purposes; it need not be made to the NRC.

Q. 273.   It would appear that once a quarter, an individual could spend 40 hours on shift under the direction of the licensed operators. And the facility could certify that he had done so, and that his status in the requal program was cur-rent. And by doing so, he could maintain an active license by spending essen-tially 40 hours a quarter on shift, instead of the 56 to 60 hours specified in other parts of the Regulations? Is that true?

A. That is true, although that is not what we intend. The issue is to make it easy for people to maintain a license. And that's a decision that the facility makes with respect to the commitment of time to the requalification program. If the facility wants to commit an additional 40 hours for parallel watch standing in a control room in addition to the requalification program, so that he can be active, that's their choice. Our intent was to make the minimum seven watches at eight hours, or five watches at twelve hours, to maintain the proficiency of those who are actually directing the activities, or manipulating the controls. It's a proficiency issue, it's not a license renewal issue.

Q. 274. Are any allowances made in 55.53(f) for off-shift licensed personnel who are involved in daily operation's supervision?

A. No. They are either in active status or they are not. If they are not, their just being a daily operations manager, or an operations superintendent, does not convert them to an active status.

Q. 275. Suppose someone completes 40 hours on shift under supervision; then his clock starts again for his seven 8-hour periods. If an individual goes through this in the last month of a quarter, does he have to complete those seven 8-hour shifts before that month is up, or does he start during the next calendar quarter?

A. If he's done 40 hours of parallel watch in a quarter, he's active in that quarter. For the next calendar quarter, he would need to stand either seven 8-hour watches, or five 12-hour watches. Regaining proficiency allows him to go back into an active status to stand watch. He does not have to do both in the same quarter. That is, he does not have to serve 40 hours under instruction, plus stand seven 8-hour watches, or five 12-hour shifts in that quarter; it goes to the next one.

Q. 276. Could you clarify what you mean by "parallel watch standing?"

A. It's very similar to "being directly under the supervision of," as we use that phrase for a trainee; that is, the individual that has the watch still has the responsibility.

The person that's in the parallel situation, even though he's licensed, is not considered proficient. The regulation requires that he not manipulate the controls or direct activities except under the direct supervision of someone who has an active license.

Q. 277. Do those 40 hours have to be consecutive; i.e., eight hours a day?

A. No. It has to be 40 hours. You can have four tens or ten fours or any other combination that adds up to 40 hours; however, they must be in the same calendar quarter.

The only explicit guidance in the regulation concerns the seven 8-hour or five 12-hour shifts where a full shift means from watch relief to watch relief.

Q. 278. Can licensed Senior Operators who are not in active status perform refueling SRO duties?

A. No. Only active SROs can supervise refueling activities. If they are not active, they must stand one 8-hour shift under instruction from licensed active SROs to perform active SRO duties limited to fuel handling.

Q. 279. What leeway do you give to the facility to know that an operator has received a felony conviction?

A. Convicted felons typically go to jail, so they're not going to be at work. Also, all those granted clearance for unrestricted access have background investigations that relate to such things as convictions for felonies. You will have access to the information from that source, too.

Q. 280. But the facility will not necessarily know within 30 days?

A. It is the operator who is required to let us know in 30 days, as a condition of the license.

Q. 281. So, we don't assume any liability for not notifying you within 30 days?

A. If you don't know, and you didn't have a reasonable basis to know, we're not going to hold you liable for that. However, if you get a criminal history check that shows that the person has been convicted of a felony, we expect you to tell us.

Q. 282. If we submit an applicant for a license who has had a felony 15 years ago, is that still reportable? If he had taken a licensing exam and was ready to receive a license, would he have to notify you within 30 days, assuming we did not know that?

A. If the individual knew that he had been convicted of a felony in the past, and he did not report that on the initial application, his application would be considered incomplete. Such an omission could be the basis for revoking his license, since he would have withheld information.

Q. 283. Why is the applicant no longer required to sign the Form 396 certifying that he or she has no felony convictions?

A. Because it is a condition of a license, per Part 55.53(g) that individuals notify us within 30 days of a conviction for a felony. So, should someone get a license who had a prior felony, he would be required to notify us of the prior felony.

Q. 284. If we were to let an individual's license go inactive, would it also be reasonable for us to let his medical requiremerts lapse?

A. No, you cannot let his medical requirements lapse. He must be medically examined each two years. That is a condition of his license, whether he maintains proficiency or not.

Q. 285. Is there is a purpose for that, if he is going to continue inactive? He is not permitted go on shift, so there seems to be little point to maintain the medical status up to date?

A. The issue is whether he is medically fit to carry out the duties of a licensed operator if you put him in a situation of watch standing to regain his proficiency. At that point, he would be permitted to manipulate the controls of the facility, and/or direct activities. The reason we extended the licensing period to six years was to make it coincide with the medical requirement, which comes up in two-year cycles.

Q. 286. Are licensees who maintain an inactive license required to participate in a requalification program to the same extent as licensees maintaining an active license?

A. Yes. A condition of their license under the new Part 55.53 (h), requires participation in the requalification program.

Q. 287. The problem is that standing the shift foreman's license does not prepare this person to go out and handle fuel, and I don't understand how doing one watch under instruction does that, how that can guarantee that he's going to be a safe person in charge of fuel handling?

A. We're talking about an SRO limited to fuel handling, not an SRO with an unlimited license here. So if a guy has an SRO license and he's an active SRO, he can be used as an SRO with no other duties but to handle fuel, or be the supervisor in charge of fuel handling, with no other duties. If he's a senior with a limited license, he's in a different category, because he can't be used as an SRO. So any active SRO could be a fuel handler senior, but if he is an active fuel handler and then he doesn't handle any fuel for awhile, or for some reason he doesn't use his license, then he has to only stand one watch, or one eight-hour shift with an SRO who is an active SRO, or an SRO with a limited fuel handler, and then he has met that certification again.

The only adjustments we've made in the rule for fuel handlers are that, in order to become active, they only have to stand one parallel shift, which would make it much quicker and easier than the 40 parallel shift, and that the requal program is limited only to those aspects of the plant operation to which their license is limited.

Q. 288. With respect to the requirements for maintaining operating proficiency, can a licensed STA (SRO License) who is standing the "STA Watch" get credit for SRO proficiency?

A. No.

Q. 289. We had a concern on restoration of an inactive license as a full-scope SRO license, and we wanted to use that individual for fuel handling during refueling. Would that individual as a full-scope license have to go through the 40 hours of concurrent duties, or just eight hours of concurrent duties?

A. It would only take eight hours under parallel watch with a person whose license is active, whether that's another licensee limited to fuel handling only, or it's a senior reactor operator.

Q. 290. When will the quarter for shift standing start when the new rule is implemented?

A. For accountability purposes the first complete calendar quarter after the rule is implemented must meet the seven shift/quarter requirement.

Q. 291. Does completion of 7 days on shift in one position such as shift engineer, allow the individual to perform duties in another position on shift for which he is also qualified?

A. If shift engineer is a Tech Spec position required to hold a SRO license, then performing in the seven-8 hour shifts, per 55.53(e) would permit the licensee to perform duties as either an SRO or RO.

Q. 292. Do technical advisors or licensed instructors require an active license, if they must maintain a license for technical specifications or FSAR?

A. They may need a license per the Technical Specifications, FSAR etc., but it does not have to be "active" per the Regulation unless the individual is required to assume a position onshift that the Technical Specifications identify as a licensed shift manning requirement.

Q. 293. If an operator gets his license during a calendar quarter, how is he to meet the seven shifts per quarter requirement?

A. For the initial calendar quarter for which a license is issued, he is considered to have met the proficiency requirements by virtue of having passed the exam. Thus, the "actively performing" requirement will commence in the first calendar quarter after he receives the license.

Requalification and Renewal (Statement of Considerations)

Q. 294. The regulation says that sometime during that six-year period, a candidate will get a test. That may be the first year through the sixth year, but the next time he is renewed, it may be as much as 11 years apart. Is that correct?

A. No. In the Statement of Considerations, II(H)(4), the last sentence says, "The NRC will administer these requalification written examinations and operating tests on a random basis, so that no operator or senior operator will go longer than six years without being examined by the NRC once a six-year license is issued." That's a direction from the Commission to the staff. That's the same way we handle the clarification of the INPO status, in the Statement of Considerations that goes with the Rule, describing intent. Some operators will receive more than one NRC-administered exam during the term of their license in order to comply with the Commission's direction to the staff.

Renewal of Licenses (Subpart H, Section 55.57)

Q. 295. At what point will the six-year cycle start for present license holders?

A. It will start with the first license issuance after May 26th. We do not intend to amend the present licenses. So on May 25th, someone will get a two-year license. On May 26th, that individual would receive a six-year license.

Q. 296. I have 107 licenses expiring over the next two years for which NRC requal exams are not taken. Where do they stand?

A. The renewal of the two-year license is governed by the rules under which they were given their original license, so no NRC exam is required.

Q. 297. We've gone from a situation where at the end of the examination conducted by NRC, the results were discussed with the utility, to a situation presently where the results are not discussed until the license certificate is signed off and the results have been reviewed at the Region. In combining requalification exams administered by NRC with initial license exams administered by NRC, will the examiners, upon an indication that a candidate for renewal was a potential failure as a result of the operating portion of the exam, discuss that information with the utility, or will you allow that person to go back on shift pending the complete review? And how do you expect this to affect the turn-around time when we're significantly increasing the number of exams to be evaluated?

A. We can't predict how it will affect the turn-around time. Hopefully we will have the resources to do it within the existing time frame. From the point of view of a licensing decision, no decision has been made until the paper is signed. In other words, it is only a recommendation until the point that either the license or the failure has been approved by the branch chief, by the licensing authority.

We're prohibited from discussing predecisional information. That's why we do not give preliminary results either on site or from the regional office.

REQUALIFICATION AND RENEWAL

Obviously, if the examiner believes that it's a safety issue if an individual returns to shift, it's incumbent upon him to notify the licensee. We would not leave the site with a safety issue pending. However, when we leave the site, we don't always know whether an individual has passed or failed all portions of the examination (written, oral, and simulator).

Q. 298. What is written evidence of the applicant's experience and how is this supplied?

A. Written evidence will be the same as it is now; as it is reported on relevant portions of Form 398.

Q. 299. What is the evidence that the applicant has discharged the license responsibilities competently and safely, and how is this information provided?

A. The utility certifies that the individual has performed in accordance with the terms and conditions of his license, and that he has performed satisfactorily. It is for you to determine how that performance has been, through whatever mechanisms you want to use; whether it be performance evaluations, or other information that you have in your company files related to that individual.

Q. 300. In reviewing past performance under Section 55.57, you said earlier that an NRC letter or a letter of reprimand might be part of what you'd evaluate. Does this mean a letter of reprimand specifically from NRC, or one from the site itself?

A. An NRC review would be based upon two things: the certification from the company, and any official enforcement actions taken against the individual that are in his official docket file. It does not include information that has not been formally transmitted to the individual under his license, as it must be a completed action. The fact that an individual is under investigation by the NRC may not result in something going into his file. It only goes into his file when we complete an enforcement action and he receives a letter. It's a formal notification, and there is guidance as to what is permitted in the docket file and what is not. Essentially, anything in the NRC docket file has already been presented to that candidate, whether it be an examination grading report result, or an enforcement action.

Q. 301. If someone never operates the controls, and he gets a license, that license is renewable. Why do we then report the number of hours one operates the facility on a renewal?

A. Although we will renew a license of an individual who has not stood watch, that information may be helpful in making judgments on renewal applications in which the individuals did not fully meet all 55.57(b) requirements to the letter. For example, an individual may have been unable to attend every requal class because he was participating in a management course. The number of operational hours for this person may influence our decision regarding his renewal.

Q. 302. When it's time to renew the license of our shift engineers, can their license be renewed in an inactive status, without another examination, if they have maintained all of their requal requirements?

A. For anyone who holds a license, he must be kept current in the requalification program; he must be medically fit, and he must have been examined at some time by NRC during the course of that six-year license. The requalification examination requirements are applicable independent of active/inactive status.

Q. 303. If a licensee is not maintaining an active license in accordance with 55.53(f) at the time of license expiration, what are the requirements for renewal?

A. If he is not maintaining an active license, he still must meet all of the requirements for renewal in 55.57(b). However, he does not have to be active to get his license renewed. He must be, most importantly, current in the requalification program, but he does not have to be active to have his license renewed.

Q. 304. In order to obtain license renewal you must be examined by the NRC at least once during the six-year life of the license. What is the extent of this examination: written, operating, both, either?

A. With respect to format, the requalification exam will parallel the initial exam, i.e., it will include both a written and operating test. The content of requalification exams will be based on the facility's learning objectives provided that these objectives are satisfactory.

Q. 305. Section 55.57 states that license renewal is going to be based on having passed the comprehensive requal exam and operating test administered by the Commission during the term of a six-year license. I believe that you have interpreted that to mean that an exam will be given at least once every six years?

A. Yes, that's what the Commission has stated. The Commission has directed the staff to examine operators at least once each six years, and that's why we know that some people may have an exam more than once in six years.

Q. 306. What percentage of people will you examine at a time?

A. At least 16 percent per year, because we've got to examine 100 percent in six years. In fact, it will be greater than 16 percent because of the randomness involved in ensuring that candidates don't have prior knowledge of when we are coming in to examine them.

Q. 307. How far in advance will an individual licensee be notified by the Commission of his scheduled examination date?

A. Ten days, minimum; 6 weeks, maximum.

Q. 308. Do you need to take examination to renew a two-year license?

A. No. The rule is very specific: You need an examination by the NRC only for the renewal of a six-year license.

Q. 309. I have some renewal submittals that will have to be submitted before the May 26th date, but the renewal is not until after. Do I submit them under the existing rules for them to come back as a six-year license?

A. The Form 398 that you use until May 26, 1987 is the same one that's in effect today. Even, though you submit that version of the form, if we issue a license after the 26th, it will be a six-year license. Any applications submitted after May 26th should be on the new Form 398 with the new Form 396.

Q. 310. Will the people presently holding two-year licenses have to reapply at the expiration of the two years or will they be automatically extended to the six-year cycle?

A. They need to reapply prior to the expiration date of their current license.

Q. 311. Considering that every utility has or will have an accredited retraining program, what is the justification for the random selection, which would include the possibility of having more than one exam in a six-year period, versus the possibility of doing an orderly schedule to include only one exam in that same six-year period?

A. It is NRC's mandate to ensure that all licensed operators maintain a satisfactory level of proficiency at all times. As such, the required exam is intended to serve as a "spot-check" to verify that that level of proficiency is in fact being maintained. Further, we want to ensure that operators can demonstrate this level of competence without special preparation outside of the normal required training program. The Commissioners believe that this is best accomplished by randomly selecting the operators to sit for the required exam.

To the extent possible, we will coordinate the exam schedule with your regular cycles. But if we have reason to believe that there is something wrong with the program, or we have other indications of problems, we will conduct examinations at times other than during your requalification cycle.

Q. 312. How can the Commission administer a comprehensive written exam once during the six-year cycle if the utility is administering their written exam spread out over a segmented period?

A. As stated above, the Commission's mandate is to ensure a satisfactory level of operator proficiency at all times. It is the facility licenses's responsibility to ensure that their required program, although segmented, maintains this level of proficiency throughout the training cycle.

Q. 313. Who will schedule and track each licensed operator to ensure he has had an NRC exam prior to renewal?

A. That's NRC's responsibility. It will be tracked in the Regions by the docket files on each individual which will contain the last NRC-administered requal exam.

Q. 314. How soon can someone be re-examined after failing an NRC exam?

A. We have resources for two visits to a facility per year. If the individual fails and is getting close to the point for renewal, we would evaluate on a case-by-case basis whether our resources permit us to go back and give another examination before the next regularly scheduled exam.

If he's within, say, six months of renewal, and that's when he's targeted to come up for an exam, that's a pretty good indicator that he's going to be taking an exam at that next cycle before his license renewal.

Q. 315. In the past, if an operator failed the requal exam, he would go into an accelerated requal program normally administered by the utility. Is that going to remain the same, and, once he completes the accelerated requal and the examination by the utility, would that be acceptable as far as meeting the requirement of passing the NRC-administered exam?

A. No. There are two different questions there. The first deals with the acceptability of the facility's accelerated retraining program to return that individual to licensed duties, and this depends upon the status of your requalification program. If your requalification program is deemed satisfactory, then you have the capabilities under your program of dealing with the failure of a requalification examination.

The second concerns satisfying the requirement for a six-year reexamination. The Commission has directed the staff to administer a requalification examination to each licensee during the six-year term of the license. If he fails and you have a program that has been deemed satisfactory, you can retrain him and return him to shift duties; however, he must successfully pass an NRC-administered requalification examination before renewal of his license.

Q. 316. Is the appeal process for the requal examination the same as the initial exam? If so, there are two problems. One is the individual's own self-respect if he fails that exam and he feels he should not have. The other problem is that our program is being judged against the results of that requal exam. If there's something that we feel was amiss during the exam, we should have a method of recourse in having that evaluated.

A. The answer is that the appeal process does apply as it relates to the administrative process. You are provided the opportunity to comment on the written examination through the normal process for any written examination.

However, the individual does not have the right to request a hearing because his license has not been taken away. He still has a license. He can request an administrative review by the Division Director in the Region and a review at NRC Headquarters if there is a potential for the exam results to preclude his license renewal.

If we were to deny the renewal of his license and he was contesting the failure of that exam administratively, he would have the right to a hearing because we had not granted the license renewal. So in that context, he would be eligible to request a hearing on the denial of his application for a license renewal.

Q. 317. Why weren't the utilities allowed to make public comments on 10 CFR 55.57(b)(2)(iv), license renewal requirements?

A. The Commission decided to add Section 55.57(b)(2)(iv) between the time of the proposed and final rules to allow it to examine licensees during a 6-year license period. This decision was an outgrowth of comments on the proposed rule and is consistent with the Commission's Policy Statement on Training and

Qualifications, and with Section 306 of the Nuclear Waste Policy Act. Part of the reason for that decision is that we indicated in the policy statement on training and qualifications that we would use the requalification examination as a mechanism for judging the validity of the industry-accredited training program process. The Commission is continuing to do that.

We have moved out of the training review and are instead judging the ability of the individual to perform after training. We make that judgment through an examining process. That's the reason for it. The Commission has indicated their policy both through the policy statement, which was publicly noticed and available, and through a continuation of staff practice.

The Commission tied it to renewal to ensure that there was a clear understanding on the part of all operators that this was required, and to eliminate the question of "Why me," because in the past, when the staff selected operators for examination, there was always a question of, "How did I get chosen, why not someone else?" In this case, it's clear that it applies to all licensed operators who hold a six-year license.

Q. 318. Will future NRC requalification exams given in conjunction with replacement tests be modified replacement tests as in the past?

A. NRC requalification examinations are developed to evaluate the adequacy of the facility licensee's requalification program. Where replacement training program and requalification training program objectives overlap, duplication of questions is acceptable.

Q. 319. Since it is six years before any renewals will require the completion of an NRC exam, when will the process of "10-day notice exams" get started?

A. As of the effective date of the rule. We can notify selectees up to six weeks in advance of the examination date, but in no case will less than 10 days notice be given.

Q. 320. Does the six-year license apply to nonpower reactors? Do their licensed operators require an NRC exam prior to renewing a license?

A. Operators of nonpower reactors will receive six-year licenses upon satisfactory license renewal after their current licenses expire. License renewal will be in accordance with 55.57.

Q. 321. When will the requirement for an applicant to be examined by the NRC prior to renewal be implemented?

A. That requirement will become effective for all six-year licenses granted after May 26, 1987.

Q. 322. What will the basis be for "continued need" under 55.57(b)(3)?

A. It is the facility licensee's decision as to whether there is a continued need for an operator. We will not question the judgment of facility management.

Q. 323. Can the requirements of 55.57(a)(4),(5), and (6) be certified on the Form 398?

A. Part 55.57(a)(4), assurance that the applicant has satisfactorily completed the requalification program, and 55.57(a)(5), assurance that the applicant has discharged license responsibilities competently and safely, can both be certified in Form 398. For 55.57(a)(6), certification of medical condition, a Form 396 is needed.

Requalification (Subpart H, Section 55.59)

Q.324. What is required for Commission approval of a requalification program?

A. You simply certify to us that you have an accredited program that is based on a systems approach to training, and that's sufficient.

Q. 325. In Generic Letter 87-07, page 24, it states that "The specific cycle will be approved by the NRC as part of each facility's training program." What does this refer to?

A. It covers programs which are not approved through the accreditation process.

Q. 326. On the training program approval, if you have an accredited program and you certify that you're doing an SAT process, that's one method. You also listed implementation of INPO Guideline 86-025 as another approach. Can you explain this?

A. The accreditation process has a hierarchy of requirements, the top level of which are called objectives. You must meet the intent of the objective in order to be accredited, and those are contained in INPO 85-002. The Commission has reviewed and endorsed the INPO accreditation objectives and criteria as meeting the SAT or systems approach to training. I believe there are 12 objectives.

Each objective has a number of criteria; meet the criteria and you meet the objective, but the opposite is not always the case. That is, you may not meet one criterion, but you still may meet the intent of the objective through some other mechanism. You go through the criteria and objectives for your self-evaluation.

Subordinate to those are the guidelines for licensed operator training, for maintenance training, and for other areas. One guideline is for continuing training for licensed operators (INPO 86-025); it gives information about the content appropriate for a continuing training program. It also describes how you evaluate and feed information from plant operations and performance evaluations back into the process.

You clearly do not have to cross all the t's and dot all the i's of everything that's in that guideline. That guideline, however, constitutes an acceptable method of implementing a performance-based, SAT-based continuing training program that the staff would find acceptable.

The next level below guidelines are good practices. Those are things which INPO has seen facilities do that worked particularly well for a facility, and they have provided guidance on those.

We have concluded that if you are accredited you understand what the objectives are, and how criteria are used, and what the process is for developing a systems approach to training. We think that understanding, along with recent INPO training guidelines provide an adequate basis for you to review your own programs and certify to us that your program is based upon a systems approach to training.

We believe that there are two final parts to that. You need to look at the tasks that are relevant to the job, decide which ones are appropriate for training on a continuing basis, based upon such criteria as importance of the task to the safety function and frequency of performance. Clearly, emergency procedures would fall into that category. Shift relief and turnover would be outside of that category, such that your continuing training program would not address shift relief and turnover.

If you've operated continuously between outages, you would not necessarily have performed plant startups and shutdowns. In that case, you may want to fold the startup and shutdown into the continuing training program, and do that on a simulator.

It's that type of flexibility, and reviewing and determining the content of the program which we feel is the most important attribute of the change to the regulation. It gives you the flexibility to tailor your program to the needs of the job incumbents, and to bring them up to a comparable level with the initial training programs through the INPO accreditation. That's the process we think should be followed. It doesn't mean that everything has to be done in INPO 85-026 with respect to simulator training, or INPO 85-025 with respect to continuing training. Those are guidelines, and you really need to address the issues as to how much of that should be followed or done with INPO, not with the staff. We are not in the position of reviewing and determining what constitutes INPO requirements. We want to move out of that. We will provide our comments to INPO should we see problem areas for INPO to address generically with the industry. We do not want to get into the mode of providing guidance to individual utilities on how much of an INPO document needs to be followed before the staff would accept a certification. That's for you and INPO to work out.

Q. 327. While someone is in an SRO upgrade for (say) ten months, he is not officially in the requalification program. How is that going to affect that inactive status?

A. If your upgrade program meets the objectives of your requal program, you can take credit for that. However, if there is a differential there might be some areas that are not covered at all, but are covered in a requalification program. If that individual is no longer current in requalification, to resume active status, he would have to receive the remedial training necessary to make him current with the requalification program. Simply being in the upgrade program does not, necessarily, compensate for the requalification program.

We hope that that's not an issue that we face very often, because we expect that most candidates who go into an upgrade program would receive a license as a senior operator and remain cognizant of changes, LERs, and significant events. And upon the date they receive a license, they can manipulate the controls and direct the activities of others. So, it's only when there's a period between the end of his training and the time he gets a license when you may want to use him as a reactor operator. He may have to stand some parallel watch with the reactor operator before resuming duties. And that's the point when you would have to certify that he had completed the necessary requirements of the reactor requalification program, if there are any aspects that were not covered in the SRO operating training.

Q. 328. Since Section 55.59(b) indicates that the Commission would accept additional training in lieu of a licensee's participation in the requalification program, is it acceptable for a utility to remove certain license holders from the requalification program, yet have them retain their licenses if this additional training was provided to them?

A. No. Section 55.53(h) requires completion of a requalification program as a condition of a license. In general, a licensee who is permanently removed from the requalification program no longer satisfies this condition of their license, and thus has been determined to no longer need a license by the facility licensee under Section 55.55, Expiration. Only under extenuating circumstances (e.g., special temporary assignment, extended illness, removal from shift to enter a degree program, etc.) would the provisions of Section 55.59(b) be invoked. This will be handled on a case-by-case basis.

Q. 329. There is no requirement to modify the Requalification Program documentation. We just have to follow the new rule, correct?

A. That is correct. You must follow the new Rule, or your existing program, whichever is more restrictive. But you may perform a 50.59 review to bring your existing program in conformance, and simply submit that. Or, if you need an amendment to the license, you request the amendment, and you would have an administrative change approved to put your program in conformance with the Rule.

Q. 330. Most facilities have an NRC-approved requalification program in the FSAR. For utilities that cannot certify their requalification programs, either because their requalification program has not been approved by INPO, or it has been approved and does not meet the INPO 86-25 requirements for SAT, how will we implement 10 CFR 55?

A. You will continue to follow your approved program of record, as is documented in the FSAR, until you either modify it, bring it up to the INPO guidelines in 86-25, or take some other action to modify it. That's one way of doing it. You may be able to discuss with INPO other alternatives. But you follow the program of record, as modified by the Rule.

Q. 331. What is the difference between a requalification program 24 months long followed by successive requalification programs and a continuing training program administered throughout the term of the individual's license? Does the Commission mean to imply something by use of the word "requalification" versus "continuing training?" If so, what is the distinction?

A. There is little difference between the two. We expect you on some basis to step back and take a look at the performance of your licensed operators and modify your program appropriately to reflect those areas that need continuing training. From that aspect, we chose 24 months, consistent with the previous program, to be a point at which you would take that formal look at your program.

There is no distinction except that the law used the term "requalification," and that's why we continued with that term.

Q. 332. The requalification program must be conducted for a continuous period not to exceed 24 months. What is the purpose of the 24-month limit?

A. Because it's consistent with defining a fixed-length program. Since the previous period was 24 months, we retained it.

Q. 333. Is there an intent to look at a 24-month period as an isolated section and try to meet certain requirements within a 24-month period?

A. The intent is that at the end of that period we want you to do a comprehensive evaluation of the program and decide how you need to modify it for the next cycle. If you want to do it in 12-month or 18-month cycles, that's also acceptable. If you want to tie it to refueling schedules that's also acceptable. The cycle cannot be longer than 24 months, however.

Q. 334. What is considered a "continuous period" with respect to the conduct of the requalification program?

A. It's 24 months, then you start over again for another 24 months, and then another 24 months, so that you'd have three 2-year requal cycles in the six-year license period.

Q. 335. Will the program that breaks for, say, a two-month refueling outage be considered a continuous program?

A. By "continuous" we mean that it's the same program for operators on shift as well as off shift, and it's the program as you've described it. There may be cases where you want to stop it for a period of time, where you are using segmented training and you want to teach one segment, and in the next segment you, in fact, may have some particular training in the outage that you want to cover prior to the outage.

That's the flexibility you have under the systems approach in defining your needs are and sequencing accordingly.

We want one program for all licensed operators. We don't want one schedule or program for people on shift and a different schedule or program for people who are not normal watch standers on shift.

Q. 336. Does NRC want to see a comprehensive evaluation of the program on a biennial basis?

A. Yes, at least on a biennial basis. That's the intent of the biennial qualification examination being comprehensive. Part 55 requires that the evaluation be used in determination of subsequent continuing training requirements.

Q. 337. On Page 24 of the supplementary information provided to Generic Letter 87-07 is the following statement: "The frequency of the comprehensive re-qualification written examination has been changed to a maximum of every two years." Where is this statement to be found in the text of 10 CFR 55?

A. The statement "maximum of two years" with regard to examination frequency can be derived from 10 CFR 55.59(a)(1) under "Requalification Requirements" where it says "Each licensee shall successfully complete the requalification program developed by the facility licensee that has been approved by the Commission and that the program shall be conducted for a continuous period not to exceed 24 months in duration." The next paragraph says "pass a comprehensive requalification examination and an annual operating test." So, by inference, the written examination only has to be administered on a two-year basis, where the operating test is required on an annual basis.

Q. 338. Does this statement mean that written requalification exams can occur less often than every two years?

A. No. It must be conducted concurrent with the two-year program.

Q. 339. If a utility currently has an NRC requal examination scheduled for the first week of June 1987, what will be the impact of this rule on the examination? Will the examination content be covered by the old rule, or will the content be upgraded to the requirements of the new rule? If the examination will be covering the content by the old rule, when can we expect examinations utilizing the content covered in the new rule?

A. There will be no change for the June exams because preparation of those exams has already begun. Only exams given after July 1st of this year will be able to conform to the new rule.

For clarification, there are clearly some changes in the rule that will change the examination. We don't expect that there will be changes in the content of the exam, based upon a requal program that's already been done under the current Examiner Standard, ES-601, where we are auditing individuals who have two-year licenses and auditing the company's program.

Clearly, however, the operating test portion will be documented on the new Form 157, and we will be addressing areas that are required by the regulation in constructing the examination. We aren't going to be testing on areas outside of the requal program, or the current licensing program at the facilities, but there will be some change in forms and in the documentation process. The reason for that is that those examinations are already in preparation now, and you can't do 90 days worth of work in the transition period, so we will be continuing to use the materials that were submitted prior to the effective date of the rule to construct the first few exams after the effective date of the rule, but there will be some changes in forms and processing and how it's handled.

Q. 340. Can the written requalification examination be given in several sections over a period of time or is the intent to administer one complete examination at one time?

A. If you currently have a requalification program in which you've committed to an annual comprehensive written exam, you have to continue giving that annual comprehensive written exam until you have sent in the appropriate documentation that you have an SAT-based program and that you're moving to a continuous program that is going to be conducted over a period of 24 months. That's one way of doing it, sending us a letter telling us when you are accredited and that you have a requalification program that's SAT-based.

The other alternative is what we have done in the past, which is the 50.54 change, where you would notify us that you're changing your program. So if you're committed to an annual written exam during this transition period, you have to continue to meet your commitments until you've notified us that you're changing.

Along those lines, with regard to the segmented exams, if you currently have in your program an annual comprehensive examination, then we will expect you to continue that.

If you have an accredited program and the segmented approach to evaluation is an acceptable methodology under that program, we will allow you to implement your program.

But realizing that the NRC examination will be a comprehensive examination, we expect that the program evaluations that you implement will be comprehensive in nature, also. For clarification, weekly quizzes that may be given following a week of instruction tallied together to form one exam probably would not meet the comprehensive intent of this evaluation process.

Q. 341. Written examinations for requalification will be based on initial license material. Should the exam not be limited to the scope of the approved Requalification Program?

A. The requalification exams are intended to be performance-based and operationally oriented. To the extent that they're made available to us in the submittal following the 90-day letter, we intend to use the facility licensee's learning objectives that pertain specifically to the continuing training program.

We anticipate that when you have an SAT-based requal training program, it would be modified from time to time, depending on the needs of the job incumbents. As your needs change, you would modify your program.

We anticipate that those learning objectives might be different from time to time. We would, of course, tailor our exams to those learning objectives.

Q. 342. Would it be NRC's goal to document those differences between the initial exams and the requalification exams?

A. We want you to certify that you've got a requalification program that's based upon a systems approach to training; and you should document those differences.

That's why we say that when you do the initial task analysis, you should identify that subset of tasks which are appropriate for continuing training.

We believe that to the extent you follow the INPO guidelines in 86-025, you will have done that. We believe that that's a fair representation of the type of material that should be contained in continuing training and should be used for the basis of a requalification examination.

Q. 343. Where do we find the standards and criteria for administering the comprehensive exams for the requals?

A. The standards and criteria are identified in Section 55.59, and as far as our implementation, they will be clarified in ES-601.

Q. 344. You said previously, where there is an annual operating exam and then a comprehensive written exam every two years, that the NRC exam would count for the operating portion of the examination. Why would that not also be acceptable for the written portion, if individuals were scheduled to have their written exam during that year?

A. We intend for it to be both. If NRC administers a written exam, that will substitute for the facility written; if NRC administers an operating test, that will substitute for the facility operating test for that year or for that program, whichever is appropriate.

Q. 345. Will section 55.59(a)(2) change the policy of using a licensed SRO to write/review the written requal examination? If the written examination is given every two years, would he still fulfill the requirements of this section since technically he is not taking the exam? Similarly, will the SRO who writes the performance exam, and is thus exempt from taking the exam for that year, comply with this requirement?

A. Section 55.59(a)(2) will not change the policy of using a licensed SRO to write or renew these examinations. However, it is the Commission's intent that all licensed operators be enrolled in the requalification program and take the requalification exams; further, an individual must take an exam that he did not write or review.

Q. 346. What will be the duration of the grace period for the implementation of the new 10 CFR 55?

A. The rule goes into effect on May 26, 1987. There are grace periods identified within the rule for certain aspects of the rule, and those are stated in the rule.

These include operating tests on an annual basis. If an individual is licensed on May 26, 1987, and holds a license, he must have had an operating test by May 26, 1988, within one year. For an application which you submit in the middle of that period -- after, say, six months has expired -- he may or may not have had an operating test, because you would not have been required to complete an operating test for everyone until after one year. So if it says you've got to examine annually, then one year after the effective date of the rule, everyone should have had an operating test. Another example is the comprehensive written examination to be done at least each 24 months. After the rule has been in effect for 24 months, everyone who was licensed on the first day that the rule went into effect shall have had a comprehensive examination, unless, of course, you are accredited, and then you may use a segmented exam.

Q. 347. It appears that comprehensive requalification written exams are required only every two years and operating tests are required once per year. Is this true?

A. It is true that the written examination will go to every two years unless your program commitments are more stringent. If your current program requires an annual exam and it is not an accredited program, then you will have to notify us if you intend to reduce that commitment. If it's an accredited program, then you can make the changes as appropriate.

Q. 348. Our past requal programs, for those facilities which don't have plant-referenced simulators, have not included an operating test. They have included some operating evaluations, but not a pure test in the context of the new regulation. Some of the currently licensed operators will be up for renewal immediately, as soon as the new 10 CFR 55 goes into effect. Will there be a transition period during which it would be possible to get a waiver for those operators because they will not have had an operating test? We do not have a simulator certified by NRC to conduct an operating test. And, in fact, I'm not even sure if, under the new regulation, we could use our current off-site simulator to conduct an operating test. So, how do we address renewal of licenses for the period between now and when we get our plant-referenced simulator; or will there be some time after which we will have to do an operating test?

A. During the period between the effective date of the Rule and one year following, an individual may not have yet had an annual operating test, and you may put him up for license renewal. After one year, everyone should have had an operating test. The issue of whether an operating test is on a simulation facility, or conducted as a plant walk through is a different issue.

At least the plant walk-through portion will be required. The issue of doing it on a simulation facility, that would be required by May 26th, 1991. Prior to that time, if you have certified or approved simulation facility, you would also do it on the simulator. If you are currently using a simulator, and we are conducting examinations on it, we expect you to continue to do so, and within one year of the effective date of the rule, start examining candidates using your current simulator as a part of the operating test for the requalification program. Also, you have to make sure that the documentation that you provide for that annual operating test addresses all 13 items in the new Regulation. The Form 157 is the way that we are going to check that. You can use alternate ways, but you must make sure you document all 13 items.

Q. 349. During this one-year period of transition, do we document, by exception, and ask for a waiver on our requests for renewal? Would that be the appropriate way to handle that?

A. No, that would not be necessary.

Q. 350. Must a facility administer annual operating tests to licensed operators before a certified plant referenced simulator is available?

A. Yes. Even though it may not be part of your requal program now, you have to start administering an operating exam, and if you don't have a simulator, then you would give an oral exam, a walk-through type like we do on the plant.

This is one aspect of the transition into the new rule where we are not going to look for everyone to have completed an operating test on May 26, 1987; but by May 26, 1988, everybody who's been licensed for that last year shall have completed an operating test on the facility.

We're using a more common sense approach, so if you submit an application for renewal for a candidate who has a two-year license now, and you submit it in four months, that individual may not have had an operating test, as is described in the rule, because he has not been under that rule for a year. We would still renew the license and issue him a six-year license.

After everyone has been under the rule for one year, we would not find that he had met the terms and conditions of his license if he had not had an operating test, because the operating test is to be conducted each year.

Q. 351. If an SRO directs the proper action, does that satisfy the ability to perform the actions necessary?

A. Yes.

Q. 352. We've talked about an annual operating exam to be administered by the utility. What constitutes an "operating exam?"

A. If you currently have a simulator on which you or we are conducting examinations, then you must include an oral and a simulator examination. It is not performance of practical factors in a training environment. We've had, for instance, the requirement of the Denton letter to perform certain practical factors on an annual basis. People take simulator training and perform the practical part until successful, whether it takes one, two, or three tries.

We are interested in a structured examination. We are not interested in training on the simulator. The structured examination must meet the requirements of the regulation as it relates to sampling those areas that are specified under the regulation. It is a combination on the simulator, if you have one, and in the plant. If you don't have a simulator, it must be done in the plant.

Q. 353. What constitutes by definition, an annual operating exam? In our NRC-approved requal programs we administer what is called an accident assessment exam. It's an operational type exam, documented by written examination, which tests operator knowledge and on how they can operate the plant, implement procedures, diagnose a situation, a transient, an accident, or whatever. Does this meet the annual operating exam criteria?

A. Look at what is specified in the Regulation by way of observed behavior for the operating test, and assure yourself that the way you are implementing the exams covers those 12 items for an operating test for requal. The start up shut down is the only portion that's dropped out. But control board familiarity, those kinds of things are still being assessed. You need to look at your program, and judge whether you have met those 12 items for the operating test for requal.

Q. 354. Must the annual operating exam for requalification be given in one time frame or can that also be broken up into various pieces throughout the year? It's very difficult to get everybody done in one year by the training staff.

A. For a candidate, it needs to be done at one time, but if what you are asking is that you have 30 people that need to have an operating test, and you want to spread out the 30 tests over the period of a year, the answer is yes.

But you can't take an individual and give him a walk-through today and some simulator evaluation tomorrow and then some six months from now add those three pieces up. That would not meet the intent of an annual operating test.

Q. 355. Not even if you broke up the in-plant and the simulator between the different weeks in requal, and catch them one cycle a week, get a crew in on the simulator and maybe the next time they come up, five weeks from then, get that same crew up on the plant?

A. Although we have explicitly approved such an approach for the written examination where you are using segmented tests, provided you show that the sum of the parts equals the whole in the comprehensive exam, we have not concluded that such an approach is acceptable for an operating test. Our position is that an operating test, to be effective, must be administered at one time, and must cover the 12 items in the rule as a minimum.

Q. 356. Section 55.59(a)(2) implies that the requalification program includes observations and evaluations of performance and competency by supervisors or staff members during actual abnormal and emergency procedures at the plant. Is this required?

A. This goes to part 5, evaluation, of the definition of systematic approach to training. The intent is that when the casualties are practiced on the simulator, performance would be evaluated by staff members as part of that systematic approach to training. It's not intended to have those evaluations done on the actual plant.

Q. 357. The criteria for the NRC comprehensive requalification examinations are similar to the standard criteria for an initial examination listed in 55.41 and 55.43. What is the perceived difference between the two exams?

A. The requalification exam requires a sampling of criteria. If your requalification program is based upon a systems approach to training, you will have reviewed the tasks from the initial program which are appropriate for continuing training. You will have chosen those on some criteria, such as frequency of performance, safety significance or other criteria. That's one way of determining the content of your continuing training program.

Another way is the feedback from performance in the plant: licensee event reports, and the like. Another area would include facility design changes and/or changes in procedures. Those are the subject areas that we would tend to focus on for a requalification examination.

When you move to learning objectives for your requalification program that have conditions and standards, we would use that as the basis for sampling the content of the examination.

In the meantime, because that's not fully in place yet, we are using such things as the K/A catalogs, which identify the importance of job tasks and are based upon the industry generic job task analysis. We are also using a sampling plan -- it was referred to as the "examiner handbook" -- where we sample from that catalog to ensure that we get a representative sample of the knowledge, skills and abilities -- the skills being done on the simulator--that are appropriate for an NRC examination.

We intend the initial examination to be different from the requalification examination. We will look at the two, even though we developed them in parallel; and questions which are not appropriate for a job incumbent -- questions, for instance, on watch relief and turnover or other things which he does on a repetitive basis -- would be excluded from the requalification examination.

We believe that through the informal review process of appeals, and the facility review of the written examinations, there are sufficient safeguards in place during the transition period to ensure that there was a content-valid examination that was indeed related to job performance.

From our review of examination reports from all the regions, the weaknesses concern knowledge of events that have occurred at their own plant, significant events at other similar plants, changes to design, changes to procedures, and selection of those tasks from the initial program which are relevant to training on a continuing basis. We do not help the operators if we simply repeat the initial program for continuing training. That's not the intent.

Q. 358. How are the current guidelines, which allow requalification examination site visits to be extended to every three years based on good SALP ratings or accreditation, going to interface with 100-percent requalification every six years?

A. Basically these are two different programs. One is a programmatic evaluation looking at the adequacy of the requalification program. The other deals with the Commission-directed re-examination of each licensed operator on a six-year basis. In the next couple of years, though, we don't expect it to change very much. It's going to take some time to build up a pool of six-year licenses so that we would be conducting the examinations in accordance with this regulation. So in the near term, those facilities which have better performance and have achieved INPO accreditation would have a longer period between NRC visits.

Q. 359. On the question of randomness, if in year two a candidate passes the exam, and in year four he fails, the rule says he has to pass it once during the six years. Will that stop the renewal of his license?

A. No. If he had passed one exam and failed a second one, but was re-examined by the facility after appropriate remedial training and returned to watch, he would have passed an exam and that would be the basis for the license renewal. The rule does not say the last examination administered by the NRC. It says an examination during the six-year term of the license. And we recognize that some people may have more than one.

Q. 360. What process will be used to schedule the NRC-administered written examination and operating tests during the term of a six-year license?

A. It is our intent that this will be a random test, performed on a random basis. We would try not to have double jeopardy, where an individual takes more than one NRC exam during his six-year term. But he may. We will have to coordinate with the facility. We would, in our 90-day letter, ask for lists of people who would be eligible to take the NRC exam. This would include all licensed individuals at the site. If there were individuals who had a vacation scheduled during that time, or if there were some personal hardship, we would want to know about it. We want to work with your people's needs as much as we can.

Q. 361. This question addresses the random requalification examination and the pending notification. A lot of emphasis is placed on team work and communications, even though the license is granted to an individual. Admittedly, periodically we may rotate a person within a shift due to illness or vacation, etc., but most of the people, normally three out of the four, usually remain the same. The potential exists for administering a simulator examination, potentially to four people that don't work together normally. Have we considered the potential jeopardy there, that we have created an environment contrary to the way we have been trying to teach the operators, in particular going to the plant-referenced simulators?

A. The examiner standards indicate that when selecting people from shift, you select one crew. That is the mechanism we use. And one crew is approximately 20 percent of those people on shift, unless you have a six-shift rotation instead of five. And then we look at approximately 20 percent of the operators who are not on shift, the day-shift workers.

To the extent we can, we would put them into the crews where they normally work. But when you consider all the other constraints, such as those who have six-year licenses, those who have two years, the time frame for renewal, etc., that will not always be possible. To the extent we can, we want to accommodate your personnel. We would try to coordinate the examination visits with the requalification cycles that you are already using. In fact, in the past we have allowed the facility to identify how they wanted to combine the crews. We just say these are the guys we are going to see on this schedule, and you tell us how you want to group them.

But at the same time, there is not going to be a lot of advance notice to the individual as to when he is going to be examined. It will be on the order of ten days to six weeks. Although there may be some comfort in being examined in the team environment in which training takes place, transfer between teams is a practical reality with which each operator must be equipped to deal, both in the plant and in the NRC exam.

Q. 362. Will a representative sample group of license holders be tested or will the whole license complement be tested?

A. In keeping with the Commission directive, it should be a random sample of license holders. All would be subject to exams. We would coordinate that with you if there were severe hardships but that would have to be handled on a case-by-case basis.

Q. 363. This concerns the random examinations of licensed operators. How far in advance will I know who will be examined? When will I be supplied with the list of names, saying that on this day, these people will be examined?

A. You will be notified of the examination 90 days in advance in accordance with ES-601. Typically, ten days to six weeks, prior to the examination, we will notify you of the individuals who have been randomly selected for the requalification program evaluation.

Q. 364. Will NRC notify the facility in time to facilitate preparation of the license holders before taking the requalification exam?

A. We will provide ten days to six weeks notice. It was explicit direction from the Commission to ensure that examining is done on a random basis for reasons that are associated with evaluating the continuing training program, and evaluating and ensuring that the candidate maintains proficiency and an appropriate knowledge level over the duration of his license.

We will coordinate the scheduling of examination visits with your regular requal program schedules and/or your replacement examination schedules to the extent we can. But our resources are limited. We are budgeted for two visits per year to a facility. And if you have a need for more than two to accommodate some activity, it's likely not to occur without adequate advanced planning.

And we will choose candidates from among those who have not been examined by the NRC before we select someone who already has been so examined. However, some people will be examined twice, so that those who got examined early in their cycle shouldn't make the assumption that they're not going to see the NRC again for the duration of that period.

Q. 365. In the past NRC tested requal every two years and the operators were drum-head tight until somebody was randomly selected. Then they relaxed for two or three years, depending upon whether everybody had gotten accredited. And then the cycle was repeated.

I'm under the impression that neither NUMARC, nor the operators, nor anybody else, had an opportunity to critique these particular two paragraphs prior to having seem them here. It appears to me that as a minimum, NRC is going to have to give a requal test once a year, if I have requested a hot license test once a year.

A. Your perception is quite accurate. The Statement of Considerations is the vehicle that the Commission used to provide directions to the staff on how to implement the Regulation, which has always permitted the staff to administer requalification examinations. The fact that the requalification examination has been made a condition of license renewal is new.

There was some concern in the past, of "why me?" "Why not this other guy?" By putting it in the Regulation, and indicating what the intent is, it becomes clear that everyone will, at some time during that six-year license, be examined by NRC in order to have his license renewed.

We are accepting a certification by the facility for two written tests and five operating tests per six years, but the staff will continue to examine in some cases. That is, we will simply choose not to accept the facility's certification at that time, and we will examine the individual. There may be some cases where an individual will be examined more frequently than once each six years.

Q. 366. If an operator gets his license renewed, and is tested in the first year, my arithmetic says that he can't go but one year beyond his renewal. Then, clearly, the frequency is going to be greater, by definition, than once every six years.

A. Correct. That's why we use the term at least once during a six year license.

Q. 367. These questions are related to the NRC-administered requal. Would it be possible for an individual to be selected twice during the six year period before all other individual licensees were selected once?

A. We intend to select people who have not been selected before selecting someone a second time. But that does not preclude this from happening, if we got everybody else. If we've been through all of the people with six-year licenses, and we are still sampling, it is possible for an individual to be examined twice.

Q. 368. So, it's random, but the pool from which the random selections are made gets smaller as people are selected?

A. It could get larger, based upon more six-year licenses being issued. At some point it will reach equilibrium, where everybody has a six-year license.

Q. 369. Is this a testing of the requalification program, or is it testing human beings every six years? I feel that it may have been a step backwards in raising the anxiety level of the population of operators who are going to be up tight every year. That's why I don't understand the Statement of Considerations, because I'm just concerned about those people.

A. It says that we're going to test so that nobody goes more than six years without being tested, and means that some are going to get examined more than once in six years. It's our view that if a licensed operator is going through an effective, continuing training program, then there shouldn't be any concern with that person getting an NRC exam because our exams are designed to confirm that the individual has maintained a minimum acceptable capability. If he is going through a continuing training program, our expectation is that he is way above the minimum that's acceptable.

Q. 370. I feel perfectly comfortable that our operators, and our supervisors on shift can safely operate our units. The vehicle you are using to measure the requalification program is improperly aimed at obtaining those results. If we focus the requalification program on problem areas, design changes, and events in the industry, it's fairly narrowly focused. But the exam looks at a target area beyond that, that has not been covered, for memory/recall type things, and it's unrealistic to see the operator be able to pass that, or the senior operator, or anyone else.

But if the exam were focused on what the requal program had focused on, then the focus is on target. You ought to be able to pluck an operator off shift, have him evaluated, and expect that he'll do fine. But when it's not aimed at the same material, very little probability exists of him doing well on the exam.

A. We understand your comment, and we recognize that both groups are trying to move to the point where we are using content-valid examinations to measure performance. We have a ways to go, and we are working on that. And we think you all have ways to go in describing adequately the content of the continuing training program. Eventually, we will get to the point where we have closure on the scope and content validity of a requalification examination.

Until then, there is going to be anxiety. We believe that with the administrative review process for examinations, there are adequate safeguards to ensure that improper questions can be challenged, and that the questions are appropriate to the job. We have provided some tools to do that, and they need to be used. And until we get conservative feedback both ways, and recognize that the objective is to measure that individual's performance, the imperfect tools that we are using now aren't going to get much better.

And that is a challenge to the industry, to really take a hard look at the INPO guidelines in continuing training programs, and to consider how your program is modified to meet those objectives.

We've had problems with exams in the past, and we probably will in the future. We have found problems with requal programs in the past, and we'll probably find problems with those programs in the future. But we have not taken action against individuals by way of revoking licenses, or other activities. We do expect that until remediation is provided, those who fail are removed from shift-standing duties until they are brought back up to speed.

And if they feel that the examination is unfair, they can request a review of the examination by the Regional Division Director, and they can subsequently request a review by the Director of DLPQE. We are serious about improving the quality of exams and getting them content validated.

Q. 371. What would happen if, by chance, an individual wasn't selected during the six year period?

A. The NRC intends to administer a comprehensive written exam and operating test to every licensed operator at least once during the six-year term of the license. In the unlikely event that an individual did not receive such an exam, we would take immediate steps to initiate one. However, we would have to consider that he had made a timely application for renewal, and as a result, his existing license would remain in effect. But we would not issue a new license until we had examined the individual.

Q. 372. What occurs when an individual fails the NRC-administered requalification exam?

A. First, the individual is removed from licensed duties and placed in an accelerated training program. Once he has successfully completed all remedial training, he must pass a facility-administered examination to ensure that all weaknesses have been corrected. If that facility's training program received an NRC rating of marginal or unsatisfactory, this examination may be overseen by the NRC, in keeping with the alternate approach to requalification evaluations which was recently adopted by NRC.

In addition, it should be noted that in accordance with Section 55.57, all operators must pass an NRC-administered requalification exam during the term of the six-year license. Therefore, if this individual failed the NRC-administered requalification examination and has not passed another NRC-administered exam during the term of his current six-year license, his license will not be renewed until he has passed such an examination.

Q. 373. Is there any minimum period before a person gets into the requalification pool, after getting an initial license?

A. The clock starts the day he gets his six-year license. But if we give a requalification program audit, and there are individuals on site with two year licenses in effect, they are also in the pool to be randomly selected for an evaluation of the requalification program, in accordance with Examiner's Standard 601. So, don't assume that only six-year people may be chosen.

Q. 374. Part 55.59 states that in lieu of accepting certification by the facility licensee that the licensee has passed written examinations and operating tests administered by the facility licensee, the Commission may administer comprehensive requalification written examinations and an annual operating test. Will this testing take the same form and frequency as the previously established 20 percent testing at 50 percent of the utilities in the Region?

A. Yes. It will have essentially the same form except it will now be about 16 percent of the operators at all facilities in the region every year. For clarification, you can anticipate that the operating test will resemble the one that would be given for an initial candidate, but the written exam would be geared directly to job performance. The written exam is going to have to be operationally oriented.

Q. 375. Will requalification exams be administered to non-approved requalification programs?

A. As we see it, there are no such programs. You are operating under present NRC approval under old Appendix A, new 55.59(c), the requal program, or you have an INPO-accredited SAT-based requal program. There can't be anything outside of those.

Q. 376. Prior to the issuance of this rule, people developed their requal program with two taskmasters: one, the INPO accreditation process, and the other, the relatively non-task based aspects of Appendix A. Now that the utilities have got the flexibility to withdraw or to remove the non-task based part of the old programs, which may take some time, what is the approved program in the interim? Is it the old program?

A. Yes, you must follow the NRC-approved program, which was based previously in Appendix A to Part 55, until such time as you send to us a letter which certifies that you are accredited and that your program has been based upon an SAT approach. We don't believe, however, that that is such a big task. Some of the material we required in the past falls into the kinds of things that can be used in an SAT-based program.

Whether that set constitutes 80 percent coverage or 70 percent coverage, we're not sure; but the real issue is the flexibility to design your program based upon program evaluation and feedback from on-the-job performance to factor in changes in procedure, changes in design, licensee events, industry events, and if you look at the programs that have been approved by the NRC, those have been required.

In some cases, because of the need to cover so many hours in the classroom, you've had a competition for time available to conduct training, so important items have been covered in the discretionary time left.

So we think that's a major advantage, and it's one that we would encourage you to look at carefully and to implement as quickly as you can.

You have to follow your approved program, but by May 26, 1987, that approved program has to be brought up to at least meet the requirements under the new rule. If you have an Appendix A approved program in place currently, then on May 26th, you can submit a certification that you have SAT program which now meets the requirements of the new rule, but if you do that on May 26th, to upgrade to the SAT program, the program you have in place has to comply. No matter what it is, it has to comply with the new rule on May 26, 1987.

If you do not intend to upgrade to an SAT program, you can continue to follow the format of your old program, but that old program has to meet the requirements of the new rule on May 26, 1987.

Q. 377. What is the intent of the Commission to approve specific cycles as a part of each facility's training program?

A. Once the programs are certified as SAT programs, it's not our intention to recertify these programs on any particular basis. Item No. 5 brings in the continuing process of change that should reflect the feedback from the performance evaluation of your program. The Commission will not be requesting periodic certification. You certify once and update to indicate when subsequent accreditation was achieved.

In the first round of accreditation, you have a specific date that you were accredited. Through that process you have a requirement to submit a report at two years and to be re-accredited at four years. You would simply send in another letter that says, "My programs have been again accredited," and that would be all that's required based upon the Commission's endorsement in the policy statement as it exists today.

Q. 378. By what means is a utility to certify to the Commission that their requalification program is both accredited and based upon a systems approach to training? The interpretation for implementing a systems approach to training is somewhat different by the NRC and INPO. By what specific standards is our certification for using a systems approach to training based; i. e., the NRC's criteria utilized in conducting pre/post accreditation site evaluation, or using the INPO 85-002 criteria?

A. The two are equivalent; that is, NUREG-1220 is essentially a series of questions related to each of the five elements of a systems approach to training as it's described in the policy statement. In that same policy statement, the Commission has endorsed the INPO accreditation objectives and criteria as being a systems approach to training.

The difference comes about in that INPO has 12 objectives and about 60 subordinate criteria. The Commission in the policy statement identified five elements, and the Staff has a number of questions that we use for information-gathering in our reviews. However, we would prefer that you use the INPO accreditation objectives and criteria and supporting documents; in particular, for your requalification program.

There is clearly a hierarchy of documents within the INPO program. Objectives need to be met. Criteria may or may not be met if you can still meet the objectives. Guidelines are just that--they are guidelines, an acceptable way of doing business as INPO would review it.

That is very similar to the staff's approach in doing our postaccreditation audits. We have questions that relate to each of the five elements that the Commission has endorsed. Those questions do not imply criteria. They are simply areas where we gather information. So the simple answer to the question is follow INPO.

We have seen several cases where the requalification program was not based upon a systems approach to training; rather, it was based upon a training program docketed with the NRC, that the NRC had approved. It was very prescriptive. It was, "Conduct X number of hours of classroom training, perform certain practical factors on the simulator in accordance with the Denton letter," etc. Because of a reluctance on the part of the utility to change commitments that are required by license condition or regulation, many of those programs were not changed to a systems approach.

Effective May 26th, you can remedy that prior restriction by simply sending a letter to NRC which indicates that you are accredited and that you have developed your requalification program on a systems-approach-to-training basis.

That's the most important aspect of this rule. It gives you the flexibility to control the content of continuing training based upon the needs of the individuals who have been trained, and the feedback mechanisms which are described.

Most important is Element 5 of the systems approach to training: program revision based upon evaluation of performance on the job. That's where we see the major payoff, and we think that we are giving you the flexibility that you need to fully implement the industry commitments through training and accreditation.

Q. 379. What criteria is the Commission going to use to approve programs developed using a system approach to training?

A. If you are asking the NRC to approve a requalification program that's based on a systems approach to training, we don't look forward to trying to do those kind of reviews. We'd rather see a submittal indicating that you have an INPO-accredited program, which has both initial and requalification training based on an SAT.

If you were to ask NRC to review a training program that was not INPO-accredited, that you claimed was based on a systems approach to training, we would try to use the document that we now have to evaluate that, NUREG-1220.

For clarification, if your program is accredited, and you're not a cold plant licensee, then prior to receiving an operating license we fully expect that you will use the INPO accreditation process and the guidelines that have recently been issued by INPO in their continuing training guidelines for licensed operators to develop your requalification continuing training program.

We will accept a simple statement to the effect that this has been done. We accept as fact that you have been accredited, and therefore that you understand the process of developing performance-based training. We do not expect to review such programs. I don't think INPO would like us to review programs against their criteria and to put them into that context. We are trying to, in this rulemaking, clearly differentiate between training programs, which are being handled by the industry initiatives through NUMARC and INPO, and licensing requirements and the NRC examination. We don't want to mix those two, and would probably have discussions with facilities that propose to do otherwise.

Q. 380. As far as the INPO document, 86-025, is concerned, you just say "as long as you are following the guidelines." Do you expect verbatim compliance with the guidelines, or just general compliance?

A. There is a hierarchy of criteria within the INPO program, starting with objectives. Then you have criteria guidelines. You must meet the intent of the objective. That's a "shall." When you get down to the criteria, you may not meet all of them verbatim. For some you may have alternate methods. Guidelines indicates what INPO believes would be acceptable to meet the intent of the criteria and the objectives.

Your program has mechanisms for reviewing and deciding how you put that process in place. The fact that you are accredited is evidence to us that you understand how to use that process and those guidelines. We don't need to see the details, based upon the fact that you have been through accreditation.

The principal goal for revising the requal programs is to allow feedback from operating problems, particularly licensee events, plant design changes, procedure changes, and other aspects of training for which there is a demonstrated need, and not to be constrained to X number of hours in a class, because that's what's been required in the past.

Q. 381. What if I put in 80 hours of simulator time, although INPO says 120, but we're doing okay with 80?

A. That's between you and INPO and your needs under a program which utilizes the SAT process. We have confidence in the process based on our evaluation of a number of facilities. We may get back into training programs if we see performance deficiencies on the job, through an event or through our inspection program.

We have developed guidance, the series of questions in NUREG-1220, as to how we're going to go about evaluating programs. So that you know what you consider to be fair game for us to look at. But we are not in the mode of telling INPO what to do. That's for the Accrediting Board, INPO, and the facilities to determine.

Q. 382. Will your evaluation of the training program be in accordance with the guidelines in NUREG-1220?

A. Yes. We have had a number of discussions with INPO on it, and we have been using that for our post-accreditation review.

Q. 383. Will a change to FSAR Chapter 13 (to satisfy new 10 CFR 55 requirements) be considered a decrease in the scope of an approved operator requalification program requiring prior NRC approval, in accordance with 10 CFR 50.54(i)?

A. No. That issue is addressed in the Statement of Considerations, where it indicates that this Rule supersedes all other previous requirements. Even though the Rule may have caused a decrease in the scope of your requal program it has already been sanctioned by the Commission in its approval of this Rule, provided your program is INPO accredited. If it's not, then you must follow 50.54(i); so you must determine if it has decreased in scope.

Q. 384. Applicable portions of Title 10, Chapter 1, Code of Federal Regulations are one of the lecture topics for a requalification program. Can you be more specific as to which portions of Title 10 are applicable, or is that up to the plants to determine?

A. You just cited the NRC Rules and Regulations, which includes such things as Tech Specs and amendments to licenses, and things like that. So, there are many Title 10 issues, including the radiation protection standards in Part 20. The subject matter of those lectures should be determined by the plants to satisfy the training needs of their operators.

Q. 385. Paragraph (c)(3)(i) of Part 55.59 requires certain manipulations to be performed annually. This list of manipulations differs from the list in the Harold Denton letter of March 28, 1980. Our requalification program is based on the Denton letter. How long do we have to modify our requalification program to be in compliance with the new 55.59 requirements?"

A. The rule supersedes and should include the requirements of the Harold Denton letter of March 28, 1980. If there are commitments in your program that go beyond those identified within the March 28, 1980, letter, then you will have to entertain an amendment to your Tech Specs to bring your program to that minimum level specified within the rule. Otherwise, we expect you to have a program that is modified and in compliance with rule by May 26, 1987.

Q. 386. Section 55.59(c)(3)(v) states: "A simulator may be used in meeting the requirements of paragraphs (c)(3)(i) and (3)(ii) of this section, if it reproduces the general operating characteristics of the facility involved and the arrangement of the instrumentation and the controls of the simulator is similar to that of the facility involved." Fort Calhoun will continue to use the Combustion Engineering (CE) simulator in Windsor until the plant-referenced simulator is available for training. Is the CE simulator approved for meeting the applicable requirements until such time as a referenced simulator is available? The same question applies to the discussion in Section 55.59(c)(4)(iv).

A. Yes, until May 26, 1991. This is now a part of your requalification program and will continue to be a part of your requalification program until you either have a certified or an approved simulation facility.

Q. 387. Does NRC agree with the utility interpretation that they may use the nonplant-referenced simulator as the preferred device when it comes to the requalification training program's on-the-job training control manipulations?

A. The word "preferred," we would think of as "equal." There is a nuance for the control manipulations -- the on-the-job training in items (a) through (f). In the Rule, under on-the job training, it says, "A simulator may be used in meeting the requirements of paragraps (c)(3)(i), and (c)(3)(ii) of this section, if it reproduces the general operating characteristics of the facility involved, and the arrangement of the instrumentation and controls of the simulator is similar to that of the facility involved."

This difference permits the use of the nonplant-referenced simulator for start up, shut down, and other things which are not related to casualty control, even after you have certified or received approval of your simulation facility. It specifies that you must use the certified or approved simulation facility for the operating test, and for Subparagraphs (g) through (aa) of the Section, which are the casualties.

So, you may use a simulator other than an acceptable simulation facility for control manipulations for requals. But you must use the acceptable simulation facility for casualties after May 26, 1991, or after you have been certified or received approval. It provides you some flexibility during periods when your simulation facility may not be available for routine control manipulations.

Q. 388. May a utility use a certified simulation facility for requalification training programs, such as on-the-job training in control manipulations, or must some control manipulations be performed using the plant controls?

A. If you look at the list, it just says you can't do casualties on plant controls. Items A through F in 55.59 are eligible to be performed either on the plant or with an approved or certified simulator.

These relate to start-ups and shutdowns and changes of power of more than 10 percent, manipulations which you can perform on the facility without putting it in danger. It is your option. You may either do those on the plant or on the simulator.

For the remaining items that are required annually or for the operating test, those must be done on a simulation facility. They may not be done on the plant.

Q. 389. With respect to licensed operator/senior operator requalification training, is it appropriate that utilities assume they can take credit for the required annual and biennial plant control manipulations completed on a simulation facility (nonplant referenced) if their programs have been approved by the National Nuclear Accrediting Board?

A. Yes.

Q. 390. Can a utility whose training programs have not been accredited by the National Nuclear Accrediting Board and which does not have a plant referenced simulator take credit for plant control manipulations that are performed on a nonplant referenced simulator?

A. If that's what your approved program is now, then there will be no change to that approved program until you get your own simulator, or until May 26, 1991 at which time the regulation requires that the training portion be done on a certified or approved simulation facility. There's an exception, in Section 3, "On-the-Job Training," that you may substitute your accredited program for those requirements. So if you are able to talk INPO into accepting a simulation facility other than a plant-referenced simulator, that's between you and INPO, but for the purposes of the staff's review, we would expect you to use the simulator after it has been certified if you do that before the May 26, 1991, with one minor exception, which has to do with the first six on-the-job items listed under 55.59(c)(3). In that case, you need not have a certified simulation facility or an approved facility. The words permit you to use another simulation device. Section 55.59(c)(3)(v) permits the use of a simulator which reproduces the general operating characteristics of the facility involved, if the arrangement of instrumentation and controls of the simulator are similar to those of the facility involved. It only requires the fidelity of a plant referenced simulator for the casualties.

Q. 391. Must all six manipulations listed in Paragraph (55.59)(c)(3)(i) be performed biennially, or just one of the six?

A. Items A through L must be performed annually. All the rest are performed biennially. All of the first six items must be performed, either on the plant or the simulator. The rest are casualties, that must be performed on a simulator.

Q. 392. Is it correct that Section 55.59 has now added fuel manipulations to the required items to be done annually? They are more than what's in the Harold Denton letter. We have renewals coming up during the summer of 1987, and the training program has been ongoing for the last year. There may be some manipulations that, in fact, have not been accomplished on the simulator on an annual basis by July of 1987 that 55.59 now says should have been done on an annual basis.

A. There are two parts to this answer. First, the requirements in Section 55.59(c)(3), with the exeption of the sequence, are identical to those in the Denton letter; no fuel manipulations are required. Second, although the new requirement exists, the annual manipulations don't have to be completed for everybody until the regulation has been in effect for one year.

Q. 393. In 55.59, "ON-THE-JOB-TRAINING," loss of electrical power is one of the manipulations that needs to be performed. Is that loss of off-site power or degraded power sources, such as the loss of half of your emergency bus or is it a total blackout?

A. It may be both. That is, it could be a total loss of electrical power, or it could be loss of power, particularly involving buses or consoles.

Q. 394. If we want to run those scenarios, either one would meet that?

A. That is correct. But remember that, according to that Section, you may not do casualties on the plant. The break-out in the Regulation specifies that everything below a loss of coolant event is an accident. The malfunctions and faults are done on a simulator. But the permissive part is for the other manipulations, the control manipulations, that may be done on the plant or on a simulator.

Q. 395. Must plant control manipulations during the requalification period be documented on Form 398?

A. The documentation hasn't changed for that particular item of the 398 Form. You still have to certify that the control manipulations were done. Only where there would be exceptions to the guidance in Regulatory Guide 1.8 would there need to be some amplifying comments made. For example, if you did five similar manipulations, evaluated them and concluded they were acceptable, you might want to point that out in the comments section on the Form 398.

Q. 396. If a license holder fails the written requalification exam or operating test administered by the Commission during the six-year license term and sub-sequently participates in the approved accelerated requalification program per Section 55.59(c)(4)(v), will certification of successful participation in this program be acceptable for renewal, or will a second NRC-administered exam during the six-year term be required?

A. A second NRC examination will be required. That individual can go back on shift after failing the NRC requal exam, after participating in upgrade training and passing the facility's own evaluation. However, the terms of the Regulation are that for renewal he must pass an NRC-administered exam.

Q. 397. Must licensed Operator training records be retained for the life of the plant?

A. Those that deal with the six-year license, per se, only need to be kept for six years. However, some facilities have committed to record retention require-ments in their Technical Specifications which are more restrictive than this regulation. In order to get the relief that the regulation permits, you must submit an administrative change request to amend your Technical Specifications to make the record retention requirements equal to six years or the term of the individual's license.

This Rule supersedes all previous requirements for operator licensing and training, unless you currently have a more restrictive requirement. In that case, there are two vehicles you can use. One is an amendment to the license, if a formal amendment is necessary. The other is a 50.59 review, which you can do administratively and then notify us that it has been completed when you indicate your other changes at the end of the year. In any event, you must conform to the requirements of the regulation, particularly those that are more restrictive than your current program.

Two examples immediately come to mind. Most people today have an annual written examination. The Rule would permit you to go to a two-year examination. The change to go to a two-year exam can be processed under 50.59 and it does not constitute a reduction in scope if the change is for the purpose of conforming to the regulation.

That is, the Commission, in the process of reviewing the regulation, concluded that there were compensatory measures for changing from a one-year written exam to a two-year written exam. In this case the compensatory measure is the annual operating test. So it does not fall into a reduction of scope and it does not require prior NRC approval unless it happens to be involved in an amendment to the license or the Tech Specs.

Q. 398. This is a question about documentation of exams given at the plant. Under the requal program, it says that we must keep the student's answers for the period of the license. Does this mean that we must keep those exams as quality records and keep them for the lifetime of the plant, or are you saying that we keep it for the term of the license?

A. It's for the term of the operator's license. And in this case, for example, his records would include six operating test examination forms, and three comprehensive written examinations in his individual file, until such time as his license is renewed, and then you start over again. Now, if you use a segmented examination in lieu of a comprehensive exam for each requal program, and you have more than three written exams, then that's a function of how you structure your program. You keep them only for the term of that individual license.

Q. 399. So, are you saying for any operator exams that we administer, once we are past the renewal stage, we could destroy those as long as we have quality records to back up the fact that he had the exam -- in other words, the grades, and so forth?

A. Given the fact that he was in a requalification program before, and you certified that, the answer is yes, you could put them in other quality records.

Q. 400. On initial operator exams, are we required to keep the exam itself, or can we just keep a summary that goes in the operator's history file -- a summary of his grades, and things like this? We currently keep the master exams and a copy of the answer key, but are we required to keep the individual student exams and his answers?

A. Our requirement is that the actual exam, or copies of the actual exam, be maintained for the duration of the current license. When you get that license renewed, you may eliminate that material from the files and start over.

Q. 401. So are you saying once an operator gets a license, we could do that on the initial files, too?

A. That is correct. The requirement demonstrates that you've met the requirement of the Regulation to conduct operating tests and comprehensive written examinations during the term of that particular license.

Q. 402. How are microfilm records authenticated to meet 55.59(c)(5)(ii)?

A. They are authenticated by an authorized representative of the facility.

Q. 403. Could you comment on the use of video tape as far as exam documentation. You mentioned keeping a deck log where you would recover strip charts. Would you give us some comment on the use of video tape?

A. We do not intend to use video tape or the equivalent of instant replay during an examination. The records that we are looking for are the same records that would be used for a post-trip review, essentially the same documentation. To the extent that the simulator has the ability to retain the scenario, and you can down load that to a computer tape, you could retain and use that tape.

Q. 404. I'd just like to make one comment on that. That's fine, I think, if the scenario includes a trip. If you're starting in mode four with a scenario, it's more difficult to recover those kind of parameters that you would need to recreate the scenario.

A. The problem with a TV tape is that it is incomplete. You may not hear discussions between the candidate and the examiner because of how microphones are placed. We generally stand back, but at times we are at the operator's elbow.

We have been asked on numerous occasions whether the facility would be allowed to video tape for either record purposes or training purposes. We consider it intrusive, both on the candidate and the examiner, and incomplete.

Q. 405. Most of the manipulations that are listed in the Regulation are not applicable to test and research reactors. Are we still operating under the ten manipulations in a two-year period, as we have been in the past?

A. If that was in your approved requalification program, it would remain approved.

Q. 406. Is it possible for requalification examinations administered by the NRC to be "split", such that the written and operational exams are given during different site visits?

A. This is Regional prerogative, on a case-by-case basis, with advance notice to the licensee.

Q. 407. A licensed RO is enrolled in the facility's SRO upgrade training program. NRC chooses this individual, randomly, to participate in their requal program evaluation examination. He fails the NRC administered exam, yet he is passing or has passed all portions of the upgrade program to this point.

Does he have to be withdrawn from the upgrade program, go through accelerated requal for RO requal exam failure, and be reexamined, or can he just drop RO qualification and pursue an SRO license?

A. A licensed operator must meet the requirements of the facility's requalification program which generally requires accelerated training and/or reexamination. His status in other facility managed training programs is the prerogative of facility management. If the facility elects to "drop RO qualification" for the individual under 10 CFR 55.5(a) the individual could make application for an SRO license under 10 CFR 55.31. However, the individual would not be an SRO upgrade candidate as that status assumes a active RO license.

Q. 408. Will written exams administered by NRC for requalification be totally objective, totally subjective, or some combination?

A. They will be a combination of both. Some examination questions are written with the intent of meeting the definition of an objective question. An objective question is defined as one in which: (1) there is only one correct answer; and (2) all qualified graders would agree on the amount of credit allowed for any given candidate's answer.

Q. 409. Will persons holding a two year license be included in NRC requal exams during the transition?

A. Persons with valid licenses may be included in NRC exams. However, renewals will be under 55.57 which requires the facility licensee to indicate a need for renewal of the license.

Q. 410. Please clarify paragraph 55.59(c)(4)(iii). What is being asked for?

A. The regulation requires a formalized, documented system for evaluating the performance and competency of licensed operators and senior operators. The system must include observation of on-the-job performance and evaluation of the operator's performance and competency through the use of an operating test. The operating test must include evaluation of actions taken during actual or simulated events which require the use of abnormal and emergency procedures.

Q. 411. Concerning paragraph 55.59(c)(3)(iv), what does "on a regularly scheduled basis" mean?

A. The facility licensee must establish a review schedule that will provide reasonable assurance that each licensed operator and senior operator is knowledgeable of all abnormal and emergency procedures. At a minimum, the schedule must require the review of all abnormal and emergency procedures at least once every two years.

Q. 412. Where preplanned lectures are part of the requal program, is it necessary that the licensees participate in all of these lectures, notwithstanding successful completion of the written examinations following these lectures, in order to be able to say that the licensee has met the requal program requirements on the NRC-398 application?

A. Under revised 55.59 no provisions for exemption of lectures is provided. If currently approved programs contain exemption provisions for licensed instructors the programs should continue until the programs are accredited.

INPO guideline 82-026 contains exemption provisions for instructors who teach specific subjects; however, they must attend lectures in subjects they do not teach.

Q. 413.   Paragraph 55.59(b) implies that the NRC is notified when an individual fails a comprehensive written examination or operating test. Is this a requirement?

A. The NRC does not expect to be notified if a licensed operator or senior operator fails an examination. Requalification programs have provisions for accelerated training. We expect facility management will provide the necessary retraining and reexaminations before returning to active license status an operator or senior operator who has failed a requalification examination.

Q. 414.   How will individuals who are in non-compliance with accreditated re-qualification training programs (i.e. extended illness, jury duty, etc.) be requalified?

A. Operators will be required to make-up missed portions of the requalification program and to submit evidence to the Commission of successful completion of the training.

Q. 415.   We have a program where we have licensed maintenance people as senior reactor operators limited to fuel handling. To what extent will this new rule apply to us, since in the comments preceding the rule there's mention that this is not being covered, that it's going to be covered as it is currently being done.

For the past 14 years, as long as we've had SROs limited to fuel handling, we have not been required to give operating exams. Our annual requalification exam is a written exam only.

A. For a license which is conditioned to fuel handling only, the testing and requalification program should be appropriate to the license as it's conditioned. The licensee is not permitted to operate the facility. You would therefore not be required to give him an operating test, as described in the regulation.

CONFORMING AMENDMENTS TO 10 CFR PART 50

Q. 416. The new 10 CFR 50.54(i-1) requires us to notify you of any change in the scope of our program. Since we are not defining for you what our program is now, what is it that you are looking for?

A. Let's say that you are using an NRC-approved program today, and you make a modification to that program to conform to the Regulation. Say you go from an annual written examination to a comprehensive examination each two years. You may do that pursuant to 50.59, and simply amend your FSAR at the next update. Or, preferably, you would be accredited, have completed your review of your requalification program, and confirmed it as a systems approach to training.

Both methods may be done pursuant to 50.59. They do not require amendments to licenses. It is only when you have committed to something that's a part of the licensing document. For instance, some facilities have the Denton letter incorporated in their Technical Specifications, associated with staffing on shift.

You need to look at your commitments on a case-specific basis for your utility. Our intent is that you be able to do most of those under 50.59. They would not require review and approval by the staff in advance of your implementing the change.

Q. 417. Previously Part 50.54(i) referred to a decrease in scope, frequency, or duration. Now all you are saying is scope. Is that correct?

A. Yes. The reason for that is that the Rule specifies that you shall have a duration of no longer than two years, and it must be followed. The program that you use through INPO describes content.

Q. 418. What about frequency of the parts?

A. That's covered by the systems approach to training, where you look at the task that is performed, and you decide what it is. And that's why we excluded the classroom, OJT, and examination portion of requalification given that you certify that your program is done in accordance with the systems approach to training. For clarification, although you may be giving segmented exams in your requalification program, you should be aware that if NRC conducts a requalification exam at your facility, it will be a comprehensive written exam and will include an operating test.

Q. 419. The systems approach to training in itself is subjected to revisions to the training program. Some of these changes may be considered, at least by the utility, as a reduction in scope. The statement in 50.54 is still there, where it says that Commission approval is required for a reduction in scope in a training program. How do we meet 50.54 and still comply with 55.59?

A. The key words are "except as specifically authorized by the Commission." The Commission itself, in the Policy Statement on Training and Qualification of Nuclear Power Plant Personnel, on March 20, 1985, particularly Element 5, indicates that it expects the program to be evaluated and revised as necessary, based upon job performance needs.

We recognize that if you only added and never subtracted, you would eventually get to the point where you're putting all the time into training and never doing anything on the job. We expect the evaluation to be reasonable based upon what you're doing. If you want to substitute something that's more important, the fact that you've dropped something does not constitute a reduction in scope for a systems approach to training.

We believe that's a major improvement in the whole training process. You are not locked into doing something for the next six, seven, or eight years because you committed to it in 1980. You now review it and, if it's meaningful, you perform it -- you control that evaluation process.

Q. 420. With respect to that area of 50.54 changes, which basically states that we will have a requalification program and that we cannot lessen the scope, what documents would be looked at as base documents to see whether we did or did not reduce the scope?

A. We will look at your approved requalification training program.

Q. 421. In the 50.74 requirement, you have set up some direction as to sending all correspondence for Part 55 to the Region. However, because this is a Part 50 requirement, should we be sending that to the document control desk in accordance with Part 50.4, which became effective in January of 1987? All correspondence required under Part 50 was supposed to go to the document control desk, with a copy to the Regional Administrator. Please clarify.

A. Communications under each part of the regulation have to conform to the communications requirements of that part.

Q. 422. Is the licensee definition under 50.74 the same as the licensee definition in 10 CFR 55?

A. Yes.

Q. 423. If a licensee is out of conformance with the INPO-accredited training program, is that reportable pursuant to 10 CFR 50.72 and 50.73?

A. It's not reportable to NRC, but you may need to report it to INPO, along with what you're doing to get back into conformance. It may be reportable to NRC if you have certified that someone is a graduate of an accredited program and that he has completed the program, then you find that you have not implemented the program adequately. In that instance, you may have a reporting requirement to NRC.

OPERATOR LICENSING EXAMINER STANDARDS (NUREG-1021)

Q. 424. What weight does NUREG-1021 carry?

A. The purpose of the Examiner Standards, NUREG-1021, is to ensure uniformity and consistency among the regions in the conduct of the examination process. It provides direction to the regions on how we expect them to conduct the operator licensing function. We audit the regions against that Standard. It does not impose new requirements. That is, the requirements that are addressed in the Examiner Standards flow from other documents, whether it be a Regulatory Guide, or Regulation, or other guideline.

That's why many of the changes to Examiner Standards described result from the change to the Rule, the more authoritative document. The standard contains policy on how to carry out the Rule.

Q. 425. It was mentioned that the license examiners would be filling out a simulation facility fidelity feedback report. Could we request that those reports be included in our copy of the examination packages when they are returned to us?

A. They will be. That has been incorporated into Rev. 4 to the Examiner Standards. The simulation facility fidelity feedback report is contained in Examiner Standard ES-104 "Procedures for Postexamination Activities," as section C(3), which requires that a Simulation Facility Fidelity report be prepared for each examination including simulator evaluations of candidates. The Standard also requires this report to be part of the Examination Report sent to the facility.

Q. 426. Will the Simulation Facility Fidelity Feedback Report be used to determine the status of current simulators?

A. The guidance to the examiners is that this information will be applicable only to simulation facilities that have been certified or have applied for approval. However, even today, with the present vintage of simulators, you still receive informal feedback reports in the exam review process. And that will continue. If the Examiners have a problem conducting the operating test at your simulator, you can expect some feedback, although it won't be as formal as would occur after certification or approval.

Q. 427. It was stated earlier that once Form 474 is submitted, the simulation facility is certified in accordance with ANSI/ANS 3.5, and that there are three different mechanisms that may trigger the process of further evaluation: (1) questions regarding the Form 474 submittal, (2) random visits to the facility for evaluation, and (3) the post-examination activities associated with the examination at the facility.

Would the procedures for the simulation facility evaluation feedback due by May -- specifically, ES-104 -- be specific as to the standards and criteria and mechanisms by which the examiners will make a post-examination evaluation of a facility that would then trigger the evaluation procedure?

A. No. The mechanism is intended to be essentially a simple comment sheet that might contain a comment to the effect that "During Scenario X, the simulation facility failed to perform as expected. There was no flow coast down associated with reactor coolant pumps on a loss of power."

This type of comment would be collected and evaluated. Someone would then determine whether it raised a question in our mind that would be the basis for going back and looking at the simulation facility.

It's not significantly different from comments on the simulator in the examination report -- the inspection report that's issued following an exam. If there are a number of random failures, that's the kind of information we're collecting.

There is no acceptance criteria threshold. It's the examiner's judgment. If he felt there was a problem, we're giving him a vehicle to write it down and communicate it back so that knowledgeable people can look at it and decide whether that would trigger an inspection or evaluation.

Q. 428. Typically after that type of evaluation, there's not going to be a significant amount of data by which someone away from the facility, someone who was not there at the time of the examination, could make a very objective or accurate determination as to whether there is a problem with the simulation facility or not; and I understand that there are a significant number of freezes. If, during an overpressure incident, pressure continues to rise to 3,500 pounds, then obviously there's a problem with the simulation facility, but other examples may not be so clear-cut. Therefore, there's a potential for NRC followup where, perhaps it was not warranted because of an evaluation made by someone who was not there when the event occurred.

A. That's why we're getting the feedback from the examiner who was there at the time it occurred. The facility will also receive a copy of the writeup with the inspection report, and I'm sure it will be a subject in the exit briefing with the chief examiner at the end of the exam week.

We think there are adequate mechanisms in place to alert the facility as to what the potential concern is, but most importantly, we want to get feedback on how well the simulation facility is working during an examination based upon an examiner's observation of that simulation facility.

Further, we have been increasingly requesting that facilities record data during simulator exams to the greatest extent possible so that information is available for review on a more objective scale.

Q. 429. We are required to complete training and experience blocks on Form 398 because we don't yet have an acceptable simulation facility, even though we have an INPO-accredited program. Will we still be evaluated in accordance with current ES-109 requirements?

A. Yes.

Q. 430. Under eligibility, you previously cited Examiner Standard 109. In the future an accredited program with an acceptable simulation facility may be substituted for eligibility. Examiner Standard 109 says two years of power plant experience is required. Does that requirement remain?

A. A facility with an INPO-accredited training program that utilizes a certified or approved simulation facility need not meet other experience requirements.

Revision 4 to the examiner standards revises ES 109 to conform with the Regulation.

Q. 431. Examiner Standard 109 lists the eligibility requirements for licensed operators and senior licensed operator applicants. One of these requirements is that each individual spend three months on shift as an extra man under the supervision of a licensed or senior licensed operator. Is this requirement still in effect? Where does this requirement come from, given that it is not addressed in 10 CFR 55, and the new revision supersedes previous requirements?

A. Although not a requirement, this is consistent with our past practice, and it's consistent with Reg Guide 1.8, which endorses ANSI 3.1-1981. It will be continued in ES-109. Facility licensees can ask for a waiver, and their requests will be considered.

Q. 432. Examiner Standard 109 says that training conducted as part of a license program cannot count for experience. But ANSI/ANS 3.1-1981, which is what the Commissioners have told us to use, allows related technical training to count for experience. Is ES-109 in compliance with 3.1?

A. The training time that doesn't count as experience refers to the training required by the approved license program in which the individual is participating. Related technical training refers to training he may have received in another position, such as auxiliary operator. This time may be counted, up to a certain percentage.

Q. 433. There was an article in Nuclear News, January 1987, page 42, that says the average pass rate for the industry on requalification exams administered by the NRC is 78 percent nationwide. Examiner Standard 601 says that in order for a requalification program to be evaluated as satisfactory, 80 percent or more have to pass. This indicates that the industry, nation-wide, has less than a satisfactory requal program. Do you agree?

A. No, because the statistics that Nuclear News used are somewhat questionable. Last year we evaluated 17 facilities, and 5 of them fell in the marginal or unsatisfactory category because they had substantially higher failure rates. So, a few are causing the national statistics to be different. It was similar the year before, when we had five facilities that were in the marginal or unsatisfactory category.

The program evaluation is based upon whether 80 percent or more pass. It's not based upon the average scores of the candidates taking the exam. In other words, if you examine 10 candidates, and 2 fail, you have 80 percent passing and we determine that program is satisfactory. The average score on that exam may be 78 per cent because the 2 people that failed scored in the 60s, while everybody else scored above 80.

Q. 434. Assume that NRC comes in to give the utility requalification exams, and the scores are between 60 and 80 percent and are rated marginal. After the utility modifies their program, reexamines those failures, and comes out with a satisfactory grade, does NRC change that from a marginal to acceptable program?

A. The marginal rating would be based on the examination given, in accordance with ES-601. We evaluated the program and identified individuals with weaknesses. They require remedial training, which is given. Their training will not cause us to revise our evaluation. Two years hence, when we come back and do another evaluation, hopefully 80 percent will pass at that time, and you will be evaluated as satisfactory. The original evaluation and conclusion stands until we come back and re-evaluate, either by inspection or re-examination.

Q. 435. Is that true, even if our program was modified to cover those weaknesses that you discovered?

A. Yes. Your program may, indeed, no longer be marginal. But until we come back and independently evaluate, that remains our conclusion of record.

Q. 436. So, the only way we can get that changed, is for you to come back to give another exam, is that true?

A. Yes, we come back and inspect that area, and reach a conclusion based on our inspection at that time.

Q. 437. Can we ask for such a re-evaluation?

A. Sure.

Q. 438. What limits on materials requested from the facility licensee exist, if any?

A. We will be reasonable, but there are no specific limits. Typically, we go through the list with the facility, and indicate what items we need. We are not going to ask for the whole library or every print on the facility. However, we may need more material at times than you issue to the student to learn the plant, because we have to get familiar with different plants that have slight differences from one type vendor to another. So, we may need more in-depth material.

Q. 439. We receive a copy of the written exam after it has been administered, and as part of the documentation, we are provided with the learning objectives of the source documents from which these questions were derived. For simulator examinations, could we be provided with that same documentation, since we go to the effort to develop scenarios that are based on industry events, LERs, and learning objectives that we've derived from our program so that when you design your simulator exams, they would also be based upon these same precepts?

A. We currently fill out Attachments 3 and 5 to Examiner Standard 302, which delineates the objectives that the exam events are trying to accomplish. Those have been provided to all the individuals who have failed the examination. For individuals who passed, we have provided only Attachment 3, the delineation of the overall exercise itself, malfunction by malfunction, or over-ride by override. We have not been providing Attachment 5 to individuals who pass. If you request, we can provide you a copy of Attachment 5, which contains our objectives for that examination.

Q. 440. With regard to IE Information Notice (IEIN) No. 85-101 "Applicability of 10 CFR 21 to Consulting Firms Providing Training," is training material that is found deficient reportable under 10 CFR 21?

A. The answer is yes under certain conditions. IEIN85-101 provides guidance to licensees and consultants concerning applicability of 10 CFR 21 to certain training activities provided by consultants. Further information regarding reporting requirements can be found in NUREG-0302 Rev. 1, "Remarks Presented (Questions/Answers Discussed at Public Regional Meetings to Discuss Regulations (10 CFR Part 21) for Reporting of Defects and Noncompliance."

Q. 441. Would the review of the exam to make our comments within the five working days also apply to the simulator exam?

A. The comment procedure has been limited to the written examination by the Examiner's Standards. You can comment, obviously, on our simulator exam, and we are more than willing to listen to what you have to say. But we have not been going through a formal comment procedure for the simulator exam. One of the reasons is that the simulator examination is on-going during the course of the week. And the written examination is given typically in the first day. And, usually, by the end of the week, you provide us with your written exam comments, and that expedites the grading process.

Our present practice does not solicit written comments on the simulator exam for grading purposes. Normally the dialogue established with the simulator operators (training staff) is adequate to resolve any weaknesses in the simulator scenarios prior to their execution. Otherwise, written comments are accepted during an appeal process for an individual candidate.

Appendix A

Generic Letter 87-07

MAR 19 1987

TO ALL FACILITY LICENSEES

SUBJECT: INFORMATION TRANSMITTAL OF FINAL RULEMAKING
           FOR REVISIONS TO OPERATOR LICENSING -
           10 CFR 55 AND CONFORMING AMENDMENTS
           (Generic Letter No. 87-07)

To provide information about the final revisions to 10 CFR 55, "Operators'
Licenses," and their implementation, the Commission is holding a series of
public meetings. These meetings will be held as follows:

A. April 9, 1987 for Region II
    Richard B. Russell Federal Building
    Strom Auditorium, Lower Level
    75 Spring Street, SW
    Atlanta, Georgia
    Point of Contact: Mr. Kenneth E. Brockman
                       US Nuclear Regulatory Commission, Region II
                       101 Marietta Street, Suite 3100
                       Atlanta, GA 30323
                       (404) 331-5594

B. April 14, 1987 for Regions IV and V
    Stouffer Concourse Hotel
    3801 Quebec Street
    Denver, Colorado (Across from Stapleton Airport)
    Points of Contact: Mr. Ralph Cooley
                        US Nuclear Regulatory Commission, Region IV
                        Parkway Central Plaza Building
                        611 Ryan Plaza Drive, Suite 1000
                        Arlington, TX 76011
                        (817) 860-8147

                        Mr. Phillip Morrill
                        US Nuclear Regulatory Commission, Region V
                        1450 Maria Lane, Suite 210
                        Walnut Creek, CA 94596
                        (415) 943-3740

C. April 16, 1987 for Region III
    Ramada Hotel O'Hare
    6600 N. Mannheim Road (corner of Higgins)
    Rosemont, Illinois (One mile from O'Hare Airport)
    Phone: (312) 827-5131
    Point of Contact: Mr. Thomas Burdick
                       US Nuclear Regulatory Commission, Region III
                       799 Roosevelt Road
                       Glen Ellyn, IL 60137
                       (312) 790-5566

8703190287

D. April 20, 1987 for Region I
    Hilton Hotel Valley Forge
    251 West DeKalb Pike
    King of Prussia, Pennsylvania
    Phone: (215) 337-1200
    Point of Contact: Mr. Noel F. Dudley
                       US Nuclear Regulatory Commission, Region I
                       631 Park Avenue
                       King of Prussia, PA 19406
                       (215) 337-5211

Enclosed with this letter is a double-spaced copy of the regulations and supporting information for your review prior to the public meeting. You are encouraged to forward questions to the appropriate point-of-contact, one week prior to the date of the meeting which you plan to attend. The staff intends to answer these questions and others during the meetings and will consolidate all questions and answers into a NUREG report after the meeting.

In preparation for these meetings, all licensees should pay special attention to the requirements of Sections 55.31(a) and 55.59(c) regarding both initial and requalification training and the option of substituting an accredited training program for initial and requalification training programs previously approved by NRC. This option may be implemented upon written notification to the NRC and does not require any staff review. However, because of conflicts between previous 10CFR55 Appendix A requirements and a systems approach to requalification training, it is necessary to certify that the substitute training program is both accredited and based upon a systems approach to training. The superseded training program description contained in the FSAR need not be revised until the next update required by 50.71(e).

Sincerely,

James H. Snezek /for

Harold R. Denton, Director
Office of Nuclear Reactor Regulation

Enclosure:
As stated

Appendix B

10 CFR Parts 50 and 55

Operators' Licenses and Conforming Amendments

known brucellosis in cattle for the period of 12 months preceding classification as Class Free. The Class C classification is for States or areas with the highest rate of brucellosis, with Class A and Class B in between. Restrictions on the movement of cattle are more stringent for movements from Class A States or areas compared with movements from Free States or areas, and are more stringent for movements from Class B States or areas compared with movements from Class A States or areas, and so on.

The basic standards for the different classifications of States or areas concern maintenance of: (1) A cattle herd infection rate, based on the number of herds found to have brucellosis reactors, not to exceed a stated level during 12 consecutive months; (2) a rate of infection in the cattle population, based on the percentage of brucellosis reactors found in Market Cattle Identification (MCI)—testing at stockyards and slaughtering establishments—not to exceed a stated level; (3) a surveillance system that requires testing of dairy herds, participation of all slaughtering establishments in the MCI program, identification and monitoring of herds at high risk of infection, including herds adjacent to infected herds and herds from which infected animals have been sold or received; and (4) minimum procedural standards for administering the program.

Prior to the effective date of this document, Alabama was classified as a Class B State because of the herd infection rate and the MCI reactor prevalence rate. However, a review of the brucellosis program establishes that Alabama should be changed to Class A status.

In order to attain and maintain Class A status, a State or area must (1) not exceed a cattle herd infection rate, due to field strain *Brucella abortus* of 0.25 percent or 2.5 herds per 1,000 based on the number of reactors found within the State or area during any 12 consecutive months, except in States with 10,000 or fewer herds; (2) maintain a 12 consecutive months MCI reactor prevalence rate not to exceed one reactor per 1,000 cattle tested (0.10 percent); and (3) have an approved individual herd plan in effect within 15 days of locating the source herd or recipient herd. Alabama now meets the criteria for classification as Class A.

Executive Order 12291 and Regulatory Flexibility Act

We are issuing this rule in conformance with Executive Order 12291, and we have determined that it is

not a "major rule" Based on information compiled by the Department, we have determined that this rule will have an effect on the economy of less than $100 million; will not cause a major increase in costs or prices for consumers, individual industries, Federal, State, or local government agencies, or geographic regions; and will not cause a significant adverse effect on competition, employment, investment, productivity, innovation, or on the ability of United States-based enterprises to compete with foreign-based enterprises in domestic or export markets.

For this action, the Office of Management and Budget has waived its review process required by Executive Order 12291.

Cattle moved interstate are moved for slaughter, for use as breeding stock, or for feeding. Changing the status of Alabama reduces certain testing and other requirements on the interstate movement of these cattle. However, cattle from certified brucellosis-free herds moving interstate are not affected by these changes in status. We have determined that the changes in brucellosis status made by this document will not affect market patterns and will not have a significant economic impact on those persons affected by this document.

Under these circumstances, the Administrator of the Animal and Plant Health Inspection Service has determined that this action will not have a significant economic impact on a substantial number of small entities.

Executive Order 12372

This program/activity is listed in the Catalog of Federal Domestic Assistance under No. 10.025 and is subject to the provisions of Executive Order 12372, which requires intergovernmental consultation with State and local officials. (See 7 CFR Part 3015, Subpart V.)

Emergency Action

Dr. John K. Atwell, Deputy Administrator of the Animal and Plant Health Inspection Service for Veterinary Services, has determined that an emergency situation exists, which warrants publication of this interim rule without prior opportunity for public comment. Immediate action is warranted in order to delete unnecessary restrictions on the interstate movement of certain cattle from Alabama.

Further, pursuant to administrative procedure provisions in 5 U.S.C. 533, it is found upon good cause that prior notice and other public procedures with

respect to this interim rule are impracticable and contrary to the public interest, and good cause is found for making this interim rule effective less than 30 days after the publication of this document in the Federal Register. Comments are being solicited for 60 days after publication of this document, and a final document discussing comments received and any amendments required will be published in the Federal Register as soon as possible.

List of Subjects in 9 CFR Part 78

Animal diseases, Brucellosis, Cattle, Hogs, Quarantine, Transportation.

PART 78—BRUCELLOSIS

Accordingly, 9 CFR Part 78 is amended as follows:

1. The authority citation for Part 78 continues to read as follows:

Authority: 21 U.S.C. 111–114a–1, 114g, 115, 117, 120, 121, 123–126, 134b, 134f; 7 CFR 2.17, 2.51, and 371.2(d).

§ 78.41 [Amended]

2. Section 78.41, paragraph (b) is amended by adding "Alabama" immediately before "Arizona".

3. Section 78.41, paragraph (c) is amended by removing "Alabama".

Done in Washington, DC, this 20th day of March, 1987.

B. G. Johnson,
Deputy Administrator, Veterinary Services, Animal and Plant Health Inspection Service.
[PR Doc. 87–6421 Filed 3–24–87; 8:45 am]
BILLING CODE 3410-34-M

NUCLEAR REGULATORY COMMISSION

10 CFR Parts 50 and 55

Operators' Licenses and Conforming Amendments

AGENCY: Nuclear Regulatory Commission.

ACTION: Final rule.

SUMMARY: The Nuclear Regulatory Commission is amending its regulations to (1) clarify the regulations for issuing licenses to operators and senior operators; (2) revise the requirements and scope of written examinations and operating tests for operators and senior operators, including a requirement for a simulation facility; (3) codify procedures for administering requalification examinations; and (4) describe the form and content for operator license applications. The rule is necessary to meet NRC responsibilities under Section

306 of the Nuclear Waste Policy Act of 1982.

DATES: Effective Date: May 26, 1987.
Public meeting dates: April 9, 14, 16, and 20, 1987.

ADDRESSES: Public meeting locations: Public meetings will be held to discuss implementation of the requirements of this rule. The meetings will be held as follows:

A. April 9, 1987 for Region II, Richard B. Russell Federal Building, Strom Auditorium, Lower Level, 75 Spring Street, SW., Atlanta, Georgia.

Point of Contact: Mr. Kenneth E. Brockman, U.S. Nuclear Regulatory Commission, Region II, 101 Marietta Street, Suite 3100, Altanta, GA 30323, (404) 331-5594.

B. April 14, 1987 for Regions IV and V, Stouffer Concourse Hotel, 3801 Quebec Street, Denver, Colorado (Across from Stapleton Airport).

Points of Contact: Mr. Ralph Colley, U.S. Nuclear Regulatory Commission, Region IV, Parkway Central Plaza Building, 611 Ryan Plaza Drive, Suite 1000, Arlington, TX 76011, (817) 860-8147.

Mr. Phillip Morrill, U.S. Nuclear Regulatory Commission, Region V, 1450 Maria Lane, Suite 210, Walnut Creek, CA 94596, (415) 943-3740.

C. April 16, 1987 for Region III, Ramada Hotel O'Hare, 6600 N. Mannheim Road (corner of Higgins), Rosemont, Illinois (One mile from O'Hare Airport), Phone: (312) 827-5131.

Point of Contact: Mr. Thomas Burdick, U.S. Nuclear Regulatory Commission, Region III, 799 Roosevelt Road, Glen Ellyn, IL 60137, (312) 790-5566.

D. April 20, 1987 for Region I, Hilton Hotel Valley Forge, 251 West DeKalb Pike, King of Prussia, Pennsylvania, Phone: (215) 337-1200.

Point of Contact: Mr. Noel F. Dudley, U.S. Nuclear Regulatory Commission, Region I, 631 Park Avenue, King of Prussia, PA 19406, (215) 337-5211.

Background information for the rule includes a copy of the regulatory analysis, the supporting statement for the Office of Management and Budget clearance of the information collection requirements, Regulatory Guides, ANSI/ ANS standards, NUREG-series documents, other documents discussed in this notice, and reports that contain a detailed analysis of the public comments received during the public comment period and their resolution may be examined at the NRC Public Document Room, 1717 H Street NW., Washington, DC.

A single copy of the reports concerning public comments may be obtained from Chief, Operator Licensing

Branch, Office of Nuclear Reactor Regulation, U.S. Nuclear Regulatory Commission, Washington, DC 20555, Telephone: 301-492-4868.

FOR FURTHER INFORMATION CONTACT: Chief, Operator Licensing Branch, Office of Nuclear Reactor Regulation, U.S. Nuclear Regulatory Commission, Washington, DC 20555, Telephone: (301) 492-4868.

SUPPLEMENTARY INFORMATION:

I. Background

Section 107 of the Atomic Energy Act of 1954, as amended (42 U.S.C. 2137), requires the Nuclear Regulatory Commission to prescribe uniform conditions for licensing individuals as operators of production and utilization facilities and to determine the qualifications of these individuals and to issue licenses to such individuals. The regulations implementing these requirements are set out in Part 55 of Title 10, Chapter 1, of the Code of Federal Regulations. To assist licensees and others, the Commission also has issued regulatory guides and generic letters that provide guidance on acceptable methods of meeting these regulatory requirements.

The Commission has become increasingly aware of the need to update its operator licensing regulations and related regulatory guides. These revisions are needed to clarify the extent to which simulators should be used in licensing examinations and to reflect upgraded requirements for licensed operator selection, training, and requalification programs resulting from the accident at TMI-2. Although the Commission has been actively engaged in investigating these matters, the schedule for completing these activities was further accelerated by the enactment of January 7, 1983, of the Nuclear Waste Policy Act of 1982, Pub. L. 97-425. Section 306 of that act (42 U.S.C. 10226, 96 Stat. 2201 at 2262-2263) directs the NRC to establish (1) simulator training requirements for applicants for operator licenses and for operator requalification programs, (2) requirements governing NRC administration of requalification examinations, and (3) requirements for operating tests at civilian nuclear power plant simulators.

On November 26, 1984, the Commission published proposed amendments to 10 CFR Part 55, "Operators' Licenses" in the Federal Register (49 FR 46428). These amendments proposed granting, in part, a petition for rulemaking (PRM-55-1) that was filed by KMC, Inc. PRM-55-1 is discussed more fully under Section II.B,

"Medical Requirements." A 90-day comment period expired on February 25, 1985. Comments were received from 88 respondents. An additional 47 respondents commented on the three associated regulatory guides, also issued for public comment. Reports that contain a detailed analysis of these comments and their resolution are available as indicated under **"ADDRESSES:".**

These proposed revisions to 10 CFR Part 55 were to improve the operator licensing process and to achieve the following objectives:

(1) Improve the safety of nuclear power plant operations by improving the operator licensing process and examination content,

(2) Provide the NRC with an improved basis for administering operator licensing examinations and conducting operating tests, and

(3) Respond to the specific direction given by Congress in Section 306, Nuclear Waste Policy Act of 1982, Pub. L. 97-425, to promulgate regulations and guidance in the area of examinations.

On March 20, 1985, the Commission published a Final Policy Statement on Training and Qualification of Nuclear Power Plant Personnel (50 FR 11147) that describes the Commission's current policy regarding training of operators. In addition to this policy statement, the Commission is publishing the new rules described in this notice; these rules supercede all current regulations for operator licenses. Those facility licensees that have made a commitment that is less than that required by these new rules must conform to the new rules automatically. Those facility licensees that have made a commitment different from or more than that required by these new rules for license amendments and technical specification changes, may apply to the Commission so that they can conform to these new rules. Other changes should be made in accordance with 10 CFR 50.59.

Production facilities previously included in Part 55 are not referenced in the revisions since there are no operators at production facilities currently licensed by the Commission. Although special consideration has been given to the smaller size and scope of test and research reactors the requirements in this notice apply to all utilization facilities licensed under 10 CFR Part 50, including test and research reactors. Consequently, except where specific wording has been used to note different requirements, these rules apply to test and research reactors.

II. Summary of Public Comments and Final Actions

The proposed amendments to improve the operator licensing process have been modified in response to the comments received. A summary of the public comments and, where appropriate, a description of the changes that resulted from them follows.

(A) *General Comments*—(1) *General purpose of these amendments*. Several commenters provided general support for the proposed rule. Other commenters suggested changes to clarify the purpose and exemptions sections. These sections were reworded as a result of the evaluation of these comments. In particular, the purpose of the rule indicates that terms and conditions of operators' licenses and renewal are covered. Exemption for trainees at a facility is clarified to indicate that a trainee is only exempted while participating in an NRC-approved training program to qualify for an operator license. In addition, employees involved in fuel handling are exempt if they are supervised by a licensed senior operator.

(2) *Definitions*. Many commenters were concerned with the specific definitions in the rule. A number of commenters addressed the definitions of "simulation facility" and "Plant-referenced simulator," and requested clarification of the NRC's intent for the use of such devices in the partial conduct of operating tests. Several commenters believed that only plant-referenced simulators would be permitted.

The definition of a "plant-referenced simulator" is intended to mean a simulator that meets all of the requirements of ANSI/ANS 3.5–1985, as endorsed by Regulatory Guide 1.149, "Nuclear Power Plant Simulation Facilities for Use in Operator License Examinations," (see Section V, Regulatory Guides, of this Supplementary Information).

The definition of a "simulation facility" is intended to provide for flexibility in the conduct of the simulator (non-plant-walkthrough) portion of the operating test. The intent is to permit, under circumstances specified in 10 CFR 55.45(b), the use of the plant itself, and/or a plant-referenced simulator, and/or some other type of simulation device such as a part-task or basic-principles simulator, for the conduct of the simulator portion of the operating test.

A number of commenters expressed concern that a plant, when used as a simulator, could not safely perform the full range of functions that a simulator could perform, and some commenters

requested clarification about the limitation of the conditions under which the plant could be used.

It is not the intent of NRC to permit or encourage the initiation of transients on the plant when and if the plant is used as a simulation facility. The use of the plant is envisioned as a possible approach that a facility licensee might propose to use in conjunction with another simulation device or devices, in lieu of a plant-referenced simulator. This approach might be suitable, for example, for older plants without access to plant-referenced simulators, where manipulations of the plant, to the extent consistent with plant conditions, might be used to demonstrate familiarity with the plant for which the candidate would be licensed.

Several commenters suggested that the definition of "reference plant" should not be specific to a plant and its unit. The word "unit" has been deleted from this definition, although it remains the NRC's intent that a reference plant refer to a specific docket number. For those situations in which a multi-unit plant is composed of units from the same vendor and vintage, it is likely that only one simulation facility would be required. For others, Regulatory Guide 1.149 provides specific guidance for those facility licensees that want to consider the use of one simulation facility for use at more than one nuclear power plant. This guidance is based upon existing NRC policy on the granting of multiunit operator's licenses.

(B) *Medical requirements*—(1) *Criteria for medical requirements*. Most commenters agreed with the revisions to the medical certification process, which would require, for the usual case, a brief certification by the facility licensee on Form NRC–396, as revised. Some commenters questioned the relationship of these requirements to drug and alcohol problems and programs. Other commenters were confused about who would have responsibility for determining the medical condition of an operator or applicant for an operator's license. Some comments were made about the specific language in the medical requirements regarding disqualifying conditions and commenters requested changes or clarification. Many commenters noted the need to adjust the medical requirements to the renewal cycle.

The medical requirements reflect the industry standard articulated in ANSI/ANS 3.4–1983, "Medical Certification and Monitoring of Personnel Requiring Operating Licenses for Nuclear Power

Plants."[1] The intent is to prevent the manipulation of the controls by an operator whose medical condition and general health would cause operational errors endangering public health and safety. The medical requirements rely on examination of the applicant or operator by a licensed physician who evaluates the medical conditon of the operator, based on the criteria of ANSI/ANS 3.4–1983 that is endorsed by Regulatory Guide 1.134, "Medical Evaluation of Licensed Personnel for Nuclear Power Plants," and makes recommendations to the facility's management. The facility's management is responsible for certifying the suitability of the applicant for a license. The NRC has the responsibility for making an assessment of the applicant for a license, including the applicant's medical fitness. Neither the facility nor the NRC staff will make medical judgments. When a conditional license is requested, the NRC will use a qualified medical expert to review the medical evidence submitted by the facility to make a determination. For minor conditions, such as the need to wear corrective lenses or a hearing aid. the Form NRC 396 is modified to simplify the process for obtaining a medically conditioned license. Moreover, while the biennial medical examination required under § 55.21 is intended to detect alcoholism or drug dependency or both, no reference is made in the rule to alcohol or drug problems. These issues are covered in a Policy Statement on Fitness for Duty of Nuclear Power Plant Personnel (51 FR 27921), published on August 4, 1986, by the Commission. In addition, the license renewal period is changed to 6 years to be compatible with the biennial medical examination requirements.

In July 1983, KMC, Inc., petitioned the Commission (PRM–55–1) "to simplify the procedure for the review of the medical status of applicants for operator-. . . licenses." KMC stated that the current procedures require that a detailed medical history and results of the applicant's medical examination by a licensed physician be sent to the Commission. The petitioner requested that the Commission amend its regulations to permit designated medical examiners, as defined in ANSI N546–1976, "Medical Certification and Monitoring of Personnel Requiring Operator Licenses for Nuclear Power Plants," to certify that the applicant has

---

[1] Standards discussed in this rule are available for purchase from American Nuclear Society, 555 North Kensington Avenue, La Grange Park, Illinois 60525.

been examined (using the guidance contained in ANSI N546–1976 as endorsed by Regulatory Guide 1.134) and that the applicant's general health and physical condition is not such as may cause operational errors. Under the petitioner's request the use of the current NRC Form 396 would be discontinued for utility operators and detailed medical records would be retained by the licensee's designated medical examiner. Subpart C to Part 55 responds to the KMC, Inc. petition. NRC grants its request, in part, by eliminating the requirement to submit, in usual cases, medical information for an applicant for an operator's license directly to the NRC. Instead, as described above, a certification to NRC about compliance with the health requirements in § 55.33(a)(1) would be made by the facility licensee.

(2) *Notification of incapacitation because of disability or illness.* Some confusion was noted by several commenters regarding the process to notify the Commission when an operator was incapacitated because of disability or illness. The final rule is changed to reflect more clearly the Commission's intent. That is, if, during the term of the license, an operator's medical condition changes and does not meet the requirements set forth in ANSI/ANS 3.4–1983, notification of the Commission by the facility licensee is required. At the same time, if the examining physician indicates that the condition can be accommodated as noted in § 5.1 of the ANSI/ANS 3.4–1983, a conditional license may be requested by an authorized representative of the facility licensee. Form NRC 396 must be used and supporting medical evidence must be supplied. However, the facility licensee does not have to wait for permission from the Commission before returning an operator to licensed duties, if the operator has been examined by a physician, who, using ANSI/ANS 3.4–1983 as a basis, has recommended to the facility's management that the operator can return.

(3) *Test and research reactors.* Many test and research reactor operators were concerned that the requirements in the rule changed the medical requirements for them. The rule changes only the requirements for test and research reactor facility licensees. It does not change the status quo for reactor operators, for whom ANSI/ANS–15.4–1977(N 380), "Selection and Training of Personnel for Research Reactors," requirements continue.

(C) *Applications.* Applications for an operator license require the facility

licensee to certify that there is a need for the applicant to perform assigned duties. Several commenters were concerned that the "need" was not clearly defined. The requirements are intended to simply have the facility licensee's management internally review the need for the license before the application is made. Another concern of many commenters was the relationship between industry-accredited training programs and the details regarding training and experience needed to apply to the NRC on Form NRC–398. In addition, some commenters were concerned with the definition of the phrase "learned to operate." This phrase has been deleted from § 55.31 and replaced by wording which indicates that if a candidate successfully completes the training and experience requirements to be licensed as an operator, the NRC will conduct the appropriate examination and operating test. Section 55.31(a)(5) has been added to specify the minimum number of control manipulations to be conducted by an applicant. Details regarding other training and qualification will not be required to be supplied on Form NRC–398, if these requirements are contained in an NRC-approved training program that uses a simulation facility acceptable to the NRC under § 55.45(b). Subject to continued Commission endorsement of the industry's accreditation process under the Final Policy Statement on Training and Qualification of Nuclear Power Plant Personnel (50 FR 11147; March 20, 1985), a facility licensee's training program would be approved by being accredited by the National Nuclear Accrediting Board.

(D) *Written examinations and operating tests*—(1) *Content.* Most commenters recommended that the principal means of determining the knowledge, skills, and abilities to be included in operator licensing written examinations and operating tests should be the learning objectives derived from a systematic analysis of the job performance requirements. These commenters recommended that these learning objectives form the basis and scope of examinations and tests and that other sources of information should only be used until the learning objectives are available for a facility. Conversely, some commenters questioned as premature the endorsement by NRC of a systematic analysis from which to draw the content for licensing examinations and tests. One commenter recommended that NRC

issue a document that specifically delineates what an operator is responsible for on NRC examinations and operating tests.

Systematic analysis of job performance requirements is an accepted methodology for deriving licensing examination content. The job-task analyses are being performed as part of the performance-based programs that are being implemented by facility licensees as part of the industry supported accreditation program. The learning objectives derived from these job-task analyses should form the basis for licensing written examinations and operating tests at a facility. Ultimately, the NRC testing objectives will reflect facility licensee-developed learning objectives. In the interim, while these programs are being developed and reviewed for accreditation, the NRC has activities underway to improve the content validity of NRC examinations and operating tests.

(2) *Specific wording of categories.* Many commenters made specific wording recommendations for the categories listed under content of the written examinations and operating test. These suggestions were reviewed by subject-matter experts and changes were made to clarify or improve the content categories. No major changes resulted except to two categories under the operating test. Under § 55.45, categories (12) and (13) were reworded as follows:

(12) Demonstrate the knowledge and ability as appropriate to the assigned position to assume that responsibilities associated with the safe operation of the facility.

(13) Demonstrate the applicant's ability to function within the control room team as appropriate to the assigned position, in such a way that the facility licensee's procedures are adhered to and that the limitations in its license and amendments are not violated.

(3) *Waivers.* Several commenters suggested that examinations and tests be automatically waived under specific circumstances. As the agency responsible for public health and safety with regard to nuclear facilities, the Commission cannot waive its independent assessment of operators. Waivers are based on operators previously passing all or part of a licensing examination. Details regarding the processing of waivers are addressed in NUREG–1021, "Operator Licensing Examiner Standards." *

---

* NUREG-series documents are available for public inspection and copying for a fee in the Commission's Public Document Room at 1717 H

(4) *Integrity and examinations and tests.* Although many commenters supported the addition of § 55.49, "Integrity of Examinations and Tests," they felt that the penalties in § 55.71 were excessive. Other commenters were afraid that any action might be interpreted as cheating and that the role of facility licensees in enforcement was unclear. The NRC always has prosecutorial discretion not to take enforcement action in unclear cases. The language in § 55.71 on criminal violations only covers persons who "willfully violate" the Atomic Energy Act or the NRC's regulations and does not apply to situations such as discussions after an examination is administered or when a previously administered examination is used as a practice examination.

(E) *Simulation facilities*—(1) *Application process.* Many commenters were concerned with what they termed the burdensome procedure requiring initial and subsequent application for approval to use a simulation facility. Most of these commenters felt that certification by the facility licensee to the NRC that the simulation facility met industry standards should suffice, when combined with the NRC's ability to audit the simulation facility and review the supporting documentation.

The Commission has amended the final rule to reflect the position taken in these comments. Any facility licensee that proposes to use a simulation facility that meets the definition of a plant-referenced simulator (essentially a simulator that meets the requirements of ANS–3.5, 1985, "Nuclear Power Plant Simulators for Use In Operator Training," as modified by Regulatory Guide 1.149) will be required only to certify this to the Commission, and to maintain records pertaining to performance testing results for Commission review or audit. Any facility licensee that proposes to use a simulation facility that is other than a plan-referenced simulator will be required to submit a plan detailing how the requirements of § 55.45 will be met on the alternative device or devices, followed by an application for NRC approval for use of the simulation facility. However, in response to the numerous comments received, this application process has been greatly simplified, and the requirement for a

periodic "subsequent" application has been eliminated. In support of its certification or its application, as appropriate, each facility licensee will be required to conduct periodic performance tests on its simulation facility, and maintain records pertaining to the conduct of these tests and the results obtained.

It is the Commission's intent that those facility licensees that submit a certification for a simulation facility may immediately begin use of the certified simulation facility for the conduct of operating tests at the reference plant.

(2) *Performance testing.* Many comments addressed the requirement for the conduct of a series of performance tests, in which an extensive range of tests would be conducted over a 4-year cycle, 25 percent per year. The industry standard which was in effect at the time of the proposed rulemaking, ANSI/ANS 3.5–1981, required complete simulator performance testing every four years, and R.G. 1.149 endorsed that requirement. In addition, the R.G. specified that all malfunctions which a simulation facility was capable of performing should be tested to the extent that such malfunctions could be used in the conduct of operating tests. The majority of commenters felt that the burden of conducting these tests would demand an excessive amount of time on the part of the simulation facility as well as the facility licensee's staff. Numerous suggestions were made proposing lists of performance tests thought to be appropriate, suggesting alternative formulas for the cycle of performance testing, or offering suggestions that the rule merely endorse a new version of the industry standard which was in preparation at the time.

A new version of the standard, identified as ANSI/ANS 3.5–1985, was published after the expiration of the public comment period. In response to the comments received and to the newly issued industry standard, R.G. 1.149 has been changed to endorse the new standard, with exceptions, and to include in its endorsement the specific, limited list of malfunction performance tests contained in the standard. However, although the new standard continues to require the conduct of simulator performance tests, it has deleted the requirement that these tests be conducted on a four-year cycle for the life of the simulator. Instead it has substituted an annual operability test, and now required that performance tests be conducted only upon completion of initial simulator construction and in the

event that simulator design changes result in significant simulator configuration or performance variations.

In addition, the standard is silent on the subject of periodic testing of malfunctions. The NRC endorsement of the standard in the R.G. takes exception to the deletion of periodic performance testing. The regulations will require performance testing to be conducted throughout the life of a simulation facility, on a four-year cycle, at the rate of approximately 25 percent per year.

The protection of public health and safety requires that licensed operators not only be proficient in general operations but be able to safely cope with plant transients and malfunctions. Thus a reactor operator license candidate's response to malfunctions during an operating test is an important factor in the examiner's assessment of that candidate's performance. It is also necessary to avoid misleading or negative training, which could result from the use of a simulation facility which does not correctly portray plant response to malfunctions. Therefore the ability of a simulation facility to faithfully portray plant malfunctions as well as general operability is to be verified by periodic performance testing. Such testing provides assurance that the simulation facility remains acceptable over time and continues to meet the Commission's regulations. A definition of performance testing has been added to § 55.4, and the requirements for performance testing have been clarified in the applicable paragraphs of § 55.45(b), as they apply to all simulation facilities, whether certified or approved.

(3) *Schedule.* A number of comments included criticism of the time schedules specified as being unreasonably short for submitting a simulation facility plan and for having a simulation facility in full compliance with the regulation.

The regulation has been changed to allow 1 year (versus 120 days) for a facility licensee to submit a plan detailing its approach to the simulation facility requirement; and to allow 4 years (versus 3) for its simulation facility to be in full compliance with the regulation. Those facility licensees that certify the use of a plant-referenced simulator will not have to submit a plan.

(4) *Penalty for unavailability of simulation facility.* Several comments expressed concern that the penalty was too harsh for the unavailability of a simulation facility acceptable to the Commission.

It is the Commission's intent that every facility licensee have available a simulation facility that meets the

Commission's requirements within a reasonable period of time after the effective date of the rule, and that, once available, the simulation facility be maintained and upgraded, as needed, to continue its acceptability for the conduct of operating tests. The Commission recognizes that unique circumstances may arise on a plant-specific basis that cause some deviation from the time requirements established in the rule and that, from time-to-time, a previously certified or approved simulation facility may become temporarily unacceptable for the conduct of operating tests. It is the Commission's intent to address any such situations on a case-by-case basis.

(5) *Lack of guidance for assessment.* A number of comments expressed concern that the guidance to be used by the Commission in its assessment of simulation facility adequacy was not yet available. It is the Commission's intent that no simulation facility audits will be conducted until this guidance has been fully developed and made publicly available for a minimum of 6 months.

(6) *Applicability to future facility licensees.* Several commenters questioned whether the Commission's regulations regarding simulation facilities were intended to apply to future facility licensees.

It is the Commission's intent that these regulations apply to future facility licensees as well as current facility licensees.

(7) *Test and research reactor operators.* Several test and research reactor operators were concerned that the requirements in the rule changed the licensing process for them. As stated above, the rule does not change the status quo for this category of operator. The definition of "simulation facility" in § 55.4 allows the plant to be used to meet the requirements of § 55.45(b). In addition, specific wording in § 55.45(b) permits test and research reactor facility licensees to be exempted from submitting a plan for the use of a simulation facility that is other than a plant-referenced simulator.

(F) *Licenses—(1) Special senior operator licenses.* Many commenters questioned the issuance of special senior licenses. Several argued that current instructor certification requirements were sufficient, others indicated that industry-accredited programs include instructor evaluation, and others cited the Commission's Policy Statement on Training and Qualifications of Nuclear Power Plant Personnel as conflicting with these licenses.

The Commission has deleted the provision for the issuance of special

senior operator licenses from the final rule. This action is in recognition of the industry accreditation of training programs, which includes instructor training, qualification and evaluation, and is in keeping with the intent of the Commission Policy Statement on Training and Qualifications of Nuclear Power Plant Personnel. Industry efforts in implementing instructor training, qualification and evaluation programs will be monitored as described by the Policy Statement. Moreover, senior operator licenses limited to fuel handling will continue to be issued as they are currently. However, since industry accreditation includes instructor evaluation, current NRC instructor certification will not continue at facilities with industry accreditation.

A great number of commenters had specific suggestions regarding the requirements for special senior operators. These comments are no longer applicable since the Commission has deleted these licenses from the final rule.

(2) *"Actively performing the functions of an operator or senior operator."* Although only one commenter specifically questioned the definition of "actively performing the [functions] of," a great many commenters questioned this phrase in regard to R.G. 1.8, "Personnel Qualifications and Training for Nuclear Power Plants," as it was published for public comment in conjunction with the proposed rule. From the comments made in response to the regulatory guide and other comments made regarding the provision in the rule under "Requalification," which required that an operator or senior operator be "actively and extensively engaged" as an operator or senior operator, it is clear that many commenters were confused about the degree of participation in plant operations that is required as a condition to maintain an operator's or senior operator's license. To prevent further confusion, the rule has been modified in § 55.4, "Definitions," to provide the following definition:

Actively performing the functions of an operator or senior operator" means that an individual has a position on the shift crew that requires the individual to be licensed as defined in the facility's technical specifications, and that the individual carries out and is responsible for the duties covered by that position.

In addition, several commenters were concerned that the requirements were unclear regarding the return to "active" status following a period during which a licensee has not been "actively performing the functions of an operator or senior operator" for a period of 4

months or longer. Therefore, the following requirements have been added:

If an operator has not performed licensed duties on a minimum of seven 8-hour shifts or five 12-hour shifts per quarter, before resumption of activities authorized by a license issued under these regulations, an authorized representative of the facility licensee shall certify that the qualifications and status of the licensee are current and valid, and that the licensee has completed a minimum of 40 hours of shift functions under the direction of the operator or senior operator, as appropriate, and in the position to which the individual licensee will be assigned. For licenses limited to fuel handling, one supervised shift is sufficient. Certification shall be maintained at the facility.

The revision in the wording of the rule was made so that it is no longer necessary to include the wording "actively and extensively engaged" under requalification. A licensee can now maintain licensed status by successfully completing the facility licensee's NRC-approved requalification program and passing the requalification examinations and operating tests. However, to return to active performance after a period of not participating on shift, the conditions of a license in § 55.53(f) must be met. In this manner, a licensee without current knowledge of the facility would not be able to perform shift duties.

For test and research reactors, the requirements for "actively performing the functions of an operator or senior operator" would be met with a minimum of four hours per calendar quarter. Similarly, under § 55.53(f), a minimum of six hours parallel work would be required to return to active status.

(3) *Notification of the Commission.* Some commenters noted that the Commission had no need to know about the criminal conviction of a licensee. However, § 55.53(g) is intended to cover criminal behavior. NRC is interested in felonious criminal convictions of a licensee. The NRC considers that there may be a relationship between conviction for a felony and job performance.

(G) *Expiration.* Currently, licenses expire after two years. To lessen the paperwork burdens of facility licensees and the NRC, a five year expiration was proposed. Many commenters suggested that the proposed five year expiration and renewal of licenses be adjusted to meet the biennial medical examination requirements. The renewal cycle has been changed and licenses will now expire after 6 years.

(H) *Requalification and renewal—(1) Requalification program and examination content.* A great many commenters were unclear about the relationship of the NRC requalification requirements and performance-based training programs. Moreover, many commenters urged more flexibility in the requalification cycle and more clarity in the program content requirements.

Although the requirement for NRC approval of requalification programs will remain, the list of content areas under §§55.41, 55.43 and 55.45 will be referenced in § 55.59 to clarify the issue of examination and operating test content. In addition, § 55.59(c) content requirements (formerly Appendix A to 10 CFR Part 55) can be met with a performance-based program for a facility as approved by the NRC. In its Final Policy Statement on Training and Qualification of Nuclear Power Plant Personnel, the Commission endorsed industry-accredited programs as performance based. The frequency of the comprehensive requalification written examination has been changed to a maximum of every 2 years and of the requalification operating test to once a year. The requalification program must be conducted for a continuous period not to exceed 24 months. The specific cycle will be approved by the NRC as part of each facility's training program.

(2) *"Actively and extensively engaged."* As explained above, many commenters were concerned with the implementation of the provision for "actively and extensively engaged as an operator or senior operator" as it related to renewal. This provision is deleted in the final rule. This action complements the additions § 55.53 (e) and (f) to "Conditions of Licenses."

(3) *Test and research reactors.* Several commenters were concerned that the requalification requirements for operators at this class of reactor were changed. The requirements in § 55.59(c)(7) continue the requirements of former Appendix A to 10 CFR Part 55 for test and research reactors. No change in requirements is intended.

(4) *NRC administration of requalification examinations.* Some commenters questioned the NRC administration of requalification examinations. The Commission believes that an NRC administered examination for license renewal provides assurance that an operator or senior operator can operate the controls in a safe and competent manner and that a senior operator can direct the activities of other licensed operators in a safe and competent manner. The Commission also believes that NRC administered examinations provide assurance that facility licensee administered requalification programs are

successfully maintaining the proficiency and knowledge of licensed personnel. To this end, the rule requires in § 55.57 that each applicant for renewal of a six-year license pass an NRC administered comprehensive requalification written examination and operating test at least once during each six-year license. The NRC will administer these requalification written examinations and operating tests on a random basis so that no operator or senior operator will go longer than six years without being examined by the NRC once a six-year license is issued.

(I) *Modification and revocation of licenses.* Some comments were received about the Commission's authority to modify and revoke licenses. The Commission has the authority to modify, suspend or revoke a license under the Atomic Energy Act. Moreover, inherent in the Commission's authority to modify, suspend, or revoke a license is its ability to place a licensed operator or senior operator under probation, if warranted.

(J) *Editorial.* Many commenters had non-substantive editorial changes to suggest. These comments were reviewed by an NRC technical editor and incorporated as appropriate.

(K) *Conforming amendments.* A conforming amendment, 10 CFR 50.74, requires the facility licensee to notify the Commission of a change in operator status. This amendment complements § 55.53(g).

(L) *Revision to 10 CFR 50.54 and 10 CFR 50.34(b)(8).* Revisions have been made to 10 CFR 50.34(b)(8) and 50.54 to reflect the changes made to 10 CFR Part 55.

Separate Views of Commissioner Asselstine

This rule is a good idea, but it does not go far enough. The Commission should have required all licensees to obtain plant referenced simulators. There are two reasons for this. First, I believe that section 306 of the Nuclear Waste Policy Act of 1982 (Pub. L. 97–425) requires it. Second, plant referenced simulators are an excellent way for reactor operators to practice control manipulations for the plant and to actually see how the plant would respond. This is especially important in training the operators to deal with emergency or other situations when the plant is not in its normal state. It is a much more effective teaching tool for the operators to actually manipulate controls and watch the "plant" respond than to have them merely memorize emergency procedures. Further, a simulator which is referenced to the plant on which the operator will be

licensed will be a much more effective training tool than one which is not.

The Commission decided, however, that because there might be special circumstances in some cases which would weigh against requiring that a particular utility purchase a simulator the Commission would not make it a requirement. This kind of case-specific special circumstances is precisely what our exemption procedures are intended to handle. If a licensee had appropriate justification, the Commission could always consider whether to grant an exemption to the regulation. Instead, the Commission chose to water down the regulation and require less.

Separate Views of Commissioner Bernthal

I fully support the Commission's broad objective that operators be reexamined on a regular basis. But I believe the final rule is too inflexible for good regulatory and administrative practice. NRC may indeed need to examine operators every six years; in some cases, perhaps more often. But if a licensee satisfactorily demonstrates its ability to conduct high quality, performance-based examinations in accordance with § 55 57(b)(2)(iii), such licensee performance may well justify extension or relaxation of this requirement. This approach would have been consistent with the Commission's policy of rewarding good licensee performance and focusing attention and resources on deficient performers. The Commission thus could have provided incentive to licensees and flexibility to the NRC examiner staff, and should have thereby focused NRC's limited regulatory resources where they are most urgently needed.

I also continue to believe that the time has come (given the decreased cost and increased sophistication of the technology) for all but a few small powerplants to be required to have plant reference simulators for operator training While there may be some special cases that would qualify for exemption from such a requirement, on the basis of geography and/or plant similarity, licensees could in those circumstances apply for and receive an exemption.

III. Regulatory Analysis

The regulatory analysis describes the values (benefits) and impacts (costs) of implementing the proposed regulations and guidance for operator licensing. The accuracy of these estimates in the regulatory analysis is limited by the lack of extensive data on human performance improvement associated with an improved licensing process. Where possible, quantitative measures were qualitatively compared to related information from other sources for verification. The full text of the regulatory analysis on these amendments is available for inspection in the NRC Public Document Room, 1717 H Street NW., Washington, DC. Single copies of the analysis may be obtained from Chief, Operator Licensing Branch, telephone: (301) 492-4868.

IV. Backfit Analysis

The Commission has determined that these rules are in response to section 306 of the Nuclear Waste Policy Act of 1982 and, therefore, are exempt from the backfit rule 10 CFR 50 109 (50 FR 38097).

V. Regulatory Guides

Three regulatory guides were published in draft form for public comment in conjunction with the proposed rule. These guides were intended to provide guidance on acceptable methods of implementing the revisions to the regulations. As a result of public comment and additional staff review, these three guides are being issued in final form:

(1) R G. 1.134, Revision 2, "Medical Evaluation of Licensed Personnel for Nuclear Power Plants."

(2) R.G. 1.149, Revision 2, "Nuclear Power Plant Simulation Facilities for Use in Operator License Examinations."

(3) R.G. 1.8, Revision 2, "Qualification and Training of Personnel for Nuclear Power Plants."

Copies of these guides may be purchased from the Government Printing Office at the current GPO price. Information on current GPO prices may be obtained by contacting the Superintendent of Documents, U.S. Government Printing Office, Post Office Box 37082, Washington, DC 20013-7082, telephone (202) 275-2060 or (202) 275-2171.

VI. Environmental Impact: Categorical Exclusion

The NRC has determined that this regulation is the type of action described in categorical exclusion 10 CFR 51.22(c)(1). Therefore, neither an environmental impact statement nor an environmental assessment has been prepared for this regulation.

VII. Paperwork Reduction Act Statement

This final rule amends information collection requirements that are subject to the Paperwork Reduction Act of 1980 (44 U.S.C. 3501 et seq.). These paperwork requirements were approved

by the Office of Management and Budget approval number 3150-0018.

VIII. Regulatory Flexibility Certification

As required by the Regulatory Flexibility Act of 1980, 5 U.S.C. 605(b), the Commission hereby certifies that this rule will not have a significant economic impact on a substantial number of small entities. The conforming amendment to 10 CFR Part 50 and the revision of 10 CFR Part 55 affect primarily the companies that own and operate light-water nuclear power reactors and the vendors of those reactors. They also affect individuals licensed as operators at these companies. Neither the companies that own and operate reactors nor these individuals fall within the scope of the definition of "small entity" set forth in section 501(b) of the Regulatory Flexibility Act, NRC's Size Standards adopted December 9, 1985 (50 FR 50241), or the Small Business Size Standards set out in regulations issued by the Small Business Administration in 13 CFR Part 121.

List of Subjects

10 CFR Part 50

Antitrust, Classified information, Fire prevention, Incorporation by reference, Intergovernmental relations, Nuclear power plants and reactors, Penalty, Radiation protection, Reactor siting criteria, Reporting and recordkeeping requirements.

10 CFR Part 55

Manpower training programs, Nuclear power plants and reactors, Penalty, Reporting and recordkeeping requirements.

For the reasons set out in the preamble and under the authority of the Atomic Energy Act of 1954, as amended, the Energy Reorganization Act of 1974, as amended, the Nuclear Waste Policy Act of 1982, and 5 U.S.C. 553, the NRC is adopting the following amendments to 10 CFR Part 55 and 10 CFR Part 50.

1. 10 CFR Part 55 is revised to read as follows:

PART 55—OPERATORS' LICENSES

Subpart A—General Provisions

Sec
55.1 Purpose.
55.2 Scope.
55.3 License requirements.
55.4 Definitions.
55.5 Communications.
55 6 Interpretations
55 7 Additional requirements.
55.8 Information collection requirements: OMB approval.

Subpart B—Exemptions

55 11 Specific exemptions.
55.13 General exemptions.

Subpart C—Medical Requirements

55.21 Medical examination.
55.23 Certification.
55.25 Incapacitation because of disability or illness.
55.27 Documentation.

Subpart D—Applications

55.31 How to apply.
55.33 Disposition of an initial application.
55.35 Re-applications.

Subpart E—Written Examinations and Operating Tests

55 41 Written examination: Operators.
55.43 Written examination: Senior operators.
55.45 Operating tests.
55.47 Waiver of examination and test requirements.
55.49 Integrity of examinations and tests.

Subpart F—Licenses

55.51 Issuance of licenses.
55.53 Conditions of licenses.
55.55 Expiration.
55.57 Renewal of licenses.
55.59 Requalification.

Subpart G—Modification and Revocation of Licenses

55.61 Modification and revocation of licenses.

Subpart H—Enforcement

55.71 Violations.

Authority: Secs. 107, 161, 182, 68 Stat. 839, 948, 953 as amended, sec. 234, 83 Stat. 444, as amended (42 U.S.C. 2137, 2201, 2232, 2282); secs. 201, as amended, 202, 68 Stat. 1242, as amended, 1244 (42 U.S.C. 5841, 5842).

Sections 55.41, 55.43, 55.45 and 55.59 also issued under sec. 306, Pub. L. 97-425, 96 Stat. 2262 (42 U.S C. 10226). Section 55.61 also issued under secs. 186, 187, 68 Stat. 955 (42 U.S C 2236, 2237).

For the purposes of sec. 223, 68 Stat. 958, as amended (42 U.S.C. 2273) §§ 55.3, 55.21, 55.49 and 55 53 are issued under sec. 161i, 68 Stat. 949, as amended (42 U.S.C. 2201(i)); and §§ 55.23, 55.25 and 55.53(f) are issued under sec. 161o, 68 Stat. 950, as amended (42 U.S.C. 2201(o)).

Subpart A—General Provisions

§ 55.1 Purpose.

The regulations in this part:

(a) Establish procedures and criteria for the issuance of licenses to operators and senior operators of utilization facilities licensed pursuant to the Atomic Energy Act of 1954, as amended, or section 202 of the Energy Reorganization Act of 1974, as amended, and Part 50 of this chapter,

(b) Provide for the terms and conditions upon which the Commission will issue or modify these licenses, and

(c) Provide for the terms and conditions to maintain and renew these licenses.

§ 55.2 Scope.

The regulations in this part apply to—
(a) Any individual who manipulates the controls of any utilization facility licensed pursuant to Part 50 of this chapter, and

(b) Any individual designated by a facility licensee to be responsible for directing any licensed activity of a licensed operator.

§ 55.3 License requirements.

A person must be authorized by a license issued by the Commission to perform the function of an operator or a senior operator as defined in this part.

§ 55.4 Definitions.

As used in this part:
"Act" means the Atomic Energy Act of 1954, including any amendments to the Act.

"Actively performing the functions of an operator or senior operator" means that an individual has a position on the shift crew that requires the individual to be licensed as defined in the facility's technical specifications, and that the individual carries out and is responsible for the duties covered by that position.

"Commission" means the Nuclear Regulatory Commission or its duly authorized representatives.

"Controls" when used with respect to a nuclear reactor means apparatus and mechanisms the manipulation of which directly affects the reactivity or power level of the reactor.

"Facility" means any utilization facility as defined in Part 50 of this chapter. In cases for which a license is issued for operation of two or more facilities, "facility" means all facilities identified in the license.

"Facility licensee" means an applicant for or holder of a license for a facility.

"Licensee" means an individual licensed operator or senior operator.

"Operator" means any individual licensed under this part to manipulate a control of a facility.

"Performance testing" means testing conducted to verify a simulation facility's performance as compared to actual or predicted reference plant performance.

"Physician" means an individual licensed by a State or territory of the United States, the District of Columbia or the Commonwealth of Puerto Rico to dispense drugs in the practice of medicine.

"Plant-referenced simulator" means a simulator modeling the systems of the reference plant with which the operator interfaces in the control room, including operating consoles, and which permits use of the reference plant's procedures. A plant-referenced simulator

demonstrates expected plant response to operator input, and to normal, transient, and accident conditions to which the simulator has been designed to respond.

"Reference plant" means the specific nuclear power plant from which a simulation facility's control room configuration, system control arrangement, and design data are derived.

"Senior operator" means any individual licensed under this part to manipulate the controls of a facility and to direct the licensed activities of licensed operators.

"Simulation facility" means one or more of the following components, alone or in combination, used for the partial conduct of operating tests for operators, senior operators, and candidates:
(1) The plant,
(2) A plant-referenced simulator,
(3) Another simulation device.

"Systems approach to training" means a training program that includes the following five elements:
(1) Systematic analysis of the jobs to be performed.
(2) Learning objectives derived from the analysis which describe desired performance after training.
(3) Training design and implementation based on the learning objectives.
(4) Evaluation of trainee mastery of the objectives during training.
(5) Evaluation and revision of the training based on the performance of trained personnel in the job setting.

"United States," when used in a geographical sense, includes Puerto Rico and all territories and possessions of the United States.

§ 55.5 Communications.

(a) Except as provided under a regional licensing program identified in paragraph (b) of this section, an applicant or licensee or facility licensee shall submit any communication or report concerning the regulations in this part and shall submit any application filed under these regulations to the Commission as follows:
(1) By mail addressed to—Director of Nuclear Reactor Regulation, U.S. Nuclear Regulatory Commission, Washington, DC 20555, or
(2) By delivery in person to the Commission offices at—(i) 1717 H Street NW., Washington, DC or (ii) 7920 Norfolk Avenue, Bethesda, Maryland.

(b)(1) The Director of Nuclear Reactor Regulation has delegated to the Regional Administrators of Regions I, II, III, IV, and V authority and responsibility pursuant to the regulations in this part for the issuance and renewal of licenses

for operators and senior operators of nuclear reactors licensed under 10 CFR Part 50 and located in these regions.

(2) Any application for a license or license renewal filed under the regulations in this part involving a nuclear reactor licensed under 10 CFR Part 50 and any related inquiry, communication, information, or report must be submitted by mail or in person to the Regional Administrator. The Regional Administrator or the Administrator's designee will transmit to the Director of Nuclear Reactor Regulation any matter that is not within the scope of the Regional Administrator's delegated authority.

(i) If the nuclear reactor is located in Region I, submission must be made to the Regional Administrator, Region I, U.S. Nuclear Regulatory Commission, 631 Park Avenue, King of Prussia, Pennsylvania 19406.

(ii) If the nuclear reactor is located in Region II, submission must be made to the Regional Administrator, Region II, U.S. Nuclear Regulatory Commission, 101 Marietta Street, Suite 2900, Atlanta, Georgia 30303.

(iii) If the nuclear reactor is located in Region III, submission must be made to the Regional Administrator, Region III, U.S. Nuclear Regulatory Commission, 799 Roosevelt Road, Glen Ellyn, Illinois 60137.

(iv) If the nuclear reactor is located in Region IV, submission must be made to the Regional Administrator, Region IV, U.S. Nuclear Regulatory Commission, 611 Ryan Plaza Drive, Suite 1000, Arlington, Texas 76011.

(v) If the nuclear reactor is located in Region V, submission must be made to the Regional Administrator, Region V, U.S. Nuclear Regulatory Commission, 1450 Maria Lane, Suite 210, Walnut Creek, California 94596.

§ 55.6 Interpretations.

Except as specifically authorized by the Commission in writing, no interpretation of the meaning of the regulations in this part by any officer or employee of the Commission other than a written interpretation by the General Counsel will be recognized to be binding upon the Commission.

§ 55.7 Additional requirements.

The Commission may, by rule, regulation, or order, impose upon any licensee such requirements, in addition to those established in the regulations in this part, as it deems appropriate or necessary to protect health and to minimize danger to life or property.

§ 55.8 Information collection requirements: OMB approval.

(a) The Nuclear Regulatory Commission has submitted the information collection requirements contained in this part to the Office of Management and Budget (OMB) for approval as required by the Paperwork Reduction Act of 1980 (44 U.S.C. 3501 et seq.). OMB has approved the information collection requirements contained in this part under control number 3150-0018.

(b) The approved information collection requirements contained in this part appear in §§ 55.45, 55.53, and § 55.59.

(c) This part contains information collection requirements in addition to those approved under the control number specified in paragraph (a) of this section. These information collection requirements and the control numbers under which they are approved are as follows:

(1) In §§ 55.23, 55.25, 55.27, 55.31, Form NRC-396 is approved under control number 3150-0024.

(2) In §§ 55.31, 55.35, 55.47, and 55.57, Form NRC-398 is approved under control number 3150-0090.

(3) In § 55.45, Form NRC-474 is approved under control number 3150-0138.

Subpart B—Exemptions

§ 55.11 Specific exemptions.

The Commission may, upon application by an interested person, or upon its own initiative, grant such exemptions from the requirements of the regulations in this part as it determines are authorized by law and will not endanger life or property and are otherwise in the public interest.

§ 55.13 General exemptions.

The regulations in this part do not require a license for an individual who—

(a) Under the direction and in the presence of a licensed operator or senior operator, manipulates the controls of—

(1) A research or training reactor as part of the individual's training as a student, or

(2) A facility as a part of the individual's training in a facility licensee's training program as approved by the Commission to qualify for an operator license under this part.

(b) Under the direction and in the presence of a licensed senior operator, manipulates the controls of a facility to load or unload the fuel into, out of, or within the reactor vessel.

Subpart C—Medical Requirements

§ 55.21 Medical examination.

An applicant for a license shall have a medical examination by a physician. A licensee shall have a medical examination by a physician every two years. The physician shall determine that the applicant or licensee meets the requirements of § 55.33(a)(1).

§ 55.23 Certification.

To certify the medical fitness of the applicant, an authorized representative of the facility licensee shall complete and sign Form NRC-396, "Certification of Medical Examination by Facility Licensee," available from Publication Services Section, Document Management Branch, Division of Technical Information and Document Control, U.S. Nuclear Regulatory Commission, Washington, DC 20555.

(a) Form NRC-396 must certify that a physician has conducted the medical examination of the applicant as required in § 55.21.

(b) When the certification requests a conditional license based on medical evidence, the medical evidence must be submitted on NRC Form 396 to the Commission and the Commission then makes a determination in accordance with § 55.33.

§ 55.25 Incapacitation because of disability or illness.

If, during the term of the license, the licensee develops a physical or mental condition that causes the licensee to fail to meet the requirements of § 55.21 of this part, the facility licensee shall notify the Commission within 30 days of learning of the diagnosis. For conditions for which a conditional license (as describing in § 55.33(b) of this part) is requested, the facility licensee shall provide medical certification on Form NRC 396 to the Commission (as described in § 55.23 of this part).

§ 55.27 Documentation.

The facility licensee shall document and maintain the results of medical qualifications data, test results, and each operator's or senior operator's medical history for the current license period and provide the documentation to the Commission upon request. The facility licensee shall retain this documentation while an individual performs the functions of an operator or senior operator.

Subpart D—Applications

§ 55.31 How to apply.

(a) The applicant shall:
(1) Complete Form NRC-398, "Personal Qualification Statement—

Licensee," available from Publication Services Section, Document Management Branch, Division of Technical Information and Document Control, U.S. Nuclear Regulatory Commission, Washington, DC 20555;

(2) File an original and two copies of Form NRC-398, together with the information required in paragraphs (a)(3), (4), (5) and (6) of this section, with the appropriate Regional Administrator;

(3) Submit a written request from an authorized representative of the facility licensee by which the applicant will be employed that the written examination and operating test be administered to the applicant;

(4) Provide evidence that the applicant has successfully completed the facility licensee's requirements to be licensed as an operator or senior operator and of the facility licensee's need for an operator or a senior operator to perform assigned duties. An authorized representative of the facility licensee shall certify this evidence on Form NRC-398. This certification must include details of the applicant's qualifications, and details on courses of instruction administered by the facility licensee, and describe the nature of the training received at the facility, and the startup and shutdown experience received. In lieu of these details, the Commission may accept certification that the applicant has successfully completed a Commission-approved training program that is based on a systems approach to training and that uses a simulation facility acceptable to the Commission under § 55.45(b) of this part;

(5) Provide evidence that the applicant, as a trainee, has successfully manipulated the controls of the facility for which a license is sought. At a minimum, five significant control manipulations must be performed which affect reactivity or power level. For a facility that has not completed preoperational testing and initial startup test program as described in its Final Safety Analysis Report, as amended and approved by the Commission, the Commission may accept evidence of satisfactory performance of simulated control manipulations as part of a Commission-approved training program by a trainee on a simulation facility acceptable to the Commission under § 55.45(b) of this part. For a facility which has (i) completed preoperational testing as described in its Final Safety Analysis Report, as amended and approved by the Commission, and (ii) is in an extended shutdown which precludes manipulation of the control of the facility in the control room, the Commission may process the

application and may administer the written examination and operating test required by §§ 55.41 or 55.43 and 55.45 of this part, but may not issue the license until the required evidence of control manipulations is supplied. For licensed operators applying for a senior operator license, certification that the operator has successfully operated the controls of the facility as a licensed operator shall be accepted; and

(6) Provide certification by the facility licensee of medical condition and general health on Form NRC–396, to comply with §§ 55.21, 55.23 and 55.33(a)(1).

(b) The Commission may at any time after the application has been filed, and before the license has expired, require futher information under oath or affirmation in order to enable it to determine whether to grant or deny the application or whether to revoke, modify, or suspend the license.

(c) An applicant whose application has been denied because of a medical condition or general health may submit a further medical report at any time as a supplement to the application.

(d) Each application and statement must contain complete and accurate disclosure as to all matters required to be disclosed. The applicant shall sign statements required by paragraphs (a)(1) and (2) of this section.

§ 55.33 Disposition of an initial application.

(a) *Requirements for the approval of an initial application.* The Commission will approve an initial application for a license pursuant to the regulations in this part, if it finds that—

(1) *Health.* The applicants medical condition and general health will not adversely affect the performance of assigned operator job duties or cause operational errors endangering public health and safety. The Commission will base its finding upon the certification by the facility licensee as detailed in § 55.23.

(2) *Written examination and operating test.* The applicant has passed the requisite written examination and operating test in accordance with §§ 55.41 and 55.45 or 55.43 and 55.45. These examinations and tests determine whether the applicant for an operator's license has learned to operate a facility competently and safely, and additionally, in the case of a senior operator, whether the applicant has learned to direct the licensed activities of licensed operators competently and safely.

(b) *Conditional license.* If an applicant's general medical condition does not meet the minimum standards

under § 55.33(a)(1) of this part, the Commission may approve the application and include conditions in the license to accommodate the medical defect. The Commission will consider the recommendations and supporting evidence of the facility licensee and of the examining physician (provided on Form NRC–396) in arriving at its decision.

§ 55.35 Re-applications.

(a) An applicant whose application for a license has been denied because of failure to pass the written examination or operating test, or both, may file a new application two months after the date of denial. The application must be submitted on Form NRC–398 and include a statement signed by an authorized representative of the facility licensee by whom the applicant will be employed that states in detail the extent of the applicant's additional training since the denial and certifies that the applicant is ready for re-examination. An applicant may filed a third application six months after the date of denial of the second application, and may file further successive applications two years after the date of denial of each prior application. The applicant shall submit each successive application on Form NRC–398 and include a statement of additional training.

(b) An applicant who has passed either the written examination or operating test and failed the other may request in a new application on Form NRC–398 to be excused from re-examination on the portions of the examination or test which the applicant has passed. The Commission may in its discretion grant the request, if it determines that sufficient justification is presented.

Subpart E—Written Examinations and Operating Tests

§ 55.41 Written examination: Operators.

(a) *Content.* The written examination for an operator will contain a representative selection of questions on the knowledge, skills, and abilities needed to perform licensed operator duties. The knowledge, skills, and abilities will be identified, in part, from learning objectives derived from a systematic analysis of licensed operator duties performed by each facility licensee and contained in its training program and from information in the Final Safety Analysis Report, system description manuals and operating procedures, facility license and license amendments, Licensee Event Reports, and other materials requested from the facility licensee by the Commission.

(b) The written examination for an operator for a facility will include a representative sample from among the following 14 items, to the extent applicable to the facility.

(1) Fundamentals of reactor theory, including fission process, neutron multiplication, source effects, control rod effects, criticality indications, reactivity coefficients, and poison effects.

(2) General design features of the core, including core structure, fuel elements, control rods, core instrumentation, and coolant flow.

(3) Mechanical components and design features of the reactor primary system.

(4) Secondary coolant and auxiliary systems that affect the facility.

(5) Facility operating characteristics during steady state and transient conditions, including coolant chemistry, causes and effects of temperature, pressure and reactivity changes, effects of load changes, and operating limitations and reasons for these operating characteristics.

(6) Design, components, and functions of reactivity control mechanisms and instrumentation.

(7) Design, components, and functions of control and safety systems, including instrumentation, signals, interlocks, failure modes, and automatic and manual features.

(8) Components, capacity, and functions of emergency systems.

(9) Shielding, isolation, and containment design features, including access limitations.

(10) Administrative, normal, abnormal, and emergency operating procedures for the facility.

(11) Purpose and operation of radiation monitoring systems, including alarms and survey equipment.

(12) Radiological safety principles and procedures.

(13) Procedures and equipment available for handling and disposal of radioactive materials and effluents.

(14) Principles of heat transfer thermodynamics and fluid mechanics.

§ 55.43 Written examination: Senior operators.

(a) *Content.* The written examination for a senior operator will contain a representative selection of questions on the knowledge, skills, and abilities needed to perform licensed senior operator duties. The knowledge, skills, and abilities will be identified, in part, from learning objectives derived from a systematic analysis of licensed senior operator duties performed by each facility licensee and contained in its training program and from information in the Final Safety Analysis Report, sytem description manuals and operating procedures, facility license and license amendments, Licensee Event Reports, and other materials requested from the facility licensee by the Commission.

(b) The written examination for a senior operator for a facility will include a representative sample from among the following seven items and the 14 items specified in § 55.41 of this part, to the extent applicable to the facility:

(1) Conditions and limitations in the facility license.

(2) Facility operating limitations in the technical specifications and their bases.

(3) Facility licensee procedures required to obtain authority for design and operating changes in the facility.

(4) Radiation hazards that may arise during normal and abnormal situations, including maintenance activities and various contamination conditions.

(5) Assessment of facility conditions and selection of appropriate procedures during normal, abnormal, and emergency situations.

(6) Procedures and limitations involved in initial core loading, alterations in core configuration, control rod programming, and determination of various internal and external effects on core reactivity.

(7) Fuel handling facilities and procedures.

§ 55.45 Operating tests.

(a) *Content.* The operating tests administered to applicants for operator and senior operator licenses in accordance with paragraph (b)(1) of this section are generally similar in scope. The content will be identified, in part, fiom learning objectives derived from a systematic analysis of licensed operator or senior operator duties performed by each facility licensee and contained in its training program and from information in the Final Safety Analysis Report, system description manuals and operating procedures, facility license and license amendments, Licensee Event Reports, and other materials requested from the facility licensee by the Commission. The operating test, to the extent applicable, requires the applicant to demonstrate an understanding of and the ability to perform the actions necessary to accomplish a representative sample from among the following 13 items.

(1) Perform pre-startup procedures for the facility, including operating of those controls associated with plant equipment that could affect reactivity.

(2) Manipulate the console controls as required to operate the facility between shutdown and designated power levels.

(3) Identify annunciators and condition-indicating signals and perform appropriate remedial actions where appropriate.

(4) Identify the instrumentation systems and the significance of facility instrument readings.

(5) Observe and safely control the operating behavior characteristics of the facility.

(6) Perform control manipulations required to obtain desired operating results during normal, abnormal, and emergency situations.

(7) Safely operate the facility's head removal systems, including primary coolant, emergency coolant, and decay heat removal systems, and identify the relations of the proper operation of these systems to the operation of the facility.

(8) Safely operate the facility's auxiliary and emergency systems, including operation of those controls associated with plant equipment that could affect reactivity or the release of radioactive materials to the environment.

(9) Demonstrate or describe the use and function of the facility's radiation monitoring systems, inlcuding fixed radiation monitors and alarms, portable survey instruments, and personnel monitoring equipment.

(10) Demonstrate knowledge of significant radiation hazards, including permissible levels in excess of those authorized, and ability to perform other procedures to reduce excessive levels of radiation and to guard against personnel exposure.

(11) Demonstrate knowledge of the emergency plan for the facility, including, as appropriate, the operator's or senior operator's responsibility to decide whether the plan should be executed and the duties under the plan assigned.

(12) Demonstrate the knowledge and ability as appropriate to the assigned position to assume the responsibilities associated with the safe operation of the facility.

(13) Demonstrate the applicant's ability to function within the control room team as appropriate to the assigned position, in such a way that the facility licensee's procedures are adhered to and that the limitations in its license and amendments are not violated.

(b) *Implementation*—(1) *Administration.* The operating test will be administered in a plant walkthrough and in either—

(i) A simulation facility which the Commission has approved for use after application has been made by the facility licensee, or

(ii) A simulation facility consisting solely of a plant-referenced simulator which has been certified to the Commission by the facility licensee.

(2) *Schedule for facility licensees.* (i) Within one year after the effective date of this part, each facility licensee which proposes to use a simulation facility pursuant to paragraph (b)(1)(i) of this section, except test and research reactors, shall submit a plan by which its simulation facility will be developed and by which an application will be submitted for its use.

(ii) Those facility licensees which propose to conform with paragraph (b)(1)(i) of this section, not later than 42 months after the effective date of this rule, shall submit an application for use of this simulation facility to the Commission, in accordance with paragraph (b)(4)(i) of this section.

(iii) Those facility licensees which propose to conform with paragraph (b)(1)(ii) of this section, not later than 46 months after the effective date of this rule, shall submit a certification for use of this simulation facility to the Commission on Form NRC–474, "Simulation Facility Certification," available from Publication Services Section, Document Management Branch, Division of Technical Information and Document Control, U.S. Nuclear Regulatory Commission, Washington, DC 20555, in accordance with paragraph (b)(5)(i) of this section.

(iv) The simulation facility portion of the operating test will not be administered on other than a certified or an approved simulation facility after May 26, 1991.

(3) *Schedule for facility applicants.* (i) For facility licensee applications after the effective date of this rule, except test and research reactors, the applicant shall submit a plan which identifies whether its simulation facility will conform with paragraph (b)(1)(i) or (b)(1)(ii) of this section at the time of application.

(ii) Those applicants which propose to conform with paragraph (b)(1)(i) of this section, not later than 180 days before the date when the applicant proposes that the Commission conduct operating tests, shall submit an application for use of its simulation facility to the NRC, in accordance with paragraph (b)(4)(i) of this section.

(iii) Those applicants which propose to conform with paragraph (b)(1)(ii) of this section, not later than 60 days before the date when the applicant proposes that NRC conduct operating tests, shall submit a certification for use of its simulation facility to the Commission on Form NRC–474, in accordance with paragraph (b)(5)(i) of this section.

(4) *Application for and approval of simulation facilities.* Those facility licensees which propose, in accordance with paragraph (b)(1)(i) of this section, to use a simulation facility that is other than solely a plant-referenced simulator as defined in § 55.4 shall—

(i) In accordance with the plan submitted pursuant to paragraph (b)(2)(i) or (b)(3)(i) of this section, as applicable submit an application for approval of the simulation facility to the Commission, in accordance with the schedule in paragraph (b)(2)(ii) or (b)(3)(ii) of this section, as appropriate. This application must include:

(A) A statement that the simulation facility meets the plan submitted to the Commission pursuant to paragraph (b)(2)(i) or (b)(3)(i) of this section, as applicable;

(B) A description of the components of the simulation facility which are intended to be used for each part of the operating test; and

(C) A description of the performance tests as part of the application, and the results of such tests.

(ii) The Commission will approve a simulation facility if it finds that the simulation facility and its proposed use are suitable for the conduct of operating tests for the facility licensee's reference plant, in accordance with paragraph (a) of this section.

(iii) Submit, every four years on the anniversary of the application, a report to the Commission which identifies any uncorrected performance test failures, and submit a schedule for correction of these performance test failures, if any.

(iv) Retain the results of the performance test conducted until four years after the submittal of the application under paragraph (b)(4)(i), each report pursuant to paragraph (b)(4)(iii), or any reapplication under paragraph (b)(4)(iv) of this section, as appropriate.

(v) If the Commission determines, based upon the results of performance testing, that an approved simulation facility does not meet the requirements of this part, the simulation facility may not be used to conduct operating tests.

(vi) If the Commission determines, pursuant to paragraph (b)(4)(v) of this section, that an approved simulation facility does not meet the requirements of this part, the facility licensee may again submit an application for approval. This application must include a description of corrective actions taken,

including results of completed performance testing as required for approval.

(vii) Any application or report submitted pursuant to paragraphs (b)(4)(i), (b)(4)(iii) and (b)(4)(vi) of this section must include a description of the performance testing completed for the simulation facility, and must include a description of performance tests, if different, to be conducted on the simulation facility during the subsequent four-year period, and a schedule for the conduct of approximately 25 percent of the performance tests per year for the subsequent four years.

(5) *Certification of simulation facilities*—Those facility licensees which propose, in accordance with paragraph (b)(1)(ii) of this section, to use a simulation facility consisting solely of a plant-referenced simulator as defined in § 55.4, shall—

(i) Submit a certification to the Commission that the simulation facility meets the Commission's regulations. The facility licensee shall provide this certification on Form NRC–474 in accordance with the schedule in paragraph (b)(2)(iii) or (b)(3)(iii) of this section, as applicable.

(ii) Submit, every four years on the anniversary of the certification, a report to the Commission which identifies any uncorrected performance test failures, and submit a schedule for correction of such performance test failures, if any.

(iii) Retain the results of the performance test conducted until four years after the submittal of certification under paragraph (b)(5)(i), each report pursuant to paragraph (b)(5)(ii), or recertification under paragraph (b)(5)(v) of this section, as applicable.

(iv) If the Commission determines, based upon the results of performance testing, that a certified simulation facility does not meet the requirements of this part, the simulation facility may not be used to conduct operating tests.

(v) If the Commission determines, pursuant to paragraph (b)(5)(iv) of this section, that a certified simulation facility does not meet the requirements of this part, the facility licensee may submit a recertification to the Commission on Form NRC–474. This recertification must include a description of corrective actions taken, including results of completed performance testing as required for recertification.

(vi) Any certification report, or recertification submitted pursuant to paragraph (b)(5)(i), (b)(5)(ii) or (b)(5)(v) of this section must include a description of performance testing completed for the simulation facility, and must include a description of the

performance tests, if different, to be conducted on the simulation facility during the subsequent four-year period, and a schedule for the conduct of approximately 25 percent of the performance tests per year for the subsequent four years.

§ 55.47 Waiver of examination and test requirements.

(a) On application, the Commission may waive any or all of the requirements for a written examination and operating test, if it finds that the applicant—

(1) Has had extensive actual operating experience at a comparable facility, as determined by the Commission, within two years before the date of application;

(2) Has discharged his or her responsibilities competently and safely and is capable of continuing to do so; and

(3) Has learned the operating procedures for and is qualified to operate competently and safely the facility designated in the application.

(b) The Commission may accept as proof of the applicant's past performance a certification of an authorized representative of the facility licensee or of a holder of an authorization by which the applicant was previously employed. The certification must contain a description of the applicant's operating experience, including an approximate number of hours the applicant operated the controls of the facility, the duties performed, and the extent of the applicant's responsibility.

(c) The Commission may accept as proof of the applicant's current qualifications a certification of an authorized representative of the facility licensee or of a holder of an authorization where the applicant's services will be utilized.

§ 55.49 Integrity of examinations and tests.

Applicants, licensees, and facility licensees shall not engage in any activity that compromises the integrity of any application, test, or examination required by this part.

Subpart F—Licenses

§ 55.51 Issuance of licenses.

Operator and senior operator licenses. If the Commission determines that an applicant for an operator license or a senior operator license meets the requirements of the Act and its regulations, it will issue a license in the form and containing any conditions and limitations it considers appropriate and necessary

§ 55.53 Conditions of licenses.

Each license contains and is subject to the following conditions whether stated in the license or not:

(a) Neither the license nor any right under the license may be assigned or otherwise transferred.

(b) The license is limited to the facility for which it is issued.

(c) The license is limited to those controls of the facility specified in the license.

(d) The license is subject to, and the licensee shall observe, all applicable rules, regulations, and orders of the Commission.

(e) If a licensee has not been actively performing the functions of an operator or senior operator, the licensee may not resume activities authorized by a license issued under this part except as permitted by paragraph (f) of this section. To maintain active status, the licensee shall actively perform the functions of an operator or senior operator on a minimum of seven 8-hour or five 12-hour shifts per calendar quarter. For test and research reactors, the licensee shall actively perform the functions of an operator or senior operator for a minimum of four hours per calendar quarter.

(f) If paragraph (e) of this section is not met, before resumption of functions authorized by a license issued under this part, an authorized representative of the facility licensee shall certify the following:

(1) That the qualifications and status of the licensee are current and valid; and

(2) That the licensee has completed a minimum of 40 hours of shift functions under the direction of an operator or senior operator as appropriate and in the position to which the individual will be assigned. The 40 hours must have included a complete tour of the plant and all required shift turnover procedures. For senior operators limited to fuel handling under paragraph (c) of this section, one shift must have been completed. For test and research reactors, a minimum of six hours must have been completed.

(g) The licensee shall notify the Commission within 30 days about a conviction for a felony.

(h) The licensee shall complete a requalification program as described by § 55.59.

(i) The licensee shall have a biennial medical examination.

(j) The licensee shall comply with any other conditions that the Commission may impose to protect health or to minimize danger to life or property.

§ 55.55 Expiration.

(a) Each operator license and senior operator license expires six years after the date of issuance, upon termination of employment with the facility licensee, or upon determination by the facility licensee that the licensed individual no longer needs to maintain a license.

(b) If a licensee files an application for renewal or an upgrade of an existing license on Form NRC-398 at least 30 days before the expiration of the existing license, it does not expire until disposition of the application for renewal or for an upgraded license has been finally determined by the Commission. Filing by mail or telegram will be deemed to be complete at the time the application is deposited in the mail or with a telegraph company.

§ 55.57 Renewal of licenses.

(a) The applicant for renewal of a license shall—

(1) Complete and sign Form NRC-398 and include the number of the license for which renewal is sought.

(2) File an original and two copies of Form NRC-398 with the appropriate Regional Administrator specified in § 55.5(b).

(3) Provide written evidence of the applicant's experience under the existing license and the approximate number of hours that the licensee has operated the facility.

(4) Provide a statement by an authorized representative of the facility licensee that during the effective term of the current license the applicant has satisfactorily completed the requalification program for the facility for which operator or senior operator license renewal is sought.

(5) Provide evidence that the applicant has discharged the license responsibilities competently and safely. The Commission may accept as evidence of the applicant's having met this requirement a certificate of an authorized representative of the facility licensee or holder of an authorization by which the licensee has been employed.

(6) Provide certification by the facility licensee of medical condition and general health on Form NRC-396, to comply with §§ 55.21, 55.23 and 55.27.

(b) The license will be renewed if the Commission finds that—

(1) The medical condition and the general health of the licensee continue to be such as not to cause operational errors that endanger public health and safety. The Commission will base this finding upon the certification by the facility licensee as described in § 55.23.

(2) The licensee—

(i) Is capable of continuing to competently and safely assume licensed duties;

(ii) Has successfully completed a requalification program that has been approved by the Commission as required by § 55.59; and

(iii) Has passed the requalification examinations and annual operating tests as required by § 55.59.

(iv) Has passed a comprehensive requalification written examination and operating test administered by the Commission during the term of a six-year license.

(3) There is a continued need for a licensee to operate or for a senior operator to direct operators at the facility designated in the application.

(4) The past performance of the licensee has been satisfactory to the Commission. In making its finding, the Commission will include in its evaluation information such as notices of violations or letters of reprimand in the licensee's docket.

§ 55.59 Requalification.

(a) *Requalification requirements.* Each licensee shall—

(1) Successfully complete a requalification program developed by the facility licensee that has been approved by the Commission. This program shall be conducted for a continuous period not to exceed 24 months in duration.

(2) Pass a comprehensive requalification written examination and an annual operating test.

(i) the written examination will sample the items specified in §§ 55.41 and 55.43 of this part, to the extent applicable to the facility, the licensee, and any limitation of the license under § 55.53(c) of this part.

(ii) The operating test will require the operator or senior operator to demonstrate an understanding of and the ability to perform the actions necessary to accomplish a comprehensive sample of items specified in § 55.45(a) (2) through (13) inclusive to the extent applicable to the facility.

(iii) In lieu of the Commission accepting a certification by the facility licensee that the licensee has passed written examinations and operating tests administered by the facility licensee within its Commission-approved program developed by using a systems approach to training under paragraph (c) of this section, the Commission may administer a comprehensive requalification written examination and an annual operating test.

(b) *Additional training.* If the requirements of paragraphs (a) (1) and (2) of this section are not met, the Commission may require the licensee to complete additional training and to submit evidence to the Commission of successful completion of this training before returning to licensed duties.

(c) *Requalification program requirements.* A facility licensee shall have a requalification program reviewed and approved by the Commission. The requalification program must meet the requirements of paragraphs (c) (1) through (7) of this section. In lieu of paragraphs (c) (2), (3), and (4) of this section, the Commission may approve a program developed by using a systems approach to training.

(1) *Schedule.* The requalification program must be conducted for a continuous period not to exceed two years, and upon conclusion must be promptly followed, pursuant to a continuous schedule, by successive requalification programs.

(2) *Lectures.* The requalification program must include preplanned lectures on a regular and continuing basis throughout the license period in those areas where operator and senior operator written examinations and facility operating experience indicate that emphasis in scope and depth of coverage is needed in the following subjects:

(i)   Theory and principles of operation.
(ii) General and specific plant operating characteristics.
(iii) Plant instrumentation and control systems.
(iv) Plant protection systems.
(v)   Engineered safety systems.
(vi) Normal, abnormal, and emergency operating procedures.
(vii) Radiation control and safety.
(viii) Technical specifications.
(ix) Applicable portions of Title 10, Chapter I, *Code of Federal Regulations.*

(3) *On-the-job training.* The requalification program must include on-the-job training so that—

(i) Each licensed operator of a utilization facility manipulates the plant controls and each licensed senior operator either manipulates the controls or directs the activities of individuals during plant control manipulations during the term of the licensed operator's or senior operator's license. For reactor operators and senior operators, these manipulations must consist of the following control manipulations and plant evolutions if they are applicable to the plant design. Items described in paragraphs (c)(3)(i) (A) through (L) of this section must be performed annually; all other items must be performed on a two-year cycle. However, the requalification programs must contain a commitment that each individual shall perform or participate in a combination of reactivity control manipulations based on the availability of plant equipment and systems. Those control manipulations which are not performed at the plant may be performed on a simulator. The use of the Technical Specifications should be maximized during the simulator control manipulations. Senior operator licensees are credited with these activities if they direct control manipulations as they are performed.

(A) Plant or reactor startups to include a range that reactivity feedback from nuclear heat addition is noticeable and heatup rate is established.
(B) Plant shutdown.
(C) Manual control of steam generators or feedwater or both during startup and shutdown.
(D) Boration or dilution during power operation.
(E) Significant (>10 percent) power changes in manual rod control or recirculation flow.
(F) Reactor power change of 10 percent or greater where load change is performed with load limit control or where flux, temperature, or speed control is on manual (for HTGR).
(G) Loss of coolant, including—
(1) Significant PWR steam generator leaks
(2) Inside and outside primary containment
(3) Large and small, including lead-rate determination
(4) Saturated reactor coolant response (PWR).
(H) Loss of instrument air (if simulated plant specific).
(I) Loss of electrical power (or degraded power sources).
(J) Loss of core coolant flow/natural circulation.
(K) Loss of feedwater (normal and emergency).
(L) Loss of service water, if required for safety.
(M) Loss of shutdown cooling.
(N) Loss of component cooling system or cooling to an individual component.
(O) Loss of normal feedwater or normal feedwater system failure.
(P) Loss of condenser vacuum.
(Q) Loss of protective system channel.
(R) Mispositioned control rod or rods (or rod drops).
(S) Inability to drive control rods.
(T) Conditions requiring use of emergency boration or standby liquid control system.
(U) Fuel cladding failure or high activity in reactor coolant or offgas.

(V) Turbine or generator trip.
(W) Malfunction of an automatic control system that affects reactivity.
(X) Malfunction of reactor coolant pressure/volume control system.
(Y) Reactor trip.
(Z) Main steam line break (inside or outside containment).
(AA) A nuclear instrumentation failure.

(ii) Each licensed operator and senior operator has demonstrated satisfactory understanding of the operation of the apparatus and mechanisms associated with the control manipulations in paragraph (c)(3)(i) of this section, and knows the operating procedures in each area for which the operator or senior operator is licensed.

(iii) Each licensed operator and senior operator is cognizant of facility design changes, procedure changes, and facility license changes.

(iv) Each licensed operator and senior operator reviews the contents of all abnormal and emergency procedures on a regularly scheduled basis.

(v) A simulator may be used in meeting the requirements of paragraphs (c) (3)(i) and (3)(ii) of this section, if it reproduces the general operating characteristics of the facility involved and the arrangement of the instrumentation and controls of the simulator is similar to that of the facility involved. If the simulator or simulation device is used to administer operating tests for a facility, as provided in § 55.45 (b)(1), the device approved to meet the requirements of § 55 45(b)(1) must be used for credit to be given for meeting the requirements of paragraphs (c)(3)(i) (G through AA) of this section.

(4) *Evaluation.* The requalification program must include—

(i) Comprehensive requalification written examinations and annual operating tests which determine areas in which retraining is needed to upgrade licensed operator and senior operator knowledge.

(ii) Written examinations which determine licensed operators' and senior operators' knowledge of subjects covered in the requalification program and provide a basis for evaluating their knowledge of abnormal and emergency procedures.

(iii) Systematic observation and evaluation of the performance and competency of licensed operators and senior operators by supervisors and/or training staff members, including evaluation of actions taken or to be taken during actual or simulated abnormal and emergency procedures.

(iv) Simulation of emergency or abnormal conditions that may be accomplished by using the control panel of the facility involved or by using a simulator. Where the control panel of the facility is used for simulation, the actions taken or to be taken for the emergency or abnormal condition shall be discussed; actual manipulation of the plant controls is not required. If a simulator is used in meeting the requirements of paragraph (c)(4)(iii) of this section, it shall accurately reproduce the operating characteristics of the facility involved and the arrangement of the instrumentation and controls of the simulator shall closely parallel that of the facility involved. After the provisions of § 55.45(b) have been implemented at a facility, the certified or approved simulation facility must be used to comply with this paragraph.

(v) Provisions for each licensed operator and senior operator to participate in an accelerated requalification program where performance evaluations conducted pursuant to paragraphs (c)(4) (i) through (iv) of this section clearly indicated the need.

(5) *Records.* The requalification program documentation must include the following:

(i) The facility licensee shall maintain records documenting the participation of each licensed operator and senior operator in the requalification program. The records must contain copies of written examinations administered, the answers given by the licensee, and the results of evaluations and documentation of operating tests and of any additional training administered in areas in which an operator or senior operator has exhibited deficiencies. The facility licensee shall retain these records until the operator's or senior operator's license is renewed.

(ii) Each record required by this part must be legible throughout the retention period specified by each Commission regulation. The record may be the original or a reproduced copy or a microform provided that the copy or microform is authenticated by authorized personnel and that the microform is capable of producing a clear copy throughout the required retention period.

(iii) If there is a conflict between the Commission's regulations in this part, and any license condition, or other written Commission approval or authorization pertaining to the retention period for the same type of record, the retention period specified for these records by the regulations in this part apply unless the Commission, pursuant to § 55.11, grants a specific exemption from this record retention requirement.

(6) *Alternative training programs.* The requirements of this section may be met by requalification programs conducted by persons other than the facility licensee if the requalification programs are similar to the program described in paragraphs (c) (1) through (5) of this section and the alternative program has been approved by the Commission.

(7) *Applicability to research and test reactor facilities.* To accommodate specialized modes of operation and differences in control, equipment, and operator skills and knowledge, the requalification program for each licensed operator and senior operator of a research reactor or test reactor facility must conform generally but need not be identical to the requalification program outlined in paragraphs (c) (1) through (6) of this section. Significant deviations from the requirements of paragraphs (c) (1) through (6) of this section will be permitted only if supported by written justification and approved by the Commission.

Subpart G—Modification and Revocation of Licenses

§ 55.61 Modification and revocation of licenses.

(a) The terms and conditions of all licenses are subject to amendment, revision, or modification by reason of rules, regulations, or orders issued in accordance with the Act or any amendments thereto.

(b) Any license may be revoked, suspended, or modified, in whole or in part:

(1) For any material false statement in the application or in any statement of fact required under section 182 of the Act.

(2) Because of conditions revealed by the application or statement of fact or any report, record, inspection or other means that would warrant the Commission to refuse to grant a license on an original application,

(3) For willful violation of, or failure to observe any of the terms and conditions of the Act, or the license, or of any rule, regulation, or order of the Commission, or

(4) For any conduct determined by the Commission to be a hazard to safe operation of the facility.

Subpart H—Enforcement

§ 55.71 Violations.

(a) An injunction or other court order may be obtained prohibiting any violation of any provision of:

(1) The Atomic Energy Act of 1954, as amended;

(2) Title II of the Energy Reorganization Act of 1974, as amended; or

(3) Any regulation or order issued under these Acts.

(b) A court order may be obtained for the payment of a civil penalty imposed under section 234 of the Aomic Energy Act for violation of:

(1) Sections 53, 57, 62, 63, 81, 82, 101, 103, 104, 107, or 109 of the Atomic Energy Act;

(2) Section 206 of the Energy Reorganization Act of 1974;

(3) Any rule, regulation, or order issued under these Acts;

(4) Any term, condition, or limitation of any license issued under these Acts; or

(5) For any violation for which a license may be revoked under section 186 of the Atomic Energy Act.

(c) Any person who willfully violates any provision of the Atomic Energy Act or any regulation issued under the Act, including the regulations in this part, may be guilty of a crime and, upon conviction, may be punished by fine or imprisonment, or both, as provided by law.

PART 50—DOMESTIC LICENSING OF PRODUCTION AND UTILIZATION FACILITIES

2. The authority citation for Part 50 continues to read as follows:

Authority: Secs. 103, 104, 161, 182, 183, 186, 189, 68 Stat. 936, 937, 948, 953, 954, 955, 956, as amended, sec. 234, 83 Stat. 1244, as amended (42 U.S.C. 2133, 2134, 2201, 2232, 2233, 2236, 2239, 2282); secs. 201, 202, 206, 88 Stat. 1242, 1244, 1246, as amended (42 U.S.C. 5841, 5842, 5846), unless otherwise noted.

Section 50.7 also issued under Pub. L. 95-601, sec. 10, 92 Stat. 2951 (42 U.S.C. 5851). Sections 50.58, 50.91, and 50.92 also issued under Pub. L. 97-415, 96 Stat. 2071, 2073 (42 U.S.C. 2133, 2239). Section 50.78 also issued under sec. 122, 68 Stat. 939 (42 U.S.C. 2152). Sections 50.80-50.81 also issued under sec. 184, 68 Stat. 954, as amended (42 U.S.C. 2234). Sections 50.100-50.102 also issued under sec. 186, 68 Stat. 955 (42 U.S.C. 2236).

For the purposes of sec. 223, 68 Stat. 958, as amended (42 U.S.C. 2273), §§ 50.10 (a), (b), and (c), 50.44, 50.46, 50.48, 50.54, and 50.80(a) are issued under sec. 161b, 68 Stat. 948, as amended (42 U.S.C. 2201(b)); §§ 50.10(b) and (c) and 50.54 are issued under sec. 161i, 68 Stat. 949, as amended (42 U.S.C. 2201(i)); and §§ 50.55(e), 50.59(b), 50.70, 50.71, 50.72, 50.73, and 50.78 are issued under sec. 161o, 68 Stat. 950, as amended (42 U.S.C. 2201(o)).

3. In § 50.34, paragraph (b)(8) is revised as follows:

§ 50.34 Contents of applications; technical information.

* * * * *

(b) * * *

(8) A description and plans for implementation of an operator requalification program. The operator requalification program must as a minimum, meet the requirements for those programs contained in § 55.59 of Part 55 of this chapter.

* * * * *

4. In § 50.54, paragraphs (i) and (i–1) are revised to read as follows:

§ 50.54 Conditions of licenses.

* * * * *

(i) Except as provided in § 55.13 of this chapter, the licensee may not permit the manipulation of the controls of any facility by anyone who is not a licensed operator or senior operator as provided in Part 55 of this chapter.

(i–1) Within three months after issuance of an operating license, the licensee shall have in effect an operator requalification program which must as a minimum, meet the requirements of § 55.59(c) of this chapter. Notwithstanding the provisions of § 50.59, the licensee may not, except as specifically authorized by the Commission decrease the scope of an approved operator requalification program.

* * * * *

5. Immediately following § 50.73, "Licensee Event Report System," a new § 50.74 is added as a conforming amendment to read as follows:

§ 50.74 Notification of change in operator or senior operator status.

Each licensee shall notify the Commission in accordance with § 50.4 within 30 days of the following in regard to a licensed operator or senior operator:

(a) Permanent reassignment from the position for which the licensee has certified the need for a licensed operator or senior operator under § 55.31(a)(3) of this chapter;

(b) Termination of any operator or senior operator;

(c) Disability or illness as described in § 55.25 of this chapter.

Dated at Washington, DC, this 20th day of March 1987.

For the Nuclear Regulatory Commission

John C. Hoyle,

Acting Secretary for the Commission

[FR Doc. 87–6478 Filed 3–24–87; 8:45 am]

BILLING CODE 7590–01–M

DEPARTMENT OF TRANSPORTATION

Federal Aviation Administration

14 CFR Part 39

[Docket No. 86-NM-215-AD; Amdt. 39-5568]

Airworthiness Directives; Boeing Model 747 and 757 Series Airplanes

AGENCY: Federal Aviation Administration (FAA), DOT.

ACTION: Final rule.

SUMMARY: This amendment adopts a new airworthiness directive (AD), applicable to Boeing Models 747 and 757 series airplanes, which requires inspection of the passenger door emergency power reservoir for integrity of the pressure relief rupture disk, repair, if necessary, and replacement of defective disk retainers. This amendment is prompted by numerous reports of emergency power reservoirs found to be prematurely discharged. This condition, if not corrected, would render the emergency power reservoir incapable of providing power to assist in opening the door quickly when required for emergency evacuation.

DATES: Effective May 1, 1987.

ADDRESSES: The applicable Boeing service information may be obtained from the Boeing Commercial Airplane Company, P.O. Box 3707, Seattle, Washington 98124; the applicable H.R. Textron service information may be obtained from H.R. Textron, 25200 West Rye Canyon Road, Valencia, California 91355. This information may be examined at the FAA, Northwest Mountain Region, 17900 Pacific Highway South, Seattle, Washington, or the Seattle Aircraft Certification Office, 9010 East Marginal Way South, Seattle, Washington 98168.

FOR FURTHER INFORMATION CONTACT: Mr. Pliny Brestel, Airframe Branch, ANM–120S; telephone (206) 431–1931. Mailing address: FAA, Northwest Mountain Region, 17900 Pacific Highway South, C–68966, Seattle, Washington 98168.

SUPPLEMENTARY INFORMATION: A proposal to amend Part 39 of the Federal Aviation Regulations to include an airworthiness directive which requires inspection of the passenger door emergency power reservoir on Boeing Models 747 and 757 series airplanes for integrity of the pressure relief rupture disk, repair, if necessary, and replacement of defective disk retainers, was published in the Federal Register on December 24, 1986 (51 FR 46687). The comment period for the NPRM, which ended February 16, 1987, afforded interested persons an opportunity to participate in the making of this amendment. Due consideration has been given to the comments received.

The Air Transport Association (ATA) of America, representing operators of Boeing Model 747 and 757 airplanes stated that the proposed rule requiring inspection of all 747 and 757 airplanes is not justified for those operators whose records list the serial numbers and applicable aircraft of the subject reservoirs installed. The ATA, therefore, requested that paragraph A. of the proposed rule be deleted and that the effectivity be revised to read "*Boeing*: Applies to all Model 747 and 757 series airplanes equipped with emergency power reservoirs listed in H.R. Textron Service Bulletin No. 803300–52–05." The FAA agrees that it is unnecessary to inspect the airplanes if records are available to determine the serial numbers of the reservoirs installed, and the AD has been revised accordingly; however, in absence of such records, operators must inspect for serial numbers in accordance with the applicable service bulletin.

The ATA also commented that the "NOTE" in the proposed rule which advises readers that the affected reservoirs may be installed on other airplanes should be deleted because, if adopted, will create confusion in the field since the effectivity of the proposed rule is clearly only against Boeing aircraft. The FAA concurs that the effectivity is only Boeing aircraft and specifically Models 747 and 757; however, the "NOTE" should not be deleted because, while some Boeing 747 and 757 aircraft may have been delivered without defective reservoirs, a defective reservoir could have been installed in the field since delivery. The note has been revised to reflect "Boeing Model 747 and 757 series airplanes."

The ATA also requested that the initial compliance period in paragraph A. of the proposed rule be changed from 60 to 90 days to afford those operators, who may not have records listing serial numbers of reservoirs, additional time to complete the fleet inspection to determine if they are affected by the rule. The ATA stated that, in some instances (likely 50%), the installed reservoirs would require removal to read the serial number. Further, some operators check the reservoirs every four days and, therefore, need time to change their maintenance program to comply with the daily check requirement of paragraph B. The FAA does not concur with an extension of the initial compliance period from 60 to 90 days in that air safety and public interest

Appendix C

Regulatory Guide .1.134

Medical Evaluation of Licensed Personnel for Nuclear Power Plants

U.S. NUCLEAR REGULATORY COMMISSION

Revision 2*
April 1987

REGULATORY GUIDE

OFFICE OF NUCLEAR REGULATORY RESEARCH

REGULATORY GUIDE 1.134
(Task OL 401-5)

MEDICAL EVALUATION OF LICENSED PERSONNEL FOR NUCLEAR POWER PLANTS

A. INTRODUCTION

Sections 55 31, "How To Apply," and 55 57, "Renewal of Licenses," of 10 CFR Part 55, "Operators' Licenses," require that each initial or renewal application for an operator or senior operator license contain a medical examination certification following the form prescribed in Subpart C of Part 55, "Medical Requirements " Sections 55 33, "Disposition of Initial Application," and 55 57 state that the initial or renewal applications for these licenses will be approved if, among other things, the applicant has no medical or general health condition that might cause operational errors endangering public health and safety Paragraph (i) of § 55 53, "Conditions of Licenses," requires that an examination be conducted every 2 years.

Section 55 25, "Incapacitation Because of Disability or Illness," deals with an operator or senior operator who becomes incapacitated because of a mental or physical condition that might cause impaired judgment or motor coordination

Section 55 27, "Documentation," requires that the facility licensee document and maintain the medical qualifications data, current test results, and each operator's medical history and provide these to the NRC upon its request

This guide describes a method acceptable to the NRC staff for providing the information needed by the staff for its evaluation of the medical qualifications of applicants for initial or renewal operator or senior operator licenses for nuclear power plants and for providing notification to the NRC of an incapacitating disability or illness.

The Advisory Committee on Reactor Safeguards has been consulted concerning this guide and has concurred in the regulatory position.

Any information collection activities mentioned in this regulatory guide are contained as requirements in 10 CFR Part 55, which provides the regulatory basis for this guide The information collection requirements in 10 CFR Part 55 have been cleared under OMB Clearance No 3150-0018

B. DISCUSSION

Section 55 23, "Certification," of Subpart C, "Medical Requirements," of 10 CFR Part 55 requires that a physician examine the applicant in accordance with NRC's regulatory guidance and determine that the examinee's medical condition and general health meet the requirements for granting or renewing an operator license. The physician must send a full medical examination report to the facility licensee, which will then transmit a completed Form 396 to the NRC. The intent of these requirements is to have the facility licensee certify the health of its operators. However, the facility licensee is expected to maintain those records that may be reviewed by the NRC. Therefore, § 55.27 requires the facility licensee to document and maintain the full medical examination report, including the results of medical qualifications data, test results, and each operator's medical history In addition, § 55.27 requires the facility licensee to retain the most recent medical information as a result of the biennial physical examination and provide that information to the NRC on request The certification form would be sent by the facility licensee to the NRC

There are two instances in which medical information must be sent to the NRC One is when a conditional license based on medical evidence is requested under the provisions of paragraph 55.33(b). The second instance is when a licensed individual has become mentally or physically unable to

---

*The substantial number of changes in this revision has made it impractical to indicate the changes with lines in the margin.

---

perform job duties. In this case, the facility licensee must notify the NRC within 30 days after learning that the diagnosis has been made. The facility licensee must forward to the NRC Form 396 and medical records describing the disability. This related information is required by § 55 27 to be documented and maintained by the facility

An American National Standard developed by the American Nuclear Society, ANSI/ANS-3.4-1983, "Medical Certification and Monitoring of Personnel Requiring Operator Licenses for Nuclear Power Plants,"[1] prescribes minimum requirements necessary to determine that the medical condition and general health of nuclear reactor operators will not cause operational errors The criteria presented in this standard provide an examining physician a basis for determining whether a potentially disqualifying abnormal health condition exists. Establishing minimum health requirements should aid in more uniform medical evaluations. However, it is necessary to recognize that, although it is the physician's responsibility to identify and evaluate any potentially disqualifying medical conditions, NRC makes the final determination of the applicant's medical fitness.

---

[1]Copies may be obtained from the American Nuclear Society, 555 North Kensington Avenue, La Grange Park, Illinois 60525.

Nothing in ANSI/ANS-3.4-1983 or this guide should be construed to mean that such matters as an individual's reading habits, political or religious beliefs, or attitudes on social, economic, or political issues should be investigated or judged.

C. REGULATORY POSITION

The requirements contained in ANSI/ANS-3 4-1983, "Medical Certification and Monitoring of Personnel Requiring Operator Licenses for Nuclear Power Plants,"[1] provide a method acceptable to the NRC staff for determining the medical qualifications of applicants for initial or renewal operator or senior operator licenses.

D. IMPLEMENTATION

The purpose of this section is to provide information to applicants and licensees about the staff's plans for using this regulatory guide.

Except in those cases in which the licensee proposes an acceptable alternative method for complying with specified portions of the Commission's regulations, the methods described in the guide will be used in evaluating the part of an application for initial or renewal operator or senior operator licenses on NRC Form 396, "Certificate of Medical Examination by Facility Licensee."

VALUE/IMPACT ANALYSIS

A separate value/impact analysis has not been prepared for this regulatory guide. A value/impact analysis was included in the regulatory analysis for the amendments to 10 CFR Part 55 published on March 25, 1987, a copy of which was placed in the Public Document Room at that time. This analysis is also appropriate to Revision 2 of Regulatory Guide 1.134. A copy of the regulatory analysis is available for inspection and copying for a fee at the NRC Public Document Room, 1717 H Street NW., Washington, DC.

Appendix D

Regulatory Guide 1.149

Nuclear Power Plant Simulation Facilities for Use in Operator

License Examinations

U.S. NUCLEAR REGULATORY COMMISSION

Revision 1*
April 1987

REGULATORY GUIDE

OFFICE OF NUCLEAR REGULATORY RESEARCH

REGULATORY GUIDE 1.149
(Task OL 402-5)

NUCLEAR POWER PLANT SIMULATION FACILITIES FOR USE IN OPERATOR LICENSE EXAMINATIONS

A. INTRODUCTION

Paragraph 55.45(a) of 10 CFR Part 55, "Operators' Licenses," requires that an applicant for an operator or senior operator license demonstrate both an understanding of and the ability to perform certain essential job tasks. Paragraph 55 45(b) specifies that these operating tests will be administered, in part, either in a simulation facility consisting solely of a plant-referenced simulator that has been certified to the Commission by the facility licensee or in a simulation facility approved by the Commission after application has been made by the facility licensee.[1]

This regulatory guide describes a method acceptable to the NRC staff for complying with those portions of the Commission's regulations regarding (1) certification of a simulation facility consisting solely of a plant-referenced simulator and (2) application for prior approval of a simulation facility

The Advisory Committee on Reactor Safeguards has been consulted concerning this guide and has concurred in the regulatory position

Any information collection activities mentioned in this regulatory guide are contained as requirements in those sections of 10 CFR Part 55 that provide the regulatory basis for this guide. The information collection requirements in 10 CFR Part 55 have been cleared under Clearance No. 3150-0018 and No 3150-0138.

---

*The substantial number of changes in this revision has made it impractical to indicate the changes with lines in the margin.

[1]A simulation facility is defined in §55.4 as one or more of the following components, alone or in combination, used for the partial conduct of operating tests for operators, senior operators, and candidates: (i) the plant, (ii) a plant-referenced simulator, (iii) another simulation device.

B. DISCUSSION

Although ensuring that individuals who receive operator or senior operator licenses possess the knowledge, skills, and abilities necessary to operate the facility in a safe manner is the responsibility of facility licensees, the Nuclear Regulatory Commission must perform an independent audit of this process through its operator licensing examinations. Section 55.45, "Operating Tests," of 10 CFR Part 55 requires the candidate for a license to demonstrate (1) an understanding of and the ability to perform the actions necessary during normal, abnormal, and emergency situations, (2) the operation of systems that affect heat removal or reactivity changes, and (3) behaviors that show the individual's ability to function within the control room team in such a way that the facility licensee's procedures are adhered to and that the limitations in its license and amendments are not violated

The use of a plant-referenced simulator for testing enables the examiner to evaluate a candidate's performance in an environment closely correlated with conditions in the specific plant for which that candidate has applied for a license With major facility differences minimized between the testing and operating environments, examiners have been able to make pass-fail judgments with confidence

Although the increased use of plant-referenced simulators has provided to examiners the capability for better discrimination between success and failure in a candidate than could be achieved with non-plant-referenced simulators, the staff recognizes the existence of several factors that could suggest the use of alternative systems or devices for conducting the non-walkthrough portions of operating tests These factors

---

.nclude the cost and lead time associated with procurement or upgrading of a plant-referenced simulator. Moreover, rapidly changing technology in the simulation industry is resulting in previously unavailable options that could lead a facility licensee to seek alternative ways to meet the requirements of §55.45. ANSI/ANS-3.5-1985, "Nuclear Power Plant Simulators for Use in Operator Training"[2] (the standard), in conjunction with this regulatory guide, provides guidance in these areas.

C. REGULATORY POSITION

Requirements are set forth in ANSI/ANS-3.5-1985 for specifying minimum performance and configuration criteria for a simulator, for comparing a simulator to its reference plant, and for upgrading simulators to reflect changes to reference plant response or control room configuration These requirements provide a method acceptable to the NRC staff for a facility licensee (1) to certify a simulation facility consisting solely of a plant-referenced simulator or (2) to obtain approval of a simulation facility for use in portions of reactor operator and senior operator license examinations subject to the following:

1. The references to operator training in Section 1, "Scope," of the standard should be taken to apply to operating tests for operators, senior operators, and candidates

2. Simulation facilities as defined in §55.4 of 10 CFR Part 55, to the extent that the facility licensee applies for approval under the requirements of paragraph 55.45(b), should meet the applicable requirements of the standard.

3. The standard identifies in Section 1.1, "Background," other documents to be included as part of the standard The applicability of one of these documents, ANSI/ANS-3.1,[2] should be determined by referring to Revision 2 to Regulatory Guide 1 8, "Qualification and Training of Personnel for Nuclear Power Plants."

4. Section 5.2, "Simulator Update Design Data," requires that reference plant modifications be reviewed annually against the simulator and that the simulator update design data be revised as appropriate. This should be taken to mean that the first such annual review and update should take place within one year following the facility licensee's certification as specified in paragraph 55.45(b)(5)(i) or within 18 months following the submittal of the application for approval as specified in paragraph 55 45(b)(4)(i).

5. Section 5.4, "Simulator Testing," requires the conduct of specific tests to establish simulator performance and verify its operability. In addition to these procedures, applicable malfunctions, identified in Section 3.1.2, "Plant Malfunctions," should be periodically tested

to ensure the continued acceptability of the simulation facility. These malfunctions, if applicable to the facility, should be tested in their entirety not less than every four years, approximately 25% per year. When conducted in addition to the tests required by Section 5.4 and when subjected to the performance criteria for transient operations specified in Section 4.2, "Transient Operation," these malfunction tests provide an acceptable means of demonstrating the performance and operability of the simulation facility.

6 Appendix A to the standard, "Guide for Documenting Simulator Performance," and Appendix B to the standard, "Simulator Operability Tests," should be considered integral parts of the standard.

D. IMPLEMENTATION

The purpose of this section is to provide information to facility licensees about the NRC staff's plans for using this regulatory guide.

In accordance with the requirements in §55.45 of 10 CFR Part 55, the simulation facility portion of the operating test will not be administered on other than an approved or a certified simulation facility after:

1. The facility licensee has submitted a certification in accordance with paragraph 55.45(b)(5)(i), or

2. The staff has approved an application submitted by the facility licensee in accordance with paragraph 55.45(b)(4), or

3. May 28, 1991, whichever occurs sooner.

Until that time, the NRC will continue to give examinations for a facility licensee's reference plant in accordance with Generic Letter 82-18, "Reactor Operator and Senior Reactor Operator Requalification Examinations,"[3] October 12, 1982.

Licensees and applicants may propose means other than those specified in Section C of this guide for meeting applicable regulations. Except in those cases in which a facility licensee submits a certification for its simulation facility or proposes an acceptable alternative method for complying with specified portions of the Commission's regulations, the NRC will use the method described in this guide in the evaluation of the application for approval submitted by the facility licensee for its simulation facility. The guidance provided in Section C has been approved for use by the staff in the evaluation of all submittals as an acceptable means of complying with the Commission's regulations specified in Section A.

If a facility licensee wishes to utilize a simulation facility for more than one nuclear power plant, it must

[2]Copies may be obtained from the American Nuclear Society, 555 North Kensington Avenue, La Grange Park, IL 60525.

[3]Available for copying for a fee or inspection at the NRC Public Document Room, 1717 H Street NW., Washington, DC.

demonstrate to the NRC in its certification or in its application that the differences between the plants are not so significant that they have an impact on the ability of the simulation facility to meet the requirements and guidance of ANSI/ANS-3.5-1985 as qualified in this regulatory guide for each of the plants. This demonstration should include an analysis and summary of the differences between each plant and the simulation facility, including:

1 Facility design and systems relevant to control room personnel;

2. Technical specifications;

3. Procedures, primarily abnormal and emergency operating procedures;

4. Control room design and instrument/control location; and

5. Operational characteristics.

VALUE/IMPACT ANALYSIS

A separate value/impact analysis has not been prepared for this regulatory guide. A value/impact analysis was included in the regulatory analysis for the amendments to 10 CFR Part 55 published on March 25, 1987, a copy of which was placed in the Public Document Room at that time. This analysis is also appropriate to Revision 1 of Regulatory Guide 1.149. A copy of the regulatory analysis is available for inspection and copying for a fee at the NRC Public Document Room, 1717 H Street NW., Washington, DC.

Appendix F

Regulatory Guide 1.8

Qualification and Training of Personnel for Nuclear Power Plants

U.S. NUCLEAR REGULATORY COMMISSION

Revision 2*
April 1987

REGULATORY GUIDE

OFFICE OF NUCLEAR REGULATORY RESEARCH

REGULATORY GUIDE 1.8
(Task OL 403-5)

QUALIFICATION AND TRAINING OF PERSONNEL FOR NUCLEAR POWER PLANTS

A. INTRODUCTION

Paragraph 50.34(b)(6)(i) of 10 CFR Part 50, "Domestic Licensing of Production and Utilization Facilities," requires that an application for a license to operate a nuclear power plant include information concerning organizational structure, personnel qualifications, and related matters. Subpart D, "Applications," of 10 CFR Part 55, "Operators' Licenses," requires that operator license applications include information concerning an individual's education and experience and related matters. This regulatory guide describes a method acceptable to the NRC staff for complying with those portions of the Commission's regulations with regard to the training and qualifications of nuclear power plant personnel. Personnel of test, training, research, and mobile reactors are not covered by this regulatory guide.

The Advisory Committee on Reactor Safeguards has been consulted concerning this guide and has concurred in the regulatory position.

Any information collection activities mentioned in this regulatory guide are contained as requirements in 10 CFR Parts 50 and 55, which provide the regulatory basis for this guide. The information collection requirements in 10 CFR Part 50 have been approved under OMB Clearance No. 3150-011, those in 10 CFR Part 55, under OMB Clearance No. 3150-0018.

B. DISCUSSION

Subcommittee ANS-3, Reactor Operations, American Nuclear Society Standards Committee, developed a standard containing criteria for the qualification and training of nuclear power plant personnel. This standard was approved by the American National Standards Institute (ANSI) Committee N18, Design Criteria for Nuclear Power Plants, and designated ANSI N18.1-1971, "Selection and Training of Nuclear Power Plant Personnel." Regulatory Guide 1.8, "Personnel Selection and Training," endorsing ANSI N18.1-1971, was issued in March 1971, and Revision 1 was issued in September 1975. A revision of ANSI N18.1-1971 was subsequently approved by the ANSI Board of Standards Review and designated ANSI/ANS-3.1-1978, "Selection and Training of Nuclear Power Plant Personnel."

A first proposed Revision 2 to Regulatory Guide 1.8 endorsing ANSI/ANS-3.1-1978 was issued for public comment in February 1979. As a result of experience gained from the accident at Three Mile Island Unit 2 (TMI-2), additional public comments in the area of personnel qualifications were requested on proposed Revision 2 to Regulatory Guide 1.8 in May 1979. All of the comments from both requests were forwarded to the ANS-3 Subcommittee for its use during the development of a revision to ANSI/ANS-3.1-1978. Subsequently, Draft Standard ANS 3.1, dated December 6, 1979, incorporating the upgraded requirements was issued. In September 1980, public comments were requested on a second proposed Revision 2 to Regulatory Guide 1.8 that endorsed Draft Standard ANS 3.1. The public comments received were held in abeyance pending Commission action on proposed rules on operator qualifications and licensing in SECY 81-84, "Qualification of Reactor Operators,"[1] February 2, 1981, and SECY 81-84A, "Discussion of Revisions to Reactor Operator Qualifications,"[1] June 15, 1981. The Commission did not approve either of these proposals and directed the staff to continue to study the issue.

---

*The substantial number of changes in this revision has made it impractical to indicate the changes with lines in the margin.

[1]Copies are available for inspection or copying for a fee in the NRC Public Document Room, 1717 H Street NW., Washington, DC.

During 1981, Draft Standard ANS 3.1 was updated to factor in additional lessons learned from the TMI-2 accident and changing regulatory requirements. The standard was approved by the American Nuclear Society's Nuclear Power Plant Standards Committee (NUPPSCO) and the ANSI Board of Standards Review and was reissued as ANSI/ANS-3.1-1981, "Selection, Qualification and Training of Personnel for Nuclear Power Plants."[2] A third proposed Revision 2 of Regulatory Guide 1.8 was developed to endorse ANSI/ANS-3.1-1981 with certain additions and exceptions and was issued for public comment in January 1985. As a result of the public comments and Commission actions concerning training and qualifications, this Revision 2 of Regulatory Guide 1.8 now endorses Sections 4 3.1.1, "Shift Supervisor," 4.3.1.2, "Senior Operator," 4.5.1.2, "Licensed Operators," 4.4.8, "Shift Technical Advisor," and 4.4.4, "Radiation Protection," of ANSI/ANS-3.1-1981. Endorsement for all other positions will remain with ANSI N18.1-1971, "Selection and Training of Nuclear Power Plant Personnel." The bases for the additions and exceptions to ANSI/ANS-3.1-1981 are contained in NUREG-0737, "Clarification of TMI Action Plan Requirements,"[3] which includes the March 28, 1980 letter to all power reactor applicants and licensees regarding qualification of reactor operators, and NUREG-0094, "Guide for the Licensing of Facility Operators, Including Senior Operators,"[3] and the Commission's "Policy Statement on Engineering Expertise on Shift" (50 FR 43621). The regulatory position related to the radiation protection manager is revised from what was included in Revision 1 of Regulatory Guide 1.8 (1975). The industry has adopted the requisite qualifications in ANSI/ANS 3 1-1981, and the current change endorses that industry position.

On March 20, 1985, the Commission issued a "Policy Statement on Training and Qualification of Nuclear Power Plant Personnel" (50 FR 11147) that recognizes industry commitment to accredit training programs. In the policy statement, the NRC endorsed the training accreditation program managed by the Institute of Nuclear Power Operations (INPO) because it encompasses the elements of performance-based training and will provide the basis to ensure that personnel have qualifications commensurate with the performance requirements of their jobs. The Commission has decided to withhold action on promulgating new training and qualifications regulations during an evaluation period. During that period, NRC will continue to evaluate the results of the accreditation program to determine if the voluntary industry efforts ensure qualifications that meet or exceed the minimum standards included in this guide.

The Commission's "Policy Statement on Engineering Expertise on Shift" issued on October 28, 1985 (50 FR 43621) provides two options for meeting nuclear power plant staffing requirements (paragraph 50.54(m)(2)(i) of

10 CFR Part 50) and the requirement to have a shift technical advisor (STA) available to the shift (NUREG-0737, I.A.1.1). One option in the Policy Statement, which is preferred by the Commission, allows combining the functions of the STA with one of the required senior operators as long as specific training and education requirements are met. The other option allows for continuation of an approved independent STA program. Regulatory Position C.1.j reflects the guidance provided in this Policy Statement

C. REGULATORY POSITION

1. Positions in ANSI/ANS-3.1-1981 that Are Endorsed by this Regulatory Guide

For the positions listed in ANSI/ANS-3.1-1981, "Selection, Qualification and Training of Personnel for Nuclear Power Plants," as shift supervisor, senior operator, licensed operator, and shift technical advisor, the requirements contained in the standard provide an approach acceptable to the NRC staff for complying with the qualifications and training requirements of 10 CFR Parts 50 and 55 subject to the guidance regarding the STA function provided in the Commission's "Policy Statement on Engineering Expertise on Shift" and the clarifications, additions, and exceptions in paragraphs a through k below. For radiation protection supervisory personnel, Section 4.4.4 of the standard contains an approach acceptable for the position of radiation protection manager (RPM) subject to the following

a. In lieu of the description in Section 5.1 of ANSI/ANS-3 1-1981, cold license examinations should be defined as those that are administered before the unit has completed preoperational testing and initial operations as described in its Final Safety Analysis Report as amended and approved by the Commission. Hot examinations are those administered after this condition is attained.

b. Hot license applicants must meet the training elements in Sections 4.3.1.1.c, 4.3.1.2.c, and 4.5.1.2.c of the standard and the experience elements in Sections 4.3.1.1.b, 4.3.1.2.b, and 4.5.1.2.b of the standard. Cold license applicants are subject to the training elements identified above, but they are exempt from the experience elements.

c. Paragraph 2 of Section 4.3.1.1.a of ANSI/ANS-3.1-1981 is not applicable. An individual who meets the Commission's "Policy Statement on Engineering Expertise on Shift" is required on all shifts to provide engineering expertise (see Regulatory Position C.1.j).

d. The minimum educational requirement for shift supervisors, Section 4.3.1.1.a, and for senior operators, Section 4.3.1.2.a, is a high school diploma or equivalent.

e An applicant for a senior operator (SO) license should have 4 years of responsible power plant experience. Responsible power plant experience for an SO is defined as having actively performed as a designated

[2]Copies may be obtained from the American Nuclear Society, 555 North Kensington Avenue, LaGrange Park, IL 60525.

[3]Copies may be obtained from the Government Printing Office, Post Office Box 37082, Washington, DC 20013-7082.

control room operator (fossil or nuclear) or as a power plant staff engineer involved in the day-to-day activities of the facility during or after the final year of construction. A maximum of 2 years of responsible power plant experience may be fulfilled by academic or related technical training on a one-for-one time basis. Two years should be nuclear power plant experience. At least 6 months of the nuclear power plant experience should be at the plant for which an applicant seeks a license In addition, applicants for an SO position not holding a bachelor's degree in engineering or equivalent should have held an operator's license and should have been actively involved in the performance of licensed duties for at least 1 year.

f In addition to the requirements stated in Section 5 2 1 2 1 of ANSI/ANS-3 1-1981, classroom instruction for all license applicants should include training in the use of installed plant systems for the control and mitigation of an accident in which the core is severely damaged.

g In addition to the requirements in Section 5.2 1.3.1 of ANSI/ANS-3 1-1981, each applicant for an operator or senior operator license should serve 3 months as an extra person on shift in training for that position. These 3 months as an extra person on shift in training should include all phases of day-to-day operations under the supervision of licensed personnel.

h Control room operating experience for hot license applicants, described in Section 5 2.1.3 1 of ANSI/ANS-3 1-1981, should include manipulation of controls of the facility during a minimum of five reactivity changes. Every effort should be made to have a diversity of reactivity changes for each applicant Startups, shutdowns, large load changes, and changes in rod programming are some examples and could be accomplished by manually using such systems as rod control, chemical shim control, or recirculation flow

i All cold license applicants should participate in practical work assignments as described in Section 5.2 1.4 of ANSI/ANS-3 1-1981 for a minimum of 6 months.

j In addition to the responsibilities described in Section 4.4 8 of ANSI/ANS-3.1-1981, the STA should assume an active role in shift activities. For example, the STA should review plant logs, participate in shift turnover, and maintain awareness of plant configuration and status. The educational requirements for the STA specified in Section 4 4 8.a of ANSI/ANS-3.1-1981 are not applicable An independent STA should have a bachelor's degree or equivalent in a scientific or engineering discipline

"Actively performing STA functions" means performing at least three shifts per quarter as the STA. If an STA has not actively performed, the STA should receive training sufficient to ensure that the STA is cognizant of facility and procedure changes that occurred during the absence.

Combining the functions of a senior operator and the STA is acceptable if the provisions of the Commission's "Policy Statement on Engineering Expertise on Shift" are met. In addition to the requirements specified in Section 4.4.8.c of ANSI/ANS-3.1-1981, the STA should have specific training in the response to and analysis of plant transients and accidents and training in the relationship of accident conditions to offsite consequences and protective action strategies.

k. The radiation protection manager should have the qualifications described in Section 4.4.4 of ANSI/ANS-3.1-1981 with the clarification that 3 of the 4 years of experience in applied radiation protection should be professional-level experience.

2. Positions in ANSI/ANS N18.1-1971 that Are Endorsed by this Regulatory Guide

For positions listed in the standard other than those under Regulatory Position 1 above, the requirements contained in ANSI N18.1-1971, "Selection and Training of Nuclear Power Plant Personnel," provide an approach acceptable to the NRC staff for complying with the qualifications and training requirements of 10 CFR Parts 50 and 55.

D. IMPLEMENTATION

The purpose of this section is to provide information to applicants and licensees regarding the NRC staff's plans for using this regulatory guide.

Applicants and licensees may propose means other than those specified in Section C of this guide for meeting applicable regulations

Except in those cases in which the applicant or licensee proposes an acceptable alternative means of complying with the Commission's regulations specified in Section A, the guidance provided in Section C has been approved for use by the staff after March 31, 1988, in the evaluation of the qualifications and training requirements for (1) nuclear power plant personnel as described in applications for an operating license, (2) applicants for operator and senior operator licenses, and (3) replacement personnel in those positions in operating nuclear power plants whose training programs have not yet been accredited by an accreditation program endorsed by the NRC.

VALUE/IMPACT ANALYSIS

A separate value/impact analysis has not been prepared for this regulatory guide. A value/impact analysis was included in the regulatory analysis for the amendments to 10 CFR Part 55 published on March 25, 1987, a copy of which was placed in the Public Document Room at that time. This analysis is also appropriate to Revision 2 of Regulatory Guide 1.8. A copy of the regulatory analysis is available for inspection and copying for a fee at the NRC Public Document Room, 1717 H Street NW., Washington, DC.

NRC FORM 335
(2 84)
NRCM 1102,
3201, 3202

U S NUCLEAR REGULATORY COMMISSION

BIBLIOGRAPHIC DATA SHEET

SEE INSTRUCTIONS ON THE REVERSE

1 REPORT NUMBER (Assigned by TIDC add Vol No if any)
NUREG-1262

2 TITLE AND SUBTITLE

Answers to Questions at Public Meetings Regarding
Implementation of Title 10, Code of Federal Regulations,
Part 55 on Operators' Licenses

3 LEAVE BLANK

4 DATE REPORT COMPLETED	
MONTH	YEAR
November	1987

5 AUTHOR(S)

6 DATE REPORT ISSUED	
MONTH	YEAR
November	1987

7 PERFORMING ORGANIZATION NAME AND MAILING ADDRESS (Include Zip Code)

Division of Licensee Performance and Quality Evaluation
Office of Nuclear Reactor Regulation
U. S. Nuclear Regulatory Commission
Washington, DC 20555

8 PROJECT/TASK/WORK UNIT NUMBER

9 FIN OR GRANT NUMBER

10 SPONSORING ORGANIZATION NAME AND MAILING ADDRESS (Include Zip Code)

Division of Licensee Performance and Quality Evaluation
Office of Nuclear Reactor Regulation
U. S. Nuclear Regulatory Commission
Washington, DC 20555

11a TYPE OF REPORT

Question and Answer

b PERIOD COVERED (Inclusive dates)

12 SUPPLEMENTARY NOTES

13 ABSTRACT (200 words or less)

This document presents questions and answers based on the transcripts of four public
meetings (and from written questions submitted after the meetings) conducted from
April 9 to April 20, 1987 by the staff of the U. S. Nuclear Regulatory Commission. The
meetings discussed implementation of the Commission's final rule governing Operators'
Licenses and Conforming Amendments (10 CFR Parts 55 and 50). The rule became effective
May 26, 1987 and is intended to clarify the regulations for issuing licenses to operators
and senior operators; revise the requirements and scope of written examinations and
operating tests for operators and senior operators, including a requirement for a
simulation facility; clarify procedures for administering requalification examinations;
and describe the form and content for operator license applications.

14 DOCUMENT ANALYSIS - a KEYWORDS/DESCRIPTORS

Nuclear Power

b IDENTIFIERS/OPEN ENDED TERMS

Operator Licenses
10 CFR Parts 50 and 55
Simulation Facilities
Requalification Examinations

15 AVAILABILITY
STATEMENT

Unlimited

16 SECURITY CLASSIFICATION

(This page)

(This report)

17 NUMBER OF PAGES

18 PRICE